A New Philosophy of Social Conflict

Also Available From Bloomsbury

Bloomsbury Studies in Continental Philosophy presents cutting-edge scholarship in the field of modern European thought. The wholly original arguments, perspectives and research findings in titles in this series make it an important and stimulating resource for students and academics from across the discipline.

Breathing with Luce Irigaray, edited by Lenart Skof and Emily A. Holmes

Deleuze and Art, Anne Sauvagnargues

Deleuze and the Diagram: Aesthetic Threads in Visual Organization, Jakub Zdebik

Derrida, Badiou and the Formal Imperative, Christopher Norris

Desire in Ashes: Deconstruction, Psychoanalysis, Philosophy, edited by Simon Morgan Wortham and Chiara Alfano

Egalitarian Moments: From Descartes to Rancière, Devin Zane Shaw

Ernst Bloch and His Contemporaries, Ivan Boldyrev

The Field of Theory: The Rise and Decline of Structuralism in France, Johannes Angermuller

Gadamer's Poetics: A Critique of Modern Aesthetics, John Arthos

Heidegger, History and the Holocaust, Mahon O'Brien

Heidegger and the Emergence of the Question of Being, Jesús Adrián Escudero

Immanent Transcendence: Reconfiguring Materialism in Continental Philosophy, Patrice Haynes

Merleau-Ponty's Existential Phenomenology and the Realization of Philosophy, Bryan A. Smyth

Nietzsche and Political Thought, edited by Keith Ansell-Pearson

Nietzsche as a Scholar of Antiquity, Helmut Heit

Philosophy, Sophistry, Antiphilosophy: Badiou's Dispute with Lyotard, Matthew R. McLennan

The Poetic Imagination in Heidegger and Schelling, Christopher Yates

Post-Rationalism: Psychoanalysis, Epistemology, and Marxism in Post-War France, Tom Eyers

Revisiting Normativity with Deleuze, edited by Rosi Braidotti and Patricia Pisters

Towards the Critique of Violence: Walter Benjamin and Giorgio Agamben, Brendan Moran and Carlo Salzani

A New Philosophy of Social Conflict

Mediating Collective Trauma and Transitional Justice

Leonard C. Hawes

Bloomsbury Academic
An imprint of Bloomsbury Publishing Plc

BLOOMSBURY
LONDON • NEW DELHI • NEW YORK • SYDNEY

Bloomsbury Academic
An imprint of Bloomsbury Publishing Plc

50 Bedford Square
London
WC1B 3DP
UK

1385 Broadway
New York
NY 10018
USA

www.bloomsbury.com

BLOOMSBURY and the Diana logo are trademarks of Bloomsbury Publishing Plc

First published 2015

British Library Cataloguing-in-Publication Data
A catalogue record for this book is available from the British Library.

ISBN: HB: 978-1-47252-405-8
ePDF: 978-1-47253-061-5
ePub: 978-1-47253-265-7

Library of Congress Cataloging-in-Publication Data
A catalog record for this book is available from the Library of Congress.

Typeset by Deanta Global Publishing Services, Chennai, India

To Michelle
She knows how

Contents

Acknowledgements

The Communication Department and the College of Humanities at the University of Utah have served as my academic home since I began work on this project with a University Research Fellowship in 2003–04, during which time I was in residence at the University of Aalborg in Denmark, a seemingly unlikely place to begin work on the 1994 Rwandan genocide. Nonetheless, directly and indirectly influenced by brilliant, committed and compassionate colleagues there and in Copenhagen, I began to formulate this Deleuzean experiment. Marianne Kristiansen, then professor of Communication at Aalborg, and Jørgen Bloch-Poulsen, founder of Dialog, an action research consulting firm, made my extended stay in Denmark possible and enormously rewarding in many intended and unintended ways. It was during frequent dinners at their country home in Hjørring, and conversations late into the night about our work with difficult, seemingly impossible conflicts, that I began to make sense of the Event of 1994 – the Rwandan genocide. Many of our conversations had little to do with Rwanda and genocide, and yet that Event had been serving as a virtual touchstone for me, as I would come to realize.

Since that time, for the last decade, I have been drafting and redrafting the manuscript that became *A New Philosophy of Social Conflict*. It has been the focus of my intellectual and emotional work since my time in Denmark. When I returned to the University of Utah, I began working closely with Jim Holbrook, clinical professor of law at the S. J. Quinney School of Law. He and I have been teaching advanced negotiation, mediation and transitional justice seminars to law students and graduate students for many years. He read early drafts of the manuscript and met with me for countless hours to talk through my blind spots and my unchecked assumptions. His intellectual generosity, nuanced insight and intuitive subtlety were pivotal to the development of this project; he pushed and prodded me to extend my thinking. After he went to Iraq as Chief of Party managing the Law School's multimillion dollar contract with the U.S. State Department to provide research and advice to the Iraqi government and parliament, he continued corresponding with me about the manuscript and its relevance and applicability to his on-the-ground working circumstances in the Green Zone. He insisted on its value for making sense of violent social conflict, transitional justice and for reconciling collective trauma. He is a gift and a treasure.

Brian Polkinghorn, Distinguished Professor of Conflict and Dispute Resolution and the Wilson Elkin Professor & Executive Director of Conflict Resolution at Salisbury State University, meticulously reviewed my manuscript, even though he had more than a full plate while a Fulbright Scholar in Tel Aviv. He provided detailed suggestions, questions, corrections and critiques. He graciously agreed to re-read the entire manuscript after I revised it in accord with his suggestions. His reviews were invaluable; his influence is evident in any number of places throughout the book. He was enormously supportive and encouraging, even though, quite clearly, the book and its approach, its biases and its errors are mine and do not reflect Brian's intellectual, professional and practical contributions to the field of conflict resolution studies. I could not have hoped for a better long-distance colleague.

Larry Beall, a gifted clinical psychologist who works with trauma survivors struggling with post-traumatic stress disorder, made an invaluable contribution to my work. As Larry guided me through my own labyrinth, he became so much more than mentor; he, in his way, and Gilles Deleuze in his, opened and unfolded transcendental empiricism and virtual immanence for me. In *A Thousand Plateaus*, Deleuze and Guattari provide instructions for this work

> This is how it should be done: Lodge yourself on a stratum, experiment with the opportunities it offers, find an advantageous place on it, find potential movements of deterritorialisation, possible lines of flight, experience them, produce flow conjunctions here and there, try out continuums of intensities segment by segment, have a small plot of new land at all times (p. 161).

Larry showed me a new plot of land; he has done that for so many others.

A long list of gifted graduate students also contributed to the evolution of this project. They read, listened to, questioned and argued with me about many of the ideas that have shaped *A New Philosophy of Social Conflict*. My seminars in communication, conflict and cultural studies provided me with an opportunity to work with some of the brightest and most passionate graduate students I could have imagined. Adele Bealer works at the intersection of American Studies, Communication Studies and Environmental/Ecological Criticism; she is a brilliant theorist of the graphic novel, and a cherished intellectual companion who shares with me an abiding interest in the Gregory Bateson/Gilles Deleuze articulation. Her reading of an early draft of my manuscript added precision and insight at several pivotal joints. Michael Middleton, a critical cultural studies scholar working on grass-roots intervention projects with homeless and disenfranchized populations in the United States, has been an interested supporter of my work from its inception. They are valued colleagues and our work continues to co-evolve. Adler Egan proofread and edited the manuscript on several occasions, and his intellectual touch and ear are evident in so many of the phrases he focused and clarified.

Michelle, my marriage partner in our life together for three decades, supports me with a love I have never known before, and with a generosity of spirit beyond all reason and measure. She made this long sojourn possible and paid a huge price for it; she understood my commitment to this project even when she struggled to understand it herself. In the end, she made profound sense of it all even when I had difficulty doing so. But then, Michelle knows how to do so much of what I write about. She has been 'doing' for a long time. She sat with me over the years at our kitchen table for countless breakfast, lunch, and dinner conversations, questioning and pushing me to think more clearly and concretely at times, and at other times showing me some of the implications of my arguments that I then had an opportunity to rethink. For more than two decades, Michelle served as the director of the Conflict Resolution Graduate Certificate Program at the University of Utah in the Department of Communication. She trained hundreds of mediators now working in a wide variety of capacities.

Introduction – Transcendental Empiricism

The revaluation of violent conflict, collective trauma and transitional justice

The purpose of *A New Philosophy of Social Conflict* is to introduce a social ontology of violent social conflict, collective trauma and transitional justice. The intensity and duration of contemporary violent conflict – in particular, conflict manifesting as asymmetrical violence directed at civilian populations who live its trauma and pass those reality-effects on to people-to-come – certainly keeps pace with the planet's geometrically expanding populations. The problem is not so much a matter of working more diligently to solve conflicts as problems we know how to comprehend; it is much more a matter of reconciling the trauma that conflict produces in order to transform life for future generations. So, rather than focusing on social problems in terms of ever more rational solutions, *A New Philosophy of Social Conflict* introduces a social ontological thought experiment – a Gilles Deleuze (and at times, Félix Guattari) 'schizoanalytic' experiment – that invents a qualitatively different conceptual vocabulary and pragmatic (i.e. 'schizoanalytic') topography for rethinking the genesis of social conflict.

Formulated in terms of transitional justice, *A New Philosophy of Social Conflict* can be read as an intervention in the debates between the two dominant contemporary transitional justice regimes, that is, international criminal tribunals predicated on a model of retributive justice on the one hand, and truth and reconciliation commissions predicated on a model of restorative justice on the other. Such a thought experiment requires new concepts for the transitional justice imaginary as it struggles to comprehend contemporary social conflict, widespread asymmetrical violence and collective trauma. *A New Philosophy of Social Conflict* draws on Continental affirmative philosophy and immanent ethics, cultural and critical theory, discourse and communication studies, cybernetics and chaos theory, conflict resolution studies and trauma studies. The task is to rethink the production of violent asymmetrical social conflict, the collective trauma it produces and the ways we have of eternally returning from what Deleuze calls, in *The Logic of Sense*, the primary order of the corporeal/material depths of chaos and schizophrenia.[1] His schizoanalytic method of transcendental empiricism provides the necessary philosophical thinking to do so.

Violent social conflict has been diagnosed as collective psychosis, but because psychoanalytic thought, which has been a theoretical resource for many such interpretative projects, is not capable of imagining psychosis (the focus of psychoanalysis extends only to neurosis), psychoanalytic interpretations of violent social conflict have not been able to comprehend it or the collective trauma it creates.[2] Deleuze's transcendental empiricism and his method of schizoanalytic experimentation – given its philosophical attention to sociocultural psychosis as its model for a transcendental unconscious – is better conditioned for this project.[3] Deleuze and Guattari, in *Anti-Oedipus*, oppose schizoanalysis and its methods of experimentation to psychoanalysis and its methods of interpretation. I will have more to say about schizoanalysis and experimentation in the pages to follow, but for now, it is sufficient to understand schizoanalysis as an affirmation of the unbounded lived experience of a subject, which is a conception of a transcendental unconscious that is open to an outside, and to political, social, ecological and historical contents and forces of a body's lived experience as a subject that unfolds along a determinate but not a predetermined course.[4]

Deleuze's affirmative philosophy provides concepts for reformulating the problems of violent social conflict, collective trauma and transitional justice. I intend *A New Philosophy of Social Conflict* as a schizoanalytic experiment capable of reimagining more suitably conditioned programmes of, and processes for, engaging violent social conflict, of witnessing and reconciling collective trauma and of mediating and reconfiguring transitional justice. Deleuze's ontological philosophy of a transcendental unconscious from which verbal representation and language emerge onto a plane of empirical propositional consciousness provides the creative forms of thought and necessary concepts for much of what follows. Joe Hughes, in *Deleuze and the Genesis of Representation*, argues that *Difference and Repetition*, *The Logic of Sense* and *Anti-Oedipus* can be read productively as three different perspectives on a stable structure common to the three texts, a structure that accounts for the genesis of representation: 'there was in fact a stable structure that gave sense to the concepts involved. Each book describes the way in which this structure produces itself out of a field of materiality' (Hughes 2008, p. 156). Each text affirms and describes a pre-predicative life and the emergence of a body from a pre-individual and impersonal world into a predicative individuated world, 'from lived experience as an uneasy mixture of thought and affection to a conscious thought in which we formulate with certainty propositions regarding everything from the objects in our environment to mathematical truths' (Hughes 2008, p. 22). Whereas a psychological subject is a becoming-'I' manifested in speaking, that psychological subject and the entire tertiary order of empirical propositional consciousness presupposes a pre-positional and pre-psychological production process involving a transcendental subject.

In broad outline, Hughes argues that each of the three Deleuze texts develops an account of the genesis of representation from a different perspective, and even though each is written in a different philosophical vocabulary, there are general structural correspondences across the three books, each formulating the genesis of representation from a transcendental unconscious in stages. From a primary order of unindividuated corporeality/materiality, sensation and part-objects in collision, the dynamic genesis of desiring-production submits this discontinuous matter to three passive syntheses that together disperse and project (i.e. sublimate) it, producing a transcendental field of sense. Social-production individuates and territorializes (i.e. symbolizes) three essential relations of representation (i.e. the denoted of good sense, then the signified and the manifested of common sense), which become an empirical propositional consciousness of denotation, signification and manifestation of representation. The virtuality of sense – the fourth essential relation of representation – remains virtual and transcendental (Hughes 2008, p. 157). Given this multi-stage structure of the genesis of representation, all but the last stage is a pre-predicative, impersonal ontological account of an infant body's experience – from the infant's perspective – of escaping a primary corporeal/material order of conflicting part-objects and meaningless affect – and coming to empirical consciousness.

A New Philosophy of Social Conflict advances the following theses: Under singular and determinate conditions, empirical consciousness returns to a primary order of corporeal/material timelessness, chaos, violence and interpenetration. Under those conditions, good sense (i.e. the denoted) and common sense (i.e. the manifested and the signified) conflate and collapse into transcendental sense, which is becoming ruptured and distorted by the primary order of corporeal/material, schizophrenic depths. The transcendental surface of sensual thought, that is, the transcendental unconscious, is now unmediatedly performing the meaningless violence of a primary order – often in the name of purification – producing a corporeal/material collective schizophrenia and sociocultural violence as the sense of empirical consciousness. Violent social conflict, often asymmetrical in proportion, is produced and manifests as a return from representation and propositional consciousness back into an unindividuated schizophrenic world of part-objects, a primary order of discontinuous matter in corporeal/material communication. In the course of developing these theses, given the structural correspondences Hughes explicates, I contend that Deleuze's affirmative philosophy of transcendental empiricism provides invaluable concepts and thought-forms that resonate with and make sense of a descent into genocide.[5] Deleuze's *Bergsonism* provides a method of intuition for plumbing the depths of primary order and eternally returning, through the secondary organization of transcendental thought, to good sense and common sense that found empirical consciousness and logical propositionality (Deleuze 1991, pp. 13–35). That text also makes available the outlines of immanent ethics as a replacement for the models of transcendent morality typically invoked to judge rather than diagnose the symptomatic conditions that produce violent asymmetrical social conflict and collective trauma. Processes of minor communication machines, that is, conversing, negotiating and mediating are rethought as constitutive elements of the transitional justice experiment of the gaçaça process, including its courts, in post-genocide Rwanda.

Rwandan gaçaça courts

The gaçaça process comprised six phases: (1) the imprisonment of genocide suspects; (2) the release of selected genocide suspects into eighteen *ingando* (i.e. civic education camps) around Rwanda; (3) the genocide suspects' three-month-long programme of civic education; (4) the release of genocide suspects into their home communities; (5) the genocide suspects' trials at gaçaça; and (6) their sentencing (Clark 2010, p. 31). The process unfolded across post-genocide Rwanda from 2003 to 2010 and can be thought of as an experiment in the social-production of transitional justice to address the unimaginable injustices of a territorial assemblage that had descended into genocidal madness and collective psychosis. The experiment was designed, in effect, to conform to a novel diagram (a long-time form of local dispute resolution) whose traits of expression (i.e. conversing, arguing, negotiating and mediating) would actualize processes of transitional justice in the form of gaçaça courts whose intent was to articulate desiring-bodies (genocide suspects, survivors, victims, witnesses, government authorities) to regimes of signs (discourse formations of collective assemblages of enunciation). This experiment in post-genocide transitional justice was also intended to begin the psychic and spiritual (decidedly *not* religious) work of reconciling trauma on a massive scale. Not surprisingly, the Rwandan experiment in the social-production of transitional justice and trauma reconciliation was, and continues to be, controversial in international criminal justice circles; it was decidedly at odds with Western juridical conceptions of due process. Rather than foregrounding classical liberalism's concerns with individual rights and personal liberties, gaçaça courts foregrounded matters of power and agency, which are the primary concerns of Deleuzian politics. Much of the controversy over the administration of post-genocide transitional justice in Rwanda revolved around these significant differences.

The international criminal legal community argued that Rwanda's gaçaça courts compromised classical liberalism's conception of individual rights and the due process of law. But the social-production of both transitional justice and collective reconciliation was intended as a singular solution to a double-problem: simultaneously mediating justice transitionally and reconciling trauma collectively. Gaçaça courts were created to actualize the virtual potentiality of Rwanda's traditional-modern elements and characteristics – its legal and extra-legal objectives, methods and features – productive of uneven transitional justice, partial resolution and outlines of reconciliation. Importantly, for an articulation of truth and creation at the level of the problem (as Deleuze's Bergson set it forth in the first rule of the method of intuition, a method taken up in Chapter 3), Deleuze's transcendental empiricism, unlike classical rational empiricism, holds onto and values the concrete richness of lived experience by searching for such experience in situated historical conditions.[6]

Deleuze's empiricism is *transcendental* insofar as it attempts to deduce the conditions of the emergence of conscious experience and the genesis of empirical consciousness and representation. Consider, for example (as we will in more detail in Chapter 4), the genesis of conscious immediacy that attends saying 'I'. Rather than presupposing an *a priori* causal subject who experiences, 'Deleuze finds that the "I" only ever refers to contingent effects of interactions between events, responses, memory functions, social forces, chance happenings, belief systems, economic conditions, and so on that together make up a life' (Stagoll 2005a, p. 283). It is precisely such an 'I' that is constituted in the unfolding and emergent Rwandan gaçaça transitional justice processes. The 'I' of genocide suspects, witnesses, victims and survivors is imagined as a contingent and becoming –'I', emerging from verbal representation of a transcendental field and the good sense and common sense that founds representation. The voice of such a contingent 'I' emerges from a machinic assemblage of desiring-bodies articulating to a collective assemblage of enunciation by taking mediating turns speaking as becoming-subjects, uttering performative, distributive, integrative and transformative narrative accounts that are conjunctively consumed-consummated in the communicative processes of gaçaça courts. It is from the concrete corporeal/material events of violence that experience diverges; performative, distributive, integrative and transformative gaçaça court processes constitute the virtual potential of convergence (i.e. resolution and reconciliation of making sense) at some future point. Transcendental empiricism is the basis for a Deleuzian affirmative philosophy and a positive politics of individuality and difference, one that values agency and power as desiring-production while at the same time remaining fully aware of oppressive conditionings of social-production.

I begin by placing selected Deleuzian concepts into continuous variation with the concepts of social conflict resolution and collective trauma in order to rethink the production of transitional justice and the reconciliation of collective trauma. Transitional justice concerns itself with the problems of adjudicating claims of injustice, but doing so contingently, that is, not from sedentary and established bodies of law, but rather from nomadic, mobile and transitional standards of fairness. Left unattended and unaddressed in most instances of violent social conflict are the manifold problems of reconciling individual and collective trauma with individual and collective justice. Until relatively recently, social conflict has been theorized primarily as substantive and formal disputes over material content, that is, as disputes grounded in interpersonal, familial, local, national and international political economics of resource scarcity and value distribution, whatever those resources and values are determined to be. Individual and collective trauma, on the other hand, has been figured affectively and expressively with concepts from social work, individual therapies, counselling and clinical psychology.

A New Philosophy of Social Conflict takes up the badly analysed and supposedly interdependent problems of the social-production of transitional justice and collective reconciliation. The analytical–critical error is that transitional justice and collective reconciliation are qualitatively different phenomena; they are different in kind, not degree.[7] In accord with Deleuze's reading of Bergson, which is taken up in Chapter 3, I argue that attempts to solve the problems of social injustice and collective trauma by means of the same social machine, that is, the gaçaça process, fails in some respects and succeeds in other important ways. The social-production of transitional justice and collective reconciliation are incompatible insofar as they are different kinds of social manifestations of desiring-production, not simply different quantitative degrees of social-production. The task is to rethink asymmetrically violent social conflict and collective trauma impersonally: as escaping a primary order of chaos and violence, synthesizing, sublimating and symbolizing as transcendental thought in the process. An aleatory point (i.e. incorporeal disembodied thought, a nomadic subject) occupies empty time (Aion); more on that in Chapters 1 and 3. Our work is to think a transcendental field as active and reactive forces of co-evolving life, and as territorial assemblages in conflict in ways that supersede classic liberalism's longstanding preoccupation with individual rights and liberties. Such an experiment entails thinking about territorial assemblages composed of corporeal/materiality, regimes of signs, both active and reactive forces, and circumstances productive of both individual and collective conflict resolution and trauma reconciliation.

These are transcendental–empirical concepts that resonate with and mediate the work of activists, concepts that convoke intuitive practices necessary for designing, disseminating and implementing transitional justice trajectories (such as gaçaça courts) as well as for imagining collective assemblages of enunciation capable of reconciling collective trauma. However, the yawning divide between the production of transitional justice and collective reconciliation could not be more evident than it is here, between, on the one hand, those subjects who engage conflict and trauma in the course of daily living, as activists, survivors and victims and, on the other hand, those subjects who produce conceptual systems to train practitioners and to represent and explain results to themselves and to others. More precisely, truth, peace, justice, forgiveness, healing and reconciliation are the six transitional justice concepts that are most in need of transcendental–empirical rethinking, that is, rethinking those concepts as empirically real conditions of actual experience rather than in terms of abstract conditions of all possible experience.[8]

Rwandan genocide genealogy

For 100 days during the spring and early summer months of 1994, between 7 April and 4 July, a genocidal Event ravaged Rwanda. By G. Prunier's reckoning, three-quarters of Rwanda's Tutsi population, which was 11 per cent of the total population, were slaughtered, and tens of thousands, perhaps several hundred thousand, Tutsi fled to neighbouring countries.[9] At the time, Hutu constituted nearly 84 per cent of Rwanda's total population; Twa – pygmoid hunter gatherers – constituted about 1 per cent. According to Phil Clark, what distinguishes the Rwandan genocide from other twentieth-century genocides was the use of low-technology weaponry (machetes, clubs and spears), the mass involvement of the Hutu population in the killings, the sociocultural similarities of the Hutu perpetrators and Tutsi victims and the remarkable speed and ferocious intensity of the genocide.[10]

The hierarchical differences between Hutu, Tutsi and Twa emerged relatively slowly during the historical course of pre-colonial era Rwanda. According to one influential, quasi-historical account, the Twa arrived around AD 1000, and not long thereafter, the Bantu-speaking Hutu pastoralists arrived from eastern regions. Tutsi herdsmen began settling in Rwanda during the sixteenth century, probably coming from southern Ethiopia. According to this account, as herdsmen, Tutsi were more nomadic than Hutu pastoralists and, being better armed and organized for mobile protection, constituted a 'war machine', a force internal to and co-terminus with a non-state nomadic 'haecceity', such as the early Tutsi herdsmen. The relatively sedentary Hutu were not thought of as a war machine. Even as Tutsi clans began conquering and appropriating much of central Rwanda, the Tutsi war machine was a force external to the state; their object was not to make war in the name of a state. Nonetheless, as Tutsi increasingly territorialized central Rwanda, they were ruled by a monarch-king (*mwami*) and consolidated nomadic power into sovereign power. As collective assemblages of enunciation common to Twa, Hutu and Tutsi evolved, regimes of signs increasingly delineated these machinic assemblages of bodies, and at the same time invested the *mwami* with sovereign power (*pouvoir*).[11]

In the 'Treatise on Nomadology' in *A Thousand Plateaus*, Deleuze and Guattari take up the problem of political sovereignty and state formation, which is the moment marked by the doubly articulated investment of the despotic shaman-king and the priestly jurist-priest in the figure of the *mwami* as the two-headed function of the nascent state. By the eighteenth century, the structure of the state defined itself more clearly; power and wealth had become quantified, the latter in terms of the number of subjects controlled and the former in terms of the number of cattle possessed. Indeed, the signifier 'Tutsi' came to mean someone with a large number of subjects and/or cattle; 'Hutu' signified subordination. But those identities were permeable and their boundaries porous; becoming-'Tutsi' was possible by acquiring subjects and cattle, and conversely becoming-'Hutu' was possible by losing one's subjects and/or cattle. During the eighteenth and early nineteenth century, Tutsi began capturing Hutu land and cattle, becoming-Rwandan aristocracy and establishing a quasi-feudal class system. As Tutsi morphed from nomadic herdsmen into conquering rulers, social-production became increasingly arborescent and hierarchical with the Tutsi *mwami* and his court at the top, followed by Tutsi, Hutu and Twa arranged in descending order of status and power. Hutu became extremely impoverished. And yet, despite deep-seated resentment, there was no record of Hutu–Tutsi violence during the pre-colonial era.[12]

Rwandan colonialism began with German occupation starting in 1884; they established alliances with the ruling Tutsi, whom they recognized and identified as the 'natural rulers' of Rwanda. The Germans almost immediately came to rule Rwanda indirectly through the Tutsi *mwami*, which effectively continued the trajectory of pre-colonial centralization of Tutsi state power. Rwandan colonialism continued when, in 1919, the League of Nations mandated Belgian control of Rwanda. Belgium also favoured and perpetuated Tutsi rule, but they instituted a regime of forced Hutu labour and officially appointed Tutsi as Hutu taskmasters. In 1933, the Belgians instituted the issuance of ethnic identity cards, identifying Twa, Hutu and Tutsi. This system continued until after the genocide. In fact, identity cards were used to target Tutsi during the months of genocide. Quite obviously, the signifiers 'Tutsi' and 'Hutu' were no longer permeable categories; they had become sedentary signs triggering material-semiotic processes organizing fixed ethnic identities.[13]

Following the second World War, Belgian colonial administration was placed under UN trusteeship to assist Rwanda to move towards independence. In an effort to ensure a smooth transition of power, Belgian administrative forces began to shift allegiance from Tutsi to Hutu, offering the latter more important positions and increasingly promoting them to positions of influence. Not surprisingly, these practices produced a growing sense of Hutu confidence, solidarity and power on the one hand, and Tutsi betrayal, resentment and fear on the other. In the years preceding Rwandan independence in 1962, indeed throughout the decade of the 1960s, the first cases of mass violence between Hutu and Tutsi were recorded. In 1959, the Hutu political party, Parti du Mouvement de l'Emancipation des Bahutu (PARMEHUTU), incited mass killings of Tutsi, producing a culture of fear that stifled criticism of the state and began laying the groundwork for an unquestioning obedience that would prove to be such a powerful reactive force in the 1994 genocide. By this time, the Tutsi war machine had become incorporated as the Rwandan Patriotic Front (RPF) (Clark 2010, pp. 16–19).

During the 1960s, Tutsi fled Hutu violence to Uganda, and in October 1990, the Rwandan Patriotic Front (RPF) – descendants of the Tutsi refugees – invaded Rwanda from Uganda. In August 1993, after 3 years of fighting, Hutu government forces and the RPF signed the Arusha Peace Accords, brokered by the UN. The UN Security Council established the United Nations Assistance Mission for Rwanda (UNAMIR) with a 6-month mandate to monitor a transition to power sharing between Hutu and Tutsi military and government forces. But on 21 October 1993, Melchior Ndadye, President of Burundi, was assassinated by Tutsi forces, which ignited mass killings of Burundian Hutu, thousands of whom fled from Burundi to Rwanda, triggering fear among the Hutu that Tutsi violence would follow across the border. Along with extremist media sources, a Hutu newspaper and Rwanda's largest radio station exacerbated those fears by calling for the suppression of Rwandan Tutsi. Rwandan President Juvénal Habyarimana, with French government assistance, began training Hutu youth militias – *interahamwe* – to attack Tutsi. These attacks went largely unpunished, fostering a climate of impunity and normalizing mass violence for political ends.[14]

On the night of 6 April 1994, the plane carrying President Habyarimana and Burundian President Cyprien Ntaryamira, who were returning from diplomatic talks in Tanzania, was shot down with two missiles from near the airport, killing everyone onboard. Within an hour of the crash, *interahamwe* were stopping vehicles at roadblocks across Kigali; killing began at the roadblocks and spread into neighbourhoods, moving from house to house, targeting Tutsi, Hutu moderates and suspected Hutu collaborators. Government leaders and radio personalities broadcast hate messages on national radio, inciting widespread killing during the next few weeks. An estimated 250,000 Tutsi were slaughtered during the first 2 weeks of the genocide (Clark 2010, p. 14).[15] It became evident that the violence was a product of long-term planning on the part of the Hutu regime; the strategy was to neutralize Tutsi political opposition before launching widespread attacks against the Tutsi population at large.

On 7 April, Hutu troops overran the house of Prime Minister Agathe Uwilingiyimana, who had called for the protection of Belgian UNAMIR soldiers, but those soldiers were ordered to lay down their weapons in keeping with UNAMIR's non-intervention mandate. The Belgians followed orders, the peacekeepers were taken away and killed, and the prime minister was slaughtered in her front yard. The Belgian government called for an immediate withdrawal of all of its personnel, abandoning UNAMIR, and the United States followed suit. General Roméo Dallaire, the Canadian in command of the UN peacekeepers, called for more peacekeepers to be sent to halt the killing; instead the UN forces were reduced from 2,000 to 270 (Clark 2010, p. 15).[16] As the UN debated the parameters of its intervention, the RPF captured Kigali on 4 July, and 2 weeks later, they controlled the entire country, effectively bringing a halt to the genocide.

Phil Clark synthesizes this narrative into three forces of the genocide that are crucial to understanding the emergence and configuration of gaçaça. First, ethnic identities of Hutu, Tutsi and Twa were derived from permeable socioeconomic divisions that, under Belgian rule, became fixed and sedentary. Second, Rwandan politics were highly centralized, fostering dysfunctional levels of popular obedience towards both social and political leaders. And third, the culture of impunity that enabled the 1959 and early 1960s' mass murder of Tutsi afforded permission, if not license, to those who planned and perpetrated the 1994 genocide.[17] Clark describes the legal, political and sociocultural post-genocide self-ordering forces that configured so many of the features of the assemblages articulating bodies to signs as gaçaça transitional justice processes unfolded. The genocide had largely decimated the judicial infrastructure of Rwanda; most of its judges and lawyers had been killed or fled. The Rwandan Patriotic Front (RPF) had arrested and detained tens of thousands of genocide suspects and imprisoned them throughout Rwanda. It is alleged that on 22 April 1995, RPF forces killed between 2,000 and 8,000 Hutu civilians. The effect of this violent retribution was palpable during gaçaça proceedings; genocide suspects were fearful of returning home to participate in gaçaça court processes and Hutu were uneasy about attending and speaking out (AI Rwanda, 4 April 1996).

On 8 November 1994, the UN Security Council authorized the International Criminal Tribunal Rwanda (ICTR), modelled after the International Criminal Tribunal Yugoslavia (ICTY), to prosecute the leaders of the genocide; lower-level perpetrators were to be tried in Rwandan national courts (UN Document 955 1994). But the relations between ICTR and RPF were strained, if not overtly hostile. The ICTR wanted to prosecute RPF as well as Hutu war criminals, which angered the now governing RPF. In 2003, the ICTR appointed a new chief prosecutor, which improved relations between the ICTR and the RPF, but the RPF resented the international intrusion into its state matters, and the ICTR resented the RPF for perpetuating flawed and otherwise compromised local juridical proceedings (Clark 2010, p. 21).[18] In 1996, the Rwandan government began a massive programme to overhaul their national judicial system, training judges and lawyers and establishing courts throughout Rwanda to deal with the staggering backlog of cases involving genocide suspects (AI Index, April 2000, pp. 3–6).

Not surprisingly, post-genocide Rwanda experienced enormous political as well as legal upheaval. The RPF began centralizing and monopolizing power almost immediately after coming to power. They imposed a strong executive presidency, recomposed parliament and suppressed dissent, resulting in the resignation of the Hutu prime minister as well as several key cabinet ministers. Human rights groups reported 'disappearances' of dissidents, including some RPF members. In 2001, Rwanda began a nationwide democratization process with local elections in all Rwandan communities, but observers questioned their validity, suspecting official RPF intimidation and other irregularities. At the end of 2003, the government held a constitutional referendum in preparation for the country's first presidential and parliamentary elections, but the largest Hutu opposition party was banned on the grounds that it was spreading a genocidal ideology, and Rwanda's largest human rights organization was dissolved (Clark 2010, p. 22).[19] The RPF continued to consolidate power as it controlled most of Rwanda's political system. Another complex of contesting forces comprising the Rwanda territorial assemblage was the violence throughout the Great Lakes region, involving Democratic Republic of Congo (DRC), Zaire, Uganda, Burundi, Angola and Namibia. Following the 1994 genocide, approximately 1.5 million Hutu refugees, including many of the primary agents of the genocide, fled into Zaire in advance of invading RPF forces. Members of the *interahamwe* continued to train in Zaire refugee camps and made incursions into Rwanda with the intent of killing all Rwandan Tutsi (Clark 2010, p. 23).

A second phase of intense conflict and violence took place during August 1998 and August 2003 between Hutu and Tutsi over control of DRC's mineral mining wealth, killing nearly 2 million people. For many Rwandans, the actual and virtual effects of genocide remain immanent. Given the ever-present threat of violence from the eastern sector of DRC, Rwanda remains heavily armed, and the Rwandan government threatens a second genocide to justify its continued military presence in DRC. It was in this complex legal, political and military territorial assemblage that gaçaça – founded on principles of popular ownership and open dialogue – emerged, which would seem highly unlikely had the ruling RPF been a unified body. But there were different ideological stratifications entrenched in the ruling bloc, inciting conflict stemming from a pervasive lack of coordination and consensus. So, although government forces were intent on quashing dissent, there were also government forces supporting public dialogue and participation in gaçaça (Clark 2010, p. 25).

A gaçaça 'event'

In a Rwandan village near the Burundi border, a crowd has gathered and is facing a seated panel of elders.[20] They are being told by one of the elders, its elected president, that in their midst today is a prisoner recently released from jail, who has confessed to committing crimes of genocide in 1994, the year in which between 500,000 and 1 million Tutsi and their suspected Hutu moderate and Twa sympathizers were slaughtered in a period of 3 months. The president tells those assembled that their responsibility is to listen to anyone who saw what the released prisoner did during 1994, and to listen to families of the victims recount their narratives of trauma over losing their loved ones, after which the nine judges elected by the community will decide the case. The president asks for a moment of silence in memory of those killed during the genocide, reads the procedures guiding the meeting about to unfold, and then asks the prisoner to come forward from the crowd and address those assembled. The prisoner walks forward to stand between the line of nine judges and the assembled crowd, and begins to mumble. The president tells him to speak up. With a bowed head, the prisoner explains that he has come to confess to killing his neighbour's wife during the first week of May 1994. He tells of searching for Tutsi in the village when he came upon her in the bushes, screaming at him not to kill her. He dragged her from the bushes, threw her to the ground and slashed her twice with his machete across her neck, leaving her to die. He concludes by saying he has come today to apologize for what he has done.

After a pause, the president asks the assembly if the man's testimony is true and complete. The crowd is silent; after a lengthy pause, a man in the back stands and affirms that, yes, it is true that the man killed the woman, but he adds that the man did not tell of killing the woman's son the next day with a machete and throwing his body in a latrine. Another woman stands and affirms that she saw the prisoner kill the boy. The president asks the prisoner to respond; in a louder voice he denies killing the boy, saying he was on his way to Kigali that day and was miles away. Voices in the crowd yell 'He's lying – I saw him in the village that day' and 'I saw him too, and he killed others.' The president asks for calm and invites people to speak one at a time. Some begin to cry. The judges are taking notes as those wanting to speak do so, in turn. When everyone wishing to speak has done so, the president concludes gaçaça, informing those assembled that the elected judges will decide what crimes the prisoner has committed and that in a week's time they will announce what punishment he should receive. The assembly disperses, talking among themselves; some are weeping.

Since 2002, thousands of towns and villages throughout Rwanda have been participating in this revolutionary transitional justice court system. Gaçaça, in a very different form, had been a method for villages to resolve disputes and restore harmony. A derivation of a Kinyarwanda word for 'grass' or 'lawn', gaçaça now refers to the hearings that are conducted in community public spaces in full view for all to see.[21] It was transformed and recreated to meet the exigencies of post-genocide Rwanda, a move that generated considerable controversy, the details of which are taken up in subsequent chapters. In its contemporary post-genocide configuration, respected individuals are elected by town and village populations to hear and prosecute cases of genocide that allegedly took place in those towns and villages and in the surrounding areas. Gaçaça explicitly excludes professional judges and lawyers from participating in any official capacity. In 2001, more than 250,000 gaçaça judges were elected by communities in over 11,000 jurisdictions (Clark 2010, pp. 2–3). Gaçaça's goals were to prosecute genocide suspects and to inaugurate a process of reconciling and reconstructing sociocultural integrity and solidarity.

An 'event', as Deleuze explicates it in *The Logic of Sense*, is the product of a synthesis of forces; events signify the internal dynamic of their interactions (Deleuze 1990, pp. 64–5).[22] Event is not a condition, state or happening in and of itself; it is rather potential, immanent within a confluence of forces, a confluence of virtual parts or elements, that is, inherent possibilities that actualize in the course of their becoming a particular body or state. In the above narrative of a singular gaçaça actualization, the event is not what evidently occurs (the gaçaça proceeding through its protocol steps, from assembling to dispersing). Those features are the surface effects and passing expressions of a gaçaça's actualization; they are a particular conjuncture of bodies and circumstances. Instead of saying 'a gaçaça took place' or 'a gaçaça happened', Deleuze insists on using the infinitive form, in this case, 'to gaçaça'. Using the infinitive form makes a dynamic attribution of the predicate, that is, it asserts incorporeality distinct from both the individual bodies in attendance and the protocol judges and those assembled follow.

'To gaçaça' captures the dynamic unfolding and co-evolution of the event's actualization. Said another way, gaçaça as an event can be thought of as a dynamic, open-ended, negotiating process of a predicate, that is, the infinitive form 'to gaçaça', that which is incorporeally immanent. Every moment of any singular state of genocide is thereby potentially transformative incorporeally. As Deleuze puts it, an event is an effect or change produced in the moment of the interaction of the forces that produce it. Additionally, events are completely and entirely immanent – creative and original productions. And finally, events are pure effects; they have no goal. As such, events are dynamic changes and incorporeal transformations with no beginnings and endings; they are 'becomings', a momentary productive intensity. They are moments of potentiality, moments at which new forces emerge.

Articulation and transformative practice

I have experienced first-hand, as have many of you, the disjunctions, breaks and ruptures produced by engaging conflict escalation armed only with liberal-humanist tools of social-production crafted in the forges of innumerable shops of transcendent-rationalist Enlightenment values and principles, not knowing what actually to do in the face of threateningly violent desiring-production nor how to reconcile its traumatic consequences. Tools of social-production are too often dissociated from the immanence of empirical consciousness. They are tools designed to work on supposedly transcendent foundations, but they are conjoined instead with the primary order of corporeal/material depths and collective schizophrenia and dissociated from the rationality, conventionality, linearity, synchronicity and logical propositionality of empirical consciousness. There are pressing questions yet to be addressed – how to establish relations and sustain relationships when (1) resolution and reconciliation are unlikely; (2) there are few if any striated, hierarchical structures; (3) chaos and haecceity (i.e. a collection of an indefinite number of elements that constitutes a mobile form of partial unity, for example a mob, a flock of birds, a school of fish, a colony of ants, a cloud bank – Elias Canneti, *Crowds and Power*) best characterize what is going on; (4) processes cannot be evaluated according to rational standards of governance; (5) virtual potentiality as well as actual trajectories must be produced from conditions of scarcity; (6) factions are multiplying rather than integrating; (7) coordination is still out of reach and collaboration would be treason; (8) there is little time for strategic preparation and training; and (9) evaluation seems quaintly naïve at best, dangerously imperialistic at worst. Post-genocide Rwanda is a case study manifesting all these characteristics.

These as yet unaddressed questions have to do with the forms and substances of the discursive practices of conversing, negotiating and mediating desiring-production and social-production, arcs of intensity, forces of will, forms of resistance and expressions of resolve. Reversing subject positions of dominance and submission within an oppressive structure does little other than perpetuate the oppressive structure of dominance in structure and submission to psychic brutality. Reversals of positions do not produce structural change. In fact, forcing incumbency reversals without changing structural locations and relations of subject positions usually escalates antagonism, entrenches violence, feeds lust for revenge and traumatizes collectivities. In part as a result of an implicit acknowledgement of this double-bind, cultural studies, for example, is shifting away from colonial (i.e. oppressor and oppressed) and transgression (i.e. oppression and resistance) theoretical models towards models of articulation as transformative practice (Grossberg 1996, p. 103).

The question for conflict resolution studies and collective trauma studies concerns how to transform colonial and post-colonial transgression models of oppression and resistance, and how to imagine models of immanent articulation capable of supplementing and/or replacing models of transcendent rationality.[23] It is a thorny and perplexing theoretical and practical challenge. Cultural studies inform conflict resolution studies insofar as both are concerned with creating politically and theoretically informed intellectual practices. Stuart Hall (1996) reminds us that theory is a necessary detour on the way to more important concerns. In this respect, theory is a practical as well as an intellectual resource (i.e. theory is both *praxis* and *phronesis*). It is not so much a matter of developing, advancing and defending theoretical positions in an epistemological debate, or a Gramscian war of positions, as it is a matter of imagining discursive and non-discursive practices that refer to other ways of thinking and of engaging immanent relations of power and desire. Articulating theory to practice is crucial to the interdisciplinary projects of conflict resolution studies and collective trauma studies without hopelessly compromising transitional justice, in whatever forms and substances it is capable of manifesting. It accounts for a commitment to theory and philosophy, not as an end in itself but rather as a critical intellectual method for thinking virtuality and potentiality (and imagining other diagrams of, and programmes for, practices). Together, philosophy, theory and practice guide the design and direct the deployment of immanent practices and processes.

The territory of contingent history, memory and politics requires several theoretical and practical detours that incorporate discursive practices and performative processes. I am suggesting that conflict resolution studies and collective trauma studies assume the joint task of designing experiments for transforming oppression and transgression rather than continuing to attempt resolution via transcendence. Whereas cultural studies is committed to critical and theoretical interventions into oppression and transgression, conflict escalation and resolution studies is committed to the analysis, management and resolution of conflicts that oppression and transgression produce. The same may also characterize a growing divide between peace studies and conflict resolution studies.[24] Cultural studies assumes a more radical social-democratic and neo-Marxist political agenda for cultural politics, whereas conflict resolution studies has adopted instead the liberal-humanist (i.e. Christian-democratic) political agenda of social cohesion. These two traditions standing in opposition to each other are addressing several complementary questions. In other respects, of course, these two traditions appear to be intellectually and politically incommensurable.

A necessary theoretical detour

A preoccupation with transcendence and rationality at the expense of immanence and libidinality in conflict escalation and resolution theory and practice has led me to read closely the affirmative philosophies of ontology rather than continuing to look for transcendent potential in the negative philosophies of epistemology. The issues at stake do not turn so much on the strengths and weaknesses of particular resolution and peacebuilding methods as they do on how we imagine what we are doing with them. Transcendent-rationalists envision us entering a new historical epoch, a qualitatively different historical moment, a more libertarian moment fuelled by a growing moral concern for the individual. Individuals and identity groups supposedly are becoming the favoured units of analysis and the preferred explanations for sociopolitical developments. Not coincidentally, these are the analytic and explanatory strategies of universal human rights arguments as well.

Undervaluing collective identifications and immanent ethics while at the same time foregrounding individual identities and universal human rights is a serious philosophical, theoretical and political misstep. Collective identifications do not necessarily belong to particular topographical non-discursive spaces and discursive subject positions. And insofar as collective identifications are mobile and tactically powerful, they have important theoretical and practical implications for conflict resolution studies. Any form of universalism is simply too reductive and leaves too much out of consideration. Michael Hardt and Antonio Negri (2000, 2004) suggest that we are indeed living in another historical moment, and it is a globalized world of *Empire* and *Multitude*, not an individualistic world of local democracies.

Conflict escalation studies, imagined along lines of contingent and contextually determined machinic enterprises, become forms and substances of desiring-production and social-production.[25] They become forms and substances of both the content and the expression of desiring-production and social-production; singular events are consummated and consumed, and identifications are produced as by-products. Thinking of conflict resolution studies in terms of Deleuzian social ontology and immanent ethics facilitates the theoretical and practical as well as the virtual divergences and convergences of collective identifications conversing, negotiating, mediating and dialoguing the rhizomatic relations of community (social formations), totality (the whole way of life) and aesthetics (representational practice).[26] The significance of these relations makes good and common sense, given the conflict assemblages in and through which singular agonisms and antagonisms manifest over highly valued and contested differences.

Conflict assemblages are places where contesting forces are confronting and colliding, intersecting and transforming. Conflict escalation and resolution and peacebuilding put processes into practice that engage these agonistic and antagonistic relations – libidinal forces of desiring-production and rational forces of social-production – in order to transform their lines of flight. Rather than being solely a question of resolving conflicted differences and identities, conflict resolution studies is also a matter of articulating relations among conflicting factions, and then mapping those articulations onto the spaces and into the durations of virtuality and actuality in conflict assemblages.[27] Such a move reimagines alliances, coalitions and relationships in terms of nomadic identifications rather than in terms of sedentary identities. The scope of conflict resolution studies can be broadened considerably, resulting in something approximating a philosophy, theory, art and practice of conflict articulation or, as Mayer (2004, 2009) suggests, of conflict engagement. Such a reformulation of the relations between the global and the local is pivotal in imagining things becoming-otherwise for people-to-come.[28]

1

Becoming Conflict, Chaos and Trauma

Chapter overview

For Gilles Deleuze, the primary task of philosophy involves the creation of concepts to be able to think otherwise, that is, to think (of) philosophy differently. With Felix Guattari, in *A-O*, Deleuze creates an entirely new and at times perplexing philosophical vocabulary of concepts, only some of which will be pressed into service in these chapters in order to think differently about asymmetrically violent social conflict and its collective trauma. The rationale for doing so is to use selected portions of Deleuze's extensive oeuvre to begin to make philosophical sense of a staggeringly violent twentieth-century sociocultural Event – the 1994 Rwandan genocide, to examine it with ontological and epistemological concepts capable of fathoming the enormity of its transcendental–empirical proportions. This chapter begins with a synopsis of Deleuze's philosophical account of the transcendental unconscious and the genesis of representation. Each of the subsequent sections explicates the pivotal features of Deleuze's formulation of the transcendental unconscious, putting in place the diagram onto which, in the following chapters, the Rwandan genocide can be mapped. The overarching problem is to rethink genocide as an extreme form of asymmetrical sociocultural violence, and then to rethink post-genocide efforts to make sense of, and to come to terms with, the unspeakable travesty of it all.

The genesis of representation

Integral to our rethinking of asymmetrical violent social conflict as the product of the impress of social-production on desiring-production is Deleuze's ontological account of the genesis of representation, which Joe Hughes focuses on and explicates by reading across three of Deleuze's major texts.[1] The genesis of representation is a process immanent to social-production and desiring-production; it is the process of desiring-bodies coming to, and articulating with, regimes of signs. Initially a newborn infant can be imagined as a desiring-machine, not derogatorily in the sense of mechanistic, that is, as a mechanism, but dynamically as an ego with no consciousness yet of 'having its own body'. It comes to life in a corporeal/material primary order of extreme intensities, of at times violent sensations and chaos in a domain without meaning. In effect, the life form is an ego capable of synthesizing sensations but without a sense of 'its' body.

As this synthesizing ego escapes the primary order of corporeal/material sensation by virtue of its capacity to synthesize, it comes to awareness of partial corporeal surfaces, and then of more complete surfaces before it becomes projected (i.e. sublimated and symbolized) onto a transcendental surface of nomadic thought unconstrained by the corporeality/materiality of a body. The unconscious is said to be transcendental in the sense that thought escapes or transcends the corporeal/material body in a kind of primary dissociation. From transcendental thought an infant moves through an ontological and a logical genesis, acquiring good sense and common sense, to the third order of the genesis of representation, that is, the order of empirical consciousness and propositional logic. This genesis from the primary order of corporeal/material sensation to transcendental thought and then to empirical consciousness is a progression from the primary order of sensation to a secondary organization of sense, and finally to a tertiary order of empirical consciousness and representation, all of which Deleuze refers to as the transcendental unconscious.

Primary order

With that rather linear and all too brief synopsis of Hughes' thesis in place, consider each of its stages in greater detail to begin the process of mapping the Rwandan genocide onto this ontological account of the transcendental unconscious and the genesis of representation. The genesis of representation begins in a primary order of corporeal/material depths, an order of sensations without sense, of chaotic movements and meaningless schizoid experiences, of violent clashes of part-objects and their intense interpenetrations. This is Deleuze's understanding of a newborn infant's sensations from inside its body before the infant has any conscious conception of body, much less 'its' body. I am arguing that sociocultural dynamics of a territorial assemblage can be theorized in similar terms. The relations between corporeal/material sensations and synthesizing ego are not yet mediated by body; it is an ego without a body at this primary order of life. The synthesizing ego, by virtue of its capacity to synthesize, escapes this primary order of the corporeal/material depths of intense and meaningless sensations, submitting to three passive syntheses in a dynamic genetic progression from the primary order to a secondary organization of the transcendental unconscious (Deleuze 1990, pp. 87–9, 189).

Subtending the secondary organization of the transcendental field of sense and verbal representation, and responsible for its production, is what Hughes refers to as the primary order of corporeal/material and schizophrenic mixtures of depths. At this primordial metaphysical level, unindividuated egos clash and conflict with one another, often violently, in a world of sensation and unmediated material communication. Egos are unindividuated and without (consciousness of) bodies because as of yet they are not constituted. Our egos are among the part-objects clashing at this level. Deleuze describes this schizophrenic corporeal/material depth as a realm in which one either eats or is eaten, a compelling way of describing an immediate and unmediated domain of actions and passions (Deleuze 1990, p. 240). There is no interval or gap separating action and reaction; in fact, all actions are reactions. Early in *LS*, Deleuze describes the primary order as a domain or realm in which 'a body penetrates another and coexists with it in all of its parts, like a drop of wine in the ocean, or fire in iron' (Deleuze 1990, pp. 5–6). Later he writes that bodies 'burst and cause other bodies to burst in a universal cesspool' (Deleuze 1990, p. 187).

Considering a primary order, the secondary organization and the tertiary order as stages of the genesis of representation and empirical propositional consciousness – from the corporeal/material communication of unmediated actions and passions, to a secondary organization of transcendental thought and sense, to language and propositional empirical consciousness – Deleuze posits two different kinds of geneses. Enabling progression from the corporeal/material chaos and violence of the primary order of schizophrenic depths of this universal cesspool is a process of dynamic genesis leading from the perpetual movement of unmediated actions and passions to the production of surfaces (Deleuze 1990, p. 86, pp. 119–20). This process is a dynamic genesis insofar as it begins in a corporeal/material depth where there is only movement of unindividuated bodies that penetrate one another; there is no sense of time. Among the part-objects and material fragments being buffeted about and clashing with one another in the primordial order is a partial-body, the body as an infant experiences it, which at this genetic stage is but an ego, what Deleuze and Guattari refer to as a body-without-organs (Deleuze and Guattari 1977, pp. 9–15).

For Deleuze, this ego, this body-without-organs, is the power of synthesis, that is, spontaneous imagination. It is this power of synthesis that is its means of escaping the violence and terror of the primary order where the ego in the depths of part-objects and material fragments communicates in accord with immediate actions and passions. Hughes clarifies the two mixtures of the depths of the primary order: one mixture of solid fragments that change; the other of fluid volumes capable of melting. The first mixture is comprised of solid fragments; the second is the body-without-organs, that is, the infant's psychic body. The power of synthesis consists in the capacity for melting and welding, and what melts and welds are the material part-objects of the first mixture of solid fragments that change. The body-without-organs (i.e. that which has the capability and capacity to synthesize) synthesizes the part-objects of the primary order that are in ceaseless movement and in synthesizing them surmounts and escapes the corporeal/material depths of the primary order (Deleuze and Guattari 1982, pp. 88–9, 189, 203).

Hughes reminds us that the corporeal/material depths of the primary order are without any meaning, yet importantly, Deleuze's account of the schizophrenia, collisions and violence of the primary order anticipate the tertiary order and the problems of language. In the primary order, the meanings of the world dissolve into part-objects of noise, and every word becomes physical, immediately affecting the body. Hughes reads Deleuze here as describing 'our body's participation in the physical world, and what that participation would feel like and look like from the point of view of the body itself', specifically from an infant body's point of view.[2] Given the primordial conditions of the primary world, the formal and organized tertiary order of language and empirical consciousness is not possible. In the primary order, the ego (i.e. the body-without-organs, the capacity to synthesize) is completely passive; it has no control over what affects it, consequently, all of its actions are reactions. Hughes continues, arguing that in order for language to become possible in such conditions, the ego must escape or otherwise leave the primary world of depths and corporeal/material violence and chaos. The synthesizing ego escapes this primary order to find the freedom and the time to learn to distinguish between sounds and words. In *LS*, Deleuze writes:

> To render language possible thus signifies assuring that sounds are not confused with the sonorous bodies of things, with the sound effects of bodies, or with their actions and passions. *What renders language possible is that which separates sounds from bodies and organizes them into propositions, freeing them for their expressive functions.* (Deleuze 1990, p. 187, my emphasis)

Three passive syntheses

The dynamic genesis from primary order to secondary organization of transcendental thought consists in three synthesizing stages, the first two of which – a connective synthesis and a conjunctive synthesis – are passive. The connective synthesis produces partial surfaces for ego (i.e. body-without-organs, the power of synthesis) in a process of escaping primary order and entering into secondary organization of a transcendental field of the virtual. Ego comes to partial sense of partial surfaces of becoming-body. The partial surfaces are produced because, as Hughes writes, 'the ego living in the corporeal depths is nothing more than the power of synthesis; its body is not yet constituted' (Hughes 2008, p. 31). The surface of a body is not given *a priori*; it must be produced through the power of synthesis, that is, the ego. The second passive synthesizing stage of the dynamic genesis of representation is a conjunctive synthesis that joins an ego's partial surfaces into one complete surface, that is, a sensate body. Hughes reminds us that the production of partial surfaces of the connective synthesis corresponds to the initial escape of ego, a body-without-organs, from the determinisms of the schizophrenic depths of a violent primary order (Hughes 2008, p. 31).

Deleuze defines partial surface as 'an assemblage of both the ego, which has attained a relative independence from the part-objects of depth, and of the image that the ego contemplates' (Deleuze 1990, p. 197). As such, ego is passively contemplative of its affections and simultaneously becoming-body as it attempts to make a coherent representation of the partial objects that it passively contemplates (Hughes 2008, p. 31). Deleuze contends that this duality of the subject (i.e. passive/active) enables its escape from the depths of primary order. Ego turns attention away from the *immanence* of part-objects of corporeal/material depths and towards the *images* of part-objects, as ego articulates to partial surfaces. Thought of another way, a body-without-organs becomes a partial surface, and in doing so, the *possibility* of evolving beyond the unmediated present of affect becomes immediate reality (Deleuze, *LS*, p. 197). Hughes summarizes: 'The conjunctive synthesis gathers together partial surfaces so that they form a full body. It represents a new stage of the genesis: genital sexuality' (Hughes 2008, p. 31).

The third synthesizing stage of ego's escape from primary order, which is an active stage of the dynamic genesis, fails in its efforts to create and produce a complete and coherent image from partial objects. It is the failure of the bodily synthesis to account for its affections that leads to the creation of an incorporeal transcendental surface of a new kind of synthesis (Deleuze, *LS*, pp. 206–8). This third stage consists in a disjunctive synthesis along with a new kind of sexuality, that is, oedipal sexuality. This synthesizing ego-process attempts to bring together the first and second passive syntheses into one image. The synthesizing ego (an infant) *intends* to bring two images together in a synthesis; it actually ends by affirming their incompatibility in an affirmative or inclusive (as opposed to exclusive) disjunctive synthesis. Negating their incompatibility in an exclusive disjunctive synthesis, ego returns to primary order; the implications of this turn and return will be developed in Chapter 5. The advent of the disjunctive synthesis and the problems it produces is also the beginning of a 'metaphysical' or 'cerebral' or 'transcendental' surface. The challenge for this third – the disjunctive – synthesis is for ego to recognize the compatibility of the first two passive syntheses. Deleuze argues that the synthesis fails in its attempt to make singular sense of affections and to integrate its own history into one thought, which is always already impossible. The failure of this active synthesis pushes ego even further from the primary order of depths into a transcendental field where it becomes possible to 'make sense' of its affections. Ego loses that particular mode of organization produced by the conjunctive synthesis, which had defined it as a complete corporeal, physical surface (Hughes 2008, p. 34). However, *A New Philosophy of Social Conflict* explores the ontological consequences of the failure of this disjunctive synthesis, in effect pushing ego away from a transcendental field of thought back to primary order where it corporeally and materially, rather than transcendentally, makes sense of its affections by enacting schizo violence. But if ego proceeds to secondary organization, a surface of transcendental thought is produced, thought freed from its corporeal origins, yet still in possession of those origins.

For now, and in brief, the connective synthesis (i.e. the production of production) connects flows of desire, that is, energy and matter. The disjunctive synthesis (i.e. the production of recording) operates by registering and recording the sites of disjunctions of the flows of energy and matter, leaving marks as signs, or 'hot spots' of intensity that can be recognized and recalled as such subsequently. The concept of memory is developed more fully in Chapter 3. The conjunctive synthesis (i.e. the production of consumption-consummation) lives through the experience of the composite states of energy and matter and in the process produces identity as a by-product, and invests thought in the Event (i.e. the identity of the manifested 'I'), producing a sense of subjectivity and agency after the fact of its production. Identity produced as a self-ordering and self-reflexive by-product, however, is not experienced as a by-product of conjunctive synthesis. Instead, embodied subjects experience a manifested 'I' as the agent and source of the very flows and forces of desire that produced it. This amounts to a systematic reversal and misrecognition of content and expression (Holland 1999, pp. 33–6).

Sublimation and symbolization

Sublimation refers to how the corporeal sexual surface and the rest of the complete corporeal surface are projected at the surface of transcendental thought when the disjunctive synthesis fails to synthesize the two prior syntheses, a movement by which ego (i.e. the body-without-organs) opens itself to a transcendental surface, liberating impersonal and pre-individual singularities. When the disjunctive synthesis fails, a body dissolves and its contents are projected (i.e. they sublimate) onto a transcendental surface of thought. Part-objects that had affected the body in the primary order have become incorporeal or immaterial as they disperse on transcendental thought in a nomadic distribution. This new form of synthesis – this transcendental surface of thought – is defined by its contents, having dissociated from a dissolving body. Everything that dissolved in the process of escaping primary order is recovered and projected (i.e. sublimated) onto a surface of thought, which reorganizes it and symbolizes it. For Deleuze, symbolization refers to 'the operation through which thought reinvests with its own energy all that which occurs and is projected over the surface' (Deleuze 1990, p. 219).

Thought accomplishes this operation by reinvesting in all that occurs, and is projected with its own energy over the surface of thought in the form of Event, that is, a non-actualizable virtual sense that escapes representation because it belongs to thought and can be accomplished only by thought and in thought (Hughes 2008, p. 35). The non-actualizable part of the event – the Event – is the principle of secondary organization that comes to replace the still intact ego of the physical surface (Hughes 2008, pp. 36–7). This secondary mode of organization (i.e. what Deleuze refers to as the aleatory point, nomadic subject, the disjunctive synthesis, verbal representation, anti-production, Aion – all of which will be explicated in Chapter 3) refers to a synthesis that makes all of the sublimated fragments of our (sexual) history *communicate* or 'resonate' on the surface of thought, in effect a libidinal resonance. When the disjunctive synthesis is exclusive – either/or – conflict and violence become inevitable. Libidinality can take the form of rape and subjectivation can become oppression as the world is organized exclusively in either/or binary logics. However, thinking about the disjunctive synthesis inclusively rather than exclusively, that is, as 'inclusive disjunction,' or 'communication,' or 'resonance,' or . . ., is another way to think of the transcendental field of the virtual – secondary organization. Deleuze calls this new kind of transcendental synthesis 'eternal return' or the 'ideal synthesis of difference' (Hughes 2008, pp. 36–7).

Eternal return and counter-actualization

Sublimation and symbolization are two aspects of the eternal return and its relations to two types of becoming: the becoming of corporeal depths; and the incorporeal becoming of the metaphysical transcendental surface. The first moment of the eternal return expresses the way in which our embodied history, including our sexual history, returns primary order to the surface of thought as sublimation. The phantasm is 'the site of the eternal return' (Deleuze 1990, p. 220). The eternal return 'returns to its beginning which remained external to it; but to the extent that the beginning itself was a result, the phantasm ("the site of the eternal return") also returns to that from which the beginning had resulted (the sexuality of corporeal surfaces); and finally, little by little, it returns to the absolute origin from which everything proceeds (the depths)' (Deleuze 1990, pp. 219–20).

So, the first (1) aspect of the eternal return is the recovery of our (sexual) history on the surface of thought. The return here is to genetic origins and the way in which those origins are sublimated, and returned to the metaphysical surface. The second (2) aspect of the eternal return expresses the way in which, once on the cerebral surface, all of the events communicate with, or 'return to one another' in the Event (Deleuze 1990, p. 179). The 'return' here is the way in which each sublimated element communicates with, or returns to, all the others by virtue of the aleatory point (or nomadic subject of thought) which unites them in a synthesis. The two aspects of the eternal return have the function of liberating thought from its material origins (Hughes 2008, p. 37). But this liberation of thought from its material origins may not always succeed, and when it fails, it conditions the potential for extreme violence, collectively, even in the form of genocide. The implications of the turning and returning of a qualitatively different kind of conversing is examined in detail in Chapters 4 and 5. For now, it is important to point out that counter-actualization is the way in which thought maintains its independence from immanence (i.e. the 'interval' or 'gap').

For Deleuze, thought is extremely precarious, characterized by 'persistent fragility'. There is always the possibility that the corporeal depths or primary order and the material cause of sensations and affections will make its way to the metaphysical surface and overturn it. 'Nothing is more fragile than the surface,' a surface resting on top of the volcanic line of depths. This is a vivid and compelling characterization of the Event of the Rwandan genocide, that is, the aleatory point or nomadic subject of thought (Deleuze 1994, pp. 227, 241). Sense needs a way of holding the depths of sensations and affections at bay to maintain the independence or dissociation of thought. Creating such an interval or gap is accomplished by counter-actualization, by the non-actualizable part of the event, that is, the Event, the aleatory point and so on (Deleuze 1990, pp. 82, 168). When the depths cannot be held at bay, when the metaphysical surface is overrun by unmediated actions and passions with no interval separating excitation from reaction, common sense and good sense deterritorialize or otherwise collapse, dissolving into primary order of corporeal depths, as was compellingly the case with regard to the Rwanda genocide.

Empirical propositional consciousness – the third order of the genesis of representation – is where creative, novel and immanently ethical ways of responding to events can be actualized as conversing, negotiating, mediating and dialoguing rather than regressing into primary order of schizophrenic violence. They are minor communication machines for expanding and contracting the duration of intervals separating excitation of the brain from response of the body, that is, the interval of and for immanently ethical choice. As sublimation transfers part-objects and material fragments to the surface of thought, they become incorporeal and link up with (i.e. articulate to) the aleatory point; events are no longer determined by their material causes but are swept away in a new synthesis. They are no longer the partial objects which had affected us; they refer to one another by virtue of the communication which the aleatory point brings about. *The communication of liberated affections in the transcendental synthesis defines the impersonal transcendental field of sense* (emphasis mine). Sense is the immaterial double of the material foundation of meaningless sensation; sense is produced as an effect of the body (Hughes 2008, pp. 37–8).

It is by virtue of the failure of the disjunctive synthesis, through the dissolution of the body, that corporeal/material sensation is sublimated (i.e. is projected onto) and symbolized (i.e. is ordered and organized) as sense on the surface of the transcendental field of thought. From there, Deleuze tells us, sense is submitted to two genetic stages: the static ontological genesis consisting in the denoted of good sense and a static logical genesis consisting in the signified and the manifested of common sense. Said another way, the static ontological genesis moves from transcendental thought and virtual sense to representation (including verbal representation) through the forms of good sense and common sense. It is the process through which a mind returns self-reflexively to the corporeality/materiality of what was a primary order of unindividuated, pre-predicative, pre-personal world of affections. Moving from transcendental thought and virtual sense to tertiary order of representation, however, returns the mind to the immanence of corporeality/materiality; now, however, a mind individuates corporeality/materiality, giving it determinate form, quality and temporality (Hughes 2008, p. 40). The static ontological genesis, then, refers to this organizing of transcendental sense and the production of what actually is denoted, and the static logical genesis refers to the production of what is actually signified and manifested. The static ontological and logical geneses incorporate what has been denoted, manifested and signified into an empirical propositional consciousness of tertiary order. Deleuze tells us that the ontological and the logical geneses are opposed to one another; the signifier is the product of the logical genesis, the signified the product of the ontological genesis. The primary function of the good sense of static ontological genesis is to begin to contain and enclose the singularities sublimated to the surface of transcendental thought, containing and enclosing them, symbolizing them within a 'sedentary distribution' (Hughes 2008, p. 41).

Territorial assemblages of conflict

This section rethinks violent social conflict and collective trauma as territorial assemblages consisting in organic, semiotic, material and psychic elements. *Conflict* encompasses intense agonistic and antagonistic material and affective forces coalescing as forms and substances of at least two opposing identity formations. *Massacre*, *pogrom* and *genocide* refer to widespread, well-organized, state-sponsored and officially tolerated murder of a targeted, unarmed, non-military and non-violent population(s). Such asymmetrical violence stems from a collective history of lived experience and a projected collective memory of systematic stratified injustice, blatant discrimination, enforced scarcity and aggressive oppression. Born of threat and the fear of violence, these tendencies and forces exceed the representational capacity of linguistic, but not necessarily communicative discourse. *Chaos* is thought as a return to the unindividuated, pre-predicative, pre-individual violence and collective schizophrenia of a primary order of transcendental thought. *Representation* is thought of as the plane of immanent empirical consciousness and the logical proposition, conditioned by good sense and common sense that emerges from transcendental sense, becoming denotation, manifestation and signification as constitutive elements of representation.

Trauma is the consequence of an event or sustained series of events so intensively immanent that the primary order of corporeal/material chaos and meaningless violence is reanimated this time after the genesis of representation has emerged. The reanimated terror of the primary order ruptures the fragile surface of transcendental sense in ways that distort if not dissolve the good sense of the ontologically denoted and the common sense of the logically signified and the manifested. This damage to denotation, signification and manifestation, in turn, compromises the coherence of representation and empirical consciousness. Ego is marooned on the surface of transcendental thought with no present, imprisoned in a recurring past and a limitless future by the events of the primary order of chaos and violence that have erupted into it and foreclosed ontological, logical and chronological progression. As a consequence, those primary events are not recorded as memories; rather, they are relived repeatedly for the first time in a transcendent time with no progressive present, experienced as flashbacks and transitory psychosis. The living experience of many Rwandans participating in the processes and practices of post-genocide gaçaça transitional justice courts animates these concepts.

Unlike *systems* whose component parts are connected by relations of interiority, *assemblages* are compositions of parts whose relations are exterior relative to the parts themselves. Exterior relations, unlike interior relations, are not inherent to the constitution of the components. Rather than systems of organic properties and relations of interiority, assemblages are machinic wholes whose properties emerge from the interactions of its parts whose relations are exterior. This difference in kind between system and assemblage affords an enormously productive way of thinking of all kinds of conflicting compositions of desire and arrangements of elements whose relations of exteriority become oppositional. Those relations can always be otherwise insofar as they can be modelled as machinic assemblages whose relations of exteriority produce conflict in the process of social-production, constraining, limiting and bending desiring-production. Manuel DeLanda develops Deleuze's concept of assemblage into a philosophy of society capable of modelling all sorts of compositions of social-production. As compositions of desire, assemblages are circuitries and conduits for matter and energy flows (DeLanda 2006, pp. 5–6).

DeLanda, following Deleuze, thinks of assemblages along vertical and horizontal axes. A horizontal axis defines the variable roles an assemblage's components may play, ranging from a purely content (i.e. material) role at one extreme of the axis to a purely expressive (i.e. communicative) role at the other extreme. These roles are variable and occur in mixtures. The vertical axis defines variable processes in which the components become involved, processes that either stabilize the identity of an assemblage by increasing its degree of internal homogeneity and/or the degree of sharpness of its boundaries or destabilize its identity. Stabilizing processes are referred to as processes of territorialization; destabilizing processes have deterritorializing effects. The same assemblage can have components working simultaneously to territorialize and to deterritorialize an assemblage's identity; violent social conflict is one such example of an internally contradicting territorial assemblage. The material contents of a conflict assemblage, for example, the actions and passions of *genocidaires* and of genocide survivors, and their communicative expressions during a gaçaça court process, can both territorialize and deterritorialize affect, coherence and division.

DeLanda's specification of face-to-face conversation to exemplify the two axes of social assemblages is enormously productive for conflict resolution studies and collective trauma studies; it informs pivotal issues in the transitional justice debates (conversation and mediation as minor communication machines, are explicated in detail in Chapters 4 and 5). For now, the point to be made is that for DeLanda, expressivity (at one end of the horizontal axis of assemblages – content is at the other end) cannot be reduced to language and symbols. He distinguishes between content of conversational talk on the one hand, and forms of bodily expression such as posture, dress, facial expression, tone of voice and choice of topics, on the other. Granting that expressivity is not exclusively linguistic in the narrow sense of that term, it is nevertheless communicative. In communication studies, the articulation of the content and expression of talk constitute communication, which certainly can be thought of as social expressivity, but that formulation privileges the expression side of the horizontal axis of assemblages, forcing an exclusive disjunction between content and expression when an inclusive disjunction is called for.

Face-to-face conversations constitute the lynchpins of interpersonal assemblages that structure communities and the stratified hierarchical organizations governing cities and nation-states. This issue is addressed in more detail in Chapter 4. Assemblages of bodies, communities and organizations also consist of a wide variety of other material components: from food and physical labour to simple tools and complex machines, to buildings and neighbourhoods of actual contexts and sociocultural milieus. DeLanda does grant that face-to-face conversations are territorializations inasmuch as conversations always occur in a particular place and establish defined spatial boundaries. Conversations also refer to non-spatial processes that influence the vertical axis of assemblages, that is, conversations increase the internal homogeneity of an assemblage such as the sorting and segregation practices of Rwandan identity cards marking Hutu and Tutsi. In this sense, conversations 'work' on both axes of assemblages simultaneously, if variably, and effectuate the homogeneity and stability of territorialization, and the heterogeneity and instability of deterritorialization.

Regression and descent into violence

Logical and ontological descent from empirical consciousness and the representation of logical propositions to a transcendental sense of disembodied nomadic thought events and to meaningless primary affections and sensations of the movements of part-objects in a primary order of corporeal/material violence, and interpenetrations in the depths of individual and collective schizophrenia are always already virtually real, no matter how repugnant the thought. Deleuze is clear that there are no guarantees. The secondary organization of transcendental unconscious is delicate and extremely fragile; the transcendental surface of nomadic thought is always at risk of being overwhelmed by an eruption of the corporeal/material primary order into the sense of a transcendental surface (Deleuze 1990, p. 82). For Deleuze, transcendental sense holds the meaningless violence of the primary depth at bay and maintains the independence of thought from matter; he assigns this function to counter-actualization

(Deleuze 1990, p. 168), which is the nomadic subject, the aleatory point, that is, the non-actualizable part of an event, its transcendental sense. When counter-actualization fails and transcendental thought is breached by the violence and meaninglessness of primary depth, thought is no longer independent of materiality; the virtual conditions of collective psychosis manifest as the social-production of – in the 1994 Event in Rwanda – genocidal madness, that is, a descent into a conflation of corporeality/materiality and thought/sense.[3]

Conflating transcendental thought and corporeal materiality, and mistaking that conflation for empirical consciousness, is an ethical breach of enormous proportions. Transcendental globalization and the singular localizations of axiomatic capitalism directly and indirectly generate conflict and violence, which, in turn, shape the micropractices of machinic assemblages of desiring-bodies. The collective assemblages of macrodynamic enunciations of cultural formations, social institutions and their respective capacities vary considerably. And because of the immanence of discursive and extra-discursive practices of social conflict and collective trauma, it is never necessary to go 'elsewhere' to 'find' conflict and trauma, or to 'wait' for it to 'take place' before engaging, resolving and reconciling it. Conflict and trauma are always already immanent to daily life, they actualize wherever and whenever machinic assemblages of desiring bodies articulate to collective assemblages of enunciation.[4] Actual trajectories of conflict are products of the active and reactive forces of social-production limiting and constraining desiring-production.

Conventionally, of course, social conflict, even asymmetrical violent social conflict, is thought to be an inevitable consequence of competition generated by the consumption-consummation of scarce resources. Desire, on this account, is a function of inherent lack, that is, the desire of Freudian and Lacanian psychoanalytic theory. The logic of axiomatic capitalism (i.e. of late modern consumer and finance capitalism) subtends lack and the endless competitive struggle for survival and for the transcendent physical illusion of satisfaction, both of which are always already deferred. Freud taught us that we desire what we lack and that given *a priori* scarcity and lack, satisfaction can never be other than a partial and temporary state. But transcendental thought becomes empirical consciousness only through the static ontological genesis of good sense and the logical genesis of common sense, becoming the denotation, signification and manifestation of the actualization of subjectification and subjectivation of representation. Given the rigid logic of scarcity and lack, evolving life can do nothing other than reproduce itself. Social conflict is imagined and experienced, then, in terms of proportionality; the greater the material, semiotic, psychic, organic, inorganic and geographic scarcity, the greater the value it acquires, the more intense the competition for it becomes, the more reactively it evolves, and the more traumatic its effects, hence the reciprocal complementarity of capitalism and psychoanalysis that Deleuze and Guattari address in *A-O* and *TP*. However, '[t]he Deleuzian unconscious is not the conflictual unconscious of repressed *meanings*, but is simply the body, its affections, and its drives and syntheses' (Hughes 2008, p, 46). The unconscious is 'the natural and sensuous being' and 'the objective being of desire' (Deleuze and Guattari 1977, p. 311). Desire 'is the *subject* that is missing in desire, or desire that lacks a fixed subject' (Deleuze and Guattari 1977, p. 26). In this way, Deleuze and Guattari articulate – in the doubled sense of 'connecting' and 'expressing' – Marx's concept of labour power and Freud's concept of libido; both are modes of production in general.

Desiring-production, social-production and social conflict

The concept 'desiring-production' that Deleuze and Guattari create in *A-O* refers to the universal production of life; desiring-production is a material process of matter and energy flowing through bodies that connect and break those flows, register and record the connections and disconnections and experience them as they circulate throughout networks of production referred to as 'assemblages'. Networks of connections and disconnections, as compositions of desire, are productive of life in all its registers, from geological life, to organic life, to social life. In the social register, desire has two sides; desiring-production and social-production. Social-production is the bending and constraining of the forces of desiring-production to the contours of social life. Thought of along these lines, violent social conflict is an inherent property of social life, that is, it is the inevitable result of unregulated desiring-production becoming regulated in accord with the constraints of social-production. Desiring-production and social-production co-evolve as lived and living experience.

Eugene Holland insists that social-production and desiring-production are the two sides of desire; 'social production is purely and simply desiring-production itself under determinate conditions' (Holland 2005, pp. 65–6). Capitalism historically has separated reproduction from production at large. Reproduction is left to families; production is the public business of capitalism. Desiring-production produces virtual reality-effects by investing psychic energy; social-production produces actual reality-effects by investing corporeal/material energy. The former is libidinal, that is, transcendental unconscious, a-rational, non-linear, co-evolutional and nomadic; the latter is empirically conscious, representational, propositional, logical, linear, progressive and hierarchical. Affirming life, for Deleuze, is altogether a matter of recognizing and working both sides of desire, that is, both social-production and desiring-production, both psychical and corporeal production.[5] For Deleuze, social-production sets the limits and draws the boundaries of, and for, desiring-production. Within the boundaries of territorial assemblages, conflict and trauma are self-organizing and self-ordering processes, pitting social-production against desiring-production. Desire is both positive and productive. It is a process of nomadic thought experimentation on the surface of a transcendental field, a virtual plane of consistency and impersonal thought articulating to propositional consciousness by means of negotiating the ontological genesis of good sense, and the logical genesis of common sense, articulating them with outside social forces.[6] Libidinal forces of desire, of course, are not limited to sexuality, which it *is* in psychoanalytic models of conflict. Rather, libidinal forces of desire shape and reconfigure the transcendental surface of thought. For Hughes, it is genital emergence.[7] The intensities and densities of such active and reactive forces exceed the capabilities and capacities of discourse formations (as an element of collective assemblages of enunciation) to represent them. Desire, then, is always already abundant in the sense that it cannot be depleted even as it becomes blocked and temporarily diverted.

Desire carries along and flows through material contents of machinic assemblages of bodies, partial images, sequences of codes, traces of dreams, phantasmagorical hallucinations, mythic themes, musical refrains, aphoristic phrases, as well as strands of narratives, pieces of hearsay and all manner of transcendental thought events. Machinic assemblages of desiring-bodies and part-objects, when articulated to collective assemblages of enunciation, become subjects *for* (via subjectivation) as well as subjects *of* (via subjectification) representational discourse formations and the three essential relations of propositional logic, that is, denotation, manifestation and signification. Sense, the fourth essential relation, remains on the transcendental surface of the virtual.[8] Consisting of both corporeal/material and psychical energy, desire takes variable forms ranging between the polar extremes of paranoid-fascism and schizoid-anarchy. The paranoid pole, anchoring one extreme form of desire, is the location of closed bodies with supposedly completed identities in singular configurations of social-production, resisting and bending to desiring-production resisting change. The schizoid pole, the other extreme, fragments and dissolves bodies and objects that are taken away by flows of uncoded desire/capital. Identity dissolves into flows of fragmented and partial identifications taking partial-bodies and part-objects beyond the limitations of family and private property. At their extremes, paranoid-fascism bends to and becomes schizoid-anarchism. In effect, desiring-production and social-production are the simultaneous operations of synthesizing processes that constitute universal production operating beyond the nature/human distinction (Bonta and Protevi 2004, pp. 76–8).

Conflict is always already immanent to corporeal/material chaos and violent sensations of a primary order of schizoid depths. Transcendental thought, that is, the secondary organization of the transcendental unconscious, emerges in the process of disembodied egos psychically synthesizing and thereby escaping this primary order of pre-predicative, pre-individual, pre-personal chaos, affections and schizoid sensations, dispersing (i.e. sublimating and symbolizing) as singularities onto the surface of transcendental thought, becoming thought events.[9] The consistency of the transcendental field emerges, unfolds and co-evolves, subtending, as it does, actual empirical reality and the eternal return of pure differences – never the return of the same.[10] Violent social conflicts are actualities of social-production emerging from desiring-production of transcendental thought, that is, actual and virtual realities that co-evolve. A transcendental plane's consistent surface of pure differences is a virtual production rather than actually pre-existing, and the interconnection of singular thought events upon such a plane occurs at a speed and rhythm of duration specific to the singular changes involved. A transcendental plane, however, is not a theoretical field of some pre-existing subject or self, nor does this virtual plane of secondary organization precede syntheses brought about between events.[11]

Thinking of culture, conflict and trauma as if they were independent of one another, as if they were autonomous and freestanding phenomena, violates the concept of a transcendental field as a virtual plane of consistency. Abstracting culture, conflict and trauma from a pre-individual and impersonal transcendental field in effect sentences each concept to sedentary representations, as though unfolding and co-evolving actual social-production and virtual desiring-production could somehow themselves be transcended. Yet much of contemporary liberal-humanist thinking imagines transcendental concepts as if they are already founded on an epistemological foundation of representation that fixes their sedentary nature. Violent social conflicts and collective traumas emerge genetically from a primary order of corporeal/material schizoid depths of sensation as intensive psychic drives, tendencies and forces that are indwelling and permanently pervading properties of transcendental unconscious nomadic transversality. As a multiplicity of partial objects of sensations in dispersion that pass through passive syntheses of a dynamic genesis, those sensations emerge as singularities of a secondary organization of sense, that is, the virtual, and an empty form of time (Aion). Chapter 3 takes up the two forms of time (i.e. Chronos and Aion) in the process of developing Bergson's thinking on duration and the method of intuition. For now, it is sufficient to note that the virtual intensity of sense (i.e. the transcendental field) forms into good sense and common sense by means of a static ontological and logical genesis of individuation and social-production, becoming an empirical propositional consciousness whose formal relations are denotation, signification and manifestation – the order of language and of collective assemblages of enunciation more inclusively.[12]

In short, the desiring-production of contesting and conflicting intensities, drives and active and reactive forces of bodies articulate to collective assemblages of enunciation whose representational capacities are constituted in the formal explicit relations of denotation, signification and manifestation and in the implicit relations of virtual, transcendental sense. Denotation expresses the relation of the proposition to an external and individuated state of affairs, that is, the relation of the proposition to what it refers to (Deleuze 1990, p. 12). For example, 'Tutsi and Hutu are different kinds of people' is a linguistic proposition expressing the relation of denotation. The body that begins to speak as a (psychological as opposed to a transcendental) subject of language is a manifestation of an extremist Hutu, in this instance; that is, speaking expresses the relation of manifestation. What a speaking subject says, for example, 'Kill all the Tutsi cockroaches,' expresses the relation of signification. For Deleuze, the form of a proposition is the form of empirical consciousness (Hughes 2008, p. 22). The three explicit formal relations of a proposition, however, do not exhaust the characterization capacity of the dimensions of language. In fact, Deleuze is much less interested in those three formal explicit relations of logical propositions than he is in the fourth implicit relation, the logic of sense; that is, that which always already eludes the denotation, manifestation and signification of logical propositions in every attempt to represent it. Yet sense is that which founds and subtends all denotation, manifestation and signification – an Event, and for our purposes, as I have been referencing it here, the Event of interest is the 1994 Rwandan genocide.

The psychological subject of denotation, signification and manifestation of the tertiary order of empirical propositional consciousness presupposes pre-positional and pre-subjective processes of unconscious production – a pre-individual and impersonal transcendental field. Deleuze has several names for this transcendental field of secondary organization that subtends empirical propositional consciousness; among them are 'verbal representation' and 'sense'. For Deleuze, sense is the subtending transcendental dimension of the proposition (Hughes 2008, p. 23). The transcendental field of verbal representation, the virtual and sense is the fourth, implicit relation of the proposition (remember that denotation, signification and manifestation are the three formal explicit relations of the proposition). It is sense – verbal representation – that subtends language. In effect, 'how can I know what I think, actually think propositionally, until I hear what I say?' Hughes contends that the primary function of the secondary organization of virtual sense and verbal representation is to provide a transcendental field that is independent of the actions and passions of the corporeality/materiality of machinic assemblages of bodies (Hughes 2008, p. 23).

Intra-state-sponsored violence

Countless thousands of sedentary and settled bodies are becoming-nomads in the process of engaging with and fleeing from localized, regionalized, nationalized and internationalized violent conflicts, traumatized and 'without papers' (*sans papiers*), fleeing for their individual and collective lives. Confusing conflicts that differ quantitatively in scale (symmetrical non-violent and violent conflicts) with qualitatively different kinds of conflicts (asymmetrical violent conflicts) conditions the assumption that large-scale conflicts are somehow more significant than supposedly smaller-scale conflicts. But as will be developed in greater detail in Chapter 3, the difference in numerical scale between conflicts is a difference in degree; the difference between violent and non-violent conflict is a difference in degree as well. And the difference between symmetrical and asymmetrical conflict is a difference in degree, not a difference in kind. But violent asymmetrical conflict is a difference in kind; the systematic, organized and disciplined massacre and slaughter of an imagined category of unarmed and non-combatant bodies is qualitatively different from violent social conflict involving two armed forces that produce the same death toll. In fact, such a transcendental physical illusion constitutes a dangerous conceptual error; conflicts may be symmetrical, large or small, non-violent or violent and differ in degree. However, to experience large-scale, asymmetrical violent conflict and to live trauma anywhere is to live its immanence and consistence everywhere.

Material-semiotic conditions of violently conflicting territorial assemblages and the active and reactive forces productive of virtual and actual escalations and de-escalations of conflicts actually manifest as social machines; they may or may not be war machines. Keep in mind that Deleuze prioritizes the importance of social machines over technical machines, and that social machines are assemblages linking bodies and regimes of signs (Deleuze and Guattari 1977, p. 398). Gaçaça courts are a productive hybrid of a social machine and a technical machine; daily social life consists primarily in minor communication machinic registers, whereas legal proceedings consist primarily in major (i.e. formal) communication machinic registers. Gaçaça courts are composites of both. Registers of gaçaça minor communication machines can only be used when articulated to bodies forming parts of conflict assemblages. To engage more imaginatively with the immanence of escalating and de-escalating conflict, subsequent transitional justice and trauma reconciliation, and to rethink minor communication registers as composite machines (e.g. gaçaça courts, meetings of the Umuvumu Tree Project, and CoExist Reconciliation Centers) is to deploy social experiments and innovations 'that only secondarily allow themselves to be appropriated by the state' (Deleuze and Guattari 1987, p. 3460). Thought of as war machines, that is, as counterforces to the state's stratification, centralization and hierarchicalization of law, commerce, defence and economy, gaçaça courts, the Umuvumu Tree Project and CoExist Reconciliation Centers connect to the conflicting forces and convoluted energy flows of the self-ordering and self-organizing emergence of organic and 'non-organic life'.[13]

Our empirical example of asymmetrical intra-state violent conflict throughout these chapters will continue to be the 1994 Rwandan genocide and the post-genocide experiment with the social-production of transitional justice. That experiment is a concrete instance of desiring-bodies articulating to collective assemblages of enunciation and minor communication machines in the process of incorporeally transforming transitional justice into collective reconciliation. Gaçaça courts are a novel experiment designed to transform Rwanda materially and psychically from a deterritorializing violent conflict assemblage (following the 100-day genocide in 1994, the Tutsi RPF slaughtered thousands of Hutu in retaliation) into a reterritorializing quasi-democratic assemblage that is a becoming-democracy articulated to axiomatic capitalism. This chapter and the ones to follow explicate the implications of this thesis. The properly stated experimental task is to rethink asymmetrically violent social conflict, collective trauma and transitional justice with Deleuzian thought-forms capable of creating alternate worlds of good sense, common sense and empirically conscious logical propositions regarding genocide. Transcendental-empirical questions inquire into the virtual conditions of actuality. Minor communication machines under the authority of state governmental military forces (i.e. the Rwandan Patriotic Front, RPF) addressed the virtual and actual conditions of transitional justice and traumatic collective experience in the wake of a 100-day long massacre. What might such creative and innovative self-ordering practices look and sound like? How might such practices become actualized as trajectories of empirical consciousness and practice?

Agonism (i.e. contestation and conflict manifested primarily on planes of discourse), antagonism (i.e. conflict manifested on discursive and extra-discursive planes of actions and passions) and violent antagonism (conflict manifested primarily on planes of bodily violence) are conditioned by forces of desire, imagination, will, resistance and resolve. Different forms and substances of expression (from collective assemblages of enunciation) are capable of articulating to and with different bodies, their passions and actions (from machinic assemblages of bodies). However, intuiting actual differences in kind, currently misrecognized as differences in degree, is a method of bringing critical intelligence to such errors of thought with the potential of resolving asymmetrical violent conflict and reconciling its collective trauma (which is the focus of Chapter 3). The problem to be restated and rethought intuitively entails inventing novel ways of affirming agonism and antagonism while exercising ethical choices (rather than rendering moral judgement) with respect to traumatizing asymmetrical violence that can be engaged with active forces of desire, imagination, will, resistance and resolve (which is the focus of Chapter 5) more intuitively, imaginatively and propositionally, not necessarily more rationally, and certainly not reactively.

Empirically, ontological experiments in social conflict resolution that assume the form and substance of transitional justice institutions are relatively rare and often ineffective. Tasked with determining when discursivity is possible, when extra-discursive measures are necessary and when asymmetrical violence is called for: these determinations are of pivotal importance to conflict resolution and trauma reconciliation activist work. Ironically, avoiding antagonism, that is, attempting to transcend it, actually produces dissociation and violent antagonism, whereas affirming and engaging antagonism immanently resists violence. Agonism and antagonism are immanent elements of the social-production of daily life. The agency of desiring-production does not depend on individual or collective subjectivity; desiring-production can be characterized as agency minus subjectivity. Legitimately synthesized thought is transcendental, not dissociative, but attempts at transcendence cannot escape the immanence of empirical consciousness, nor can transcendental thought leave asymmetrical antagonistic relations and violent conditions 'behind' in the immanence of an Event supposedly transcended.

Large-scale state-sponsored asymmetrical violence increasingly targets its own civilian populations, brutally killing men, women and children – hundreds of thousands each in the Rwanda–Burundi and the Serbia/Croatia genocides, and multiple millions in Nazi Germany, Cambodia and Armenia – decimating populations, transforming survivors into refugees-becoming-diasporas, destroying urban cityscapes and savaging rural landscapes for people-yet-to-come. In the process, operational forms and substances of governmental institutions and civilian communities – and often entire states – fail, triggering devolution from quasi-democratic systems of axiomatic capitalism to barbaric despotic machines, if not to primitive territorial machines. Western media represent this kind of violence as 'ethnic conflicts' and/or 'ethnic cleansing', that is, as attempts to purify polluted populations contaminated by 'less-than-human elements'.[14] But there is nothing genetically ethnic about them, which was (and is) as true of Rwanda, Burundi, Serbia, Croatia, Armenia and Nazi Germany as it was of the pogroms, massacres and genocide in the United States with respect to the organized, officially tolerated elimination of native Americans. Framing state-sponsored, widespread, organized intra-state killing as ethnic violence poses a badly stated problematic, as will be taken up in greater detail in Chapter 3. It is much more productive to think of such pogromatic violence as stemming from physically and psychically threatened identities; almost two-thirds of the current armed conflicts can be defined as identity conflicts, and some estimates count as many as 70 current political conflicts worldwide that involve groups formally organized to promote collective identity (Regehr 1996, p. 16). Such conflicts undoubtedly are complicated by unjust distribution of resources.

John-Paul Lederach points to the post-colonial chaos of deterritorializing Eastern Europe and Central Asia following the deterritorialization of the Soviet Union, and not to the transcendent idea of ethnicity, as one of several pivotal determinants of most bloody post-colonial intra-state symmetrical and asymmetrical conflicts in Eastern Europe.[15] This is true of post-colonial Africa as well. The form and substance of pogroms of territorial conflict assemblages becoming-genocide machines are expressions of *ressentiment* and bad conscience born of colonial practices that 'divide and conquer', a structure in dominance that creates sharply defined identity groups to rationalize (the reasons for) and to justify (the truths of) the uneven distribution of valued resources to these groups, thereby instantiating an illegitimate exclusive (as opposed to inclusive) disjunctive sociocultural synthesis as a consequence of the inevitable failure of colonialism's attempted conjunctive synthesis. Identities on all planes and scales of analysis are taking form in increasingly narrow gaps within the convoluted folds and striations of post-colonial political, economic, social, cultural and religious life. In the process of liberating post-colonial thought from the colonial practices of conflating differences in degree to produce reductive and illegitimate differences in kind, violence is inevitable, but perhaps not asymmetrical violence. Antagonistic symmetrical conflict involves non-violent as well as violent contestation and struggle of at least two factions, each resisting the incursions of the other, and each framing its non-violent and violent actions and passions as defence rather than aggression. Pogroms, massacres and genocides are state-sponsored, organized and sustained asymmetrical efforts to erase a group, community or population believed to be contaminating and polluting another group, community or population. Most often, the targeted population offers up little if any violent resistance.

Bodies of conflicting territorial assemblages seek security by means of *subjectification* (i.e. being drawn to particular subject positions) and by means of *identification* (i.e. identifying with what is close to experience and with familiar narrative intensities). The illegitimate conjunctive synthesis producing a failed, illegitimate, exclusive, disjunctive sociocultural synthesis of subjectification and identification produces reductive illegitimate identities as a by-product. The consummation and consumption of subjectification and identification that produces identity also produces a sense of belonging, of being a part of something with which one has some sense of affinity and/or ownership and over which one has some sense of agency and control. Ironically, all of this entails a surrendering to the seductions of a failed transcendental sense that one nevertheless claims as one's own. Desiring-bodies are caught up in this subjectification of discursive formations and overtaken by the desiring-production of identitarian ideological narratives. State authority and its institutional infrastructures are held in place in large measure by longstanding fears of the state's monopoly on violence, that is, state-sponsored wars on communism, education, poverty, drugs, terrorism and, of course, on other nation-states. But the cynicism of these supposedly just and rational wars produces intense distrust within the populace and widespread trauma, locally and globally. The material effects of deterritorialization are multiplied by the unknowns of immanence, the fear of the Other, the pain of violence and the severity and duration of individual and collective trauma. The enemy increasingly is in the same community, frequently next door, often within the same family, in the same residence, sleeping in the same bed, hence the urgency of mapping the most salient articulations of globally and locally conflicted relations and forces. In conflict assemblages of such baffling complexity, power is not simply a function of state bureaucratic apparati. It is also a function of simultaneously deterritorializing centralization, lateralizing hierarchies, dissolving trust, betraying loyalties, shifting alliances and globalizing economies compounded by excessive and inadequate local regulations and controls. The effects of these forces complicate representation. Leaders cannot as readily control and deliver constituencies, and mechanisms for representing diverse populations become difficult, if not impossible, to institutionalize as governing machines.[16]

Political histories and memories are almost always configured by violent symmetrical and asymmetrical conflict and collective trauma, inscribed on individual and collective bodies, and registered both within and across generations. Trauma-inflected histories and memories tend to be libidinally coded and overcoded in ways that produce double-binds for rationalities punctuated by traumatizing violence. In conflict assemblages, countless numbers of bodies are extremely vulnerable (Lederach 1997, pp. 15–16). Rigid polarizations and deep divisions produce blind loyalties and the valorization and vilification of leadership. State-sponsored violence, however, oppresses everyone, albeit in very different ways. The conditions of authoritarianism and totalitarianism, for example, are always already virtually real, available for contingent articulations in regimes of signs claiming the privileges of a quasi-democratic heritage while ignoring many of the most important obligations. A consequence of these chaotic colliding forces and tensions is that conventional assumptions about governance and about the mechanisms for intervening in, and responding actively rather than reactively to, globally localized violent conflicts are proving to be ineffective. Tensions between the restrictive regional charters and international institutions and the limited set of tools available for intervening in these internal conflicts often fuel violent, primitively armed asymmetrical conflicts over cultural and religious minorities, border designations, territorial boundaries and modes of governance rooted in historically entrenched politico-historical antagonisms. A Deleuzian social ontology makes transcendental sense of empirical consciousness of this collective madness.

Immanence and transcendence

The dynamic genesis that moves from a primary order of corporeal/material schizoid depths of sensation consists in an infinite present (i.e. Chronos of the depths). The secondary organization of impersonal transcendental thought and virtual sense consists in a time with no present but with an indefinite past and future (i.e. Aion). Finally, through the static ontological and logical geneses of good sense (the denoted) and common sense (the signified and the manifested), egos – now embodied – move onto a tertiary order of the denotation, signification and manifestation of logical propositions and empirical consciousness and a return to Chronos, but now a Chronos of the logical proposition rather than a Chronos of the depths. Hughes points out that for Deleuze there are two forms of Chronos; the Chronos of the primary order of schizoid corporeal/material depths and the Chronos of the logical proposition with its properties of denotable, significatory and manifestational representation of succession. The Chronos of a primary order is defined by a physical present that cannot pass beyond an infinite present; the Chronos of the tertiary order is defined by succession, which is a present that passes in representation. Hughes argues that the Chronos of the primary order is 'unindividuated and defined by the violence of bodies acting and reacting directly on one another', whereas the Chronos of the tertiary order 'is individuated, orderly, and packed into the forms of language' (Hughes 2008, p. 26).

Packing transcendental thought into the denoted signifier of good sense and into the signified and manifested of common sense transforms thought into representations of empirical consciousness capable of communicative expression of content (i.e. manifestation of 'I', denotation of 'things' and signification of 'meanings'). Sense, that is, the non-actualizable non-representable virtual Event, remains as a secondary organization of virtual sense, whereas good sense and common sense become denoted, signified and manifested communicatively as expressions of contents by speakers.

A subject, as Rosi Braidotti argues, is a genealogical entity; a structure of affectivity with a minoritarian counter-memory capable of expressing variable degrees of affectivity and experiencing a discontinuous sense of time (Braidotti 2005, p. 238). Whereas a genealogical subject is likely to appear fragmented spatially, temporally a genealogical subject emerges with a form of consistency produced from ongoing and continuing recollection. In brief, a genealogical subject experiences the co-occurrence of a past and future of Aion and a continuous present of Chronos of the depths, which Braidotti concedes may appear schizophrenic, given the expectations of a rational, self-contained subject (Braidotti 2005, p. 239). She reminds us, however, that Deleuze's philosophy of immanence posits a transformative subject living in an active present tense of 'becoming'. Chapter 3 takes up Bergson's concept of 'duration', and the extent to which Deleuze's genealogical subject is enduring will become increasingly apparent, in the sense that such enduring is a function of virtual singularities co-evolving with actual trajectories.

The impulse to dissociate from the immanence of empirical consciousness rather than submit to the constraints of good sense and common sense and the impulse to abstract autonomous bodies from the material-semiotic obligations of logical propositions are, in effect, impulses to remain on the surface of transcendental thought and to dissolve into corporeal/material part-objects of a primary order of sociopolitical violence. Regression to a primary order rather than progression to the tertiary order abstracts and reduces immanence, representing its rhizomatic complexity as aggression, as the rational, systemic objectivity of a paranoid fascist order. It then relocates objectivity and order to other places and times, and in doing so, converts immanent ethical principles and actions into transcendent moral obligations and transgressions. Instead of representing the complexities of actual reality – the better to objectify and to 'solve' them – think of symmetrical and asymmetrical agonism and antagonism stacked on top of one another as immanent desiring-production and social-production. The problem, in other words, is thinking of ways to transform the virtual sense of transcendental thought into empirically conscious trajectories of actual reality rather than dissociating and returning to primary corporeal/material schizoid depths of chaotic, meaningless violence. Its corollary problematic is thinking of ways of re-emerging from the schizoid depths of social conflict and collective trauma, this time by means of communicative synthesizing machines rather than via genetic syntheses – that is, as connective, conjunctive and disjunctive active, as opposed to passive, communicative syntheses productive of qualitatively different nomadic trajectories of imagination on the surface of transcendental thought. Thinking otherwise, inventing virtual alternatives for good sense to denote and for common sense to signify and to manifest on the tertiary order of empirical consciousness are concerns taken up in more detail in Chapter 5.

Representing social and psychical forces and conditions at the tertiary order of propositional empirical consciousness effectively separates the libidinality projected onto the secondary organization of the virtual transcendental field from the propositionality of the tertiary order. The tertiary order codes what it can of those virtual forces as denotation, signification and manifestation. Empirical consciousness of the tertiary order becomes privileged and foregrounded in the actualization of social-production, whereas secondary organization of a transcendental field of sense remains virtual and beyond representation. After articulating to collective assemblages of enunciation in the genetic progression from the virtual to the actual – from transcendental thought to empirical consciousness – active and reactive forces and dynamic syntheses in the forms and substances of social-production struggle with one another and are always already in conflict. Transcendent representations of empirical consciousness enable the dream of a static and sedentary stability; this dream of completely exhausting the virtual by means of representing it in empirical consciousness actually conditions dissociation. Empirical propositional consciousness resists regressing beyond the secondary order, and often resists even that; there is a resistance to dissociating into partial objects of the primary order of the corporeal/material schizoid depths, a resistance that extends even to losing one's body to transcendental thought. Ironically, that resistance is what conditions vulnerability to madness, that is, to regressing into a collective psychosis of perverse good sense and the common sense of pogroms, massacres and genocide.

A New Philosophy of Social Conflict addresses some of the more troubling implications of the thinking that produces rationalized and dissociated theorizations of conflict and trauma, theorizations that remain virtual and transcendent without actualizing resolution and reconciliation. The chapters that follow are arguments for empirically conscious immanence and for praxis, that is, 'the willed action by which a theory or philosophy becomes a practical social activity' (*OED*, p. 2321). Praxis is capable, as social-production, of actualizing the virtuality of a transcendental unconscious as conflict and trauma, resolution and reconciliation. Desire, conflict, trauma and discourse are always already imbricated and thoroughly caught up in the intensities and extensities of assemblages as they assume forms and substances of actual and virtual realities of unfolding daily life. The remaining chapters extend the ontological experiments of Deleuze's transcendental empiricism to think of the virtual and actual realities of the relations of desiring-production and social-production with regard to violent social conflict and collective trauma, escalation and contagion, and de-escalation, resolution and reconciliation.

One entailment of thinking of post-genocide Rwanda as a territorial assemblage is that conflict and trauma are thought of as self-ordering capacities of assemblages; both are virtual multiplicities, that is, they both consist in patterns and thresholds of intensive processes subtending actual territorial assemblages (Deleuze 1990, pp. 104–5). The reach, complexity and density of a territorial assemblage, the scale of its stagings, the intensities of its forces and the rhythms and durations of its processes are thought of as virtual singularities as well as actual trajectories. In this respect, desire and discourse are singular in their articulations of trajectories of conflict and resolution, trauma and reconciliation. Universality, here, is not the expression of a blanket uniformity or of a totalizing generality; there are no uniform substances and forms of contents and expressions of conflict and trauma. Nor are there universal forms and substances of ways and means of engaging with and resolving conflict and reconciling trauma for de-escalating violence and for deploying post-conflict transitional justice initiatives. There is no universal consensus regarding which principles of practice to rely on or which discursive and extra-discursive practices to activate. Principles and practices, to have any pragmatic traction whatsoever, must be put into discursive and extra-discursive practice in ways that articulate to corporeal/material conditions. The perpetually open question for schizoanalysis, then, is how to mediate all of this for the sake of people-to-come.

2

Rethinking Social Conflict Theory

Chapter overview

Conflicts inevitably generate traumatic effects, and those effects are often the preconditions of subsequent conflicts; yet until recently conflict and trauma have been theorized independently. Traditionally, conflict is imagined in rational, political-economic terms, whereas trauma is conceptualized in psychological, therapeutic terms. Rwanda's post-genocide experiment with the gaçaça process attempted their integration, that is, the gaçaça process was envisioned as a machine for the social-production of transitional justice *and* for trauma reconciliation, an experiment, not surprisingly, that was criticized for its legal imperfections and praised for its social inventiveness. This chapter reviews the transcendental-empirical dilemmas that the gaçaça process was designed to address and then places several Deleuzean concepts into continuous variation with concepts of conflict resolution and trauma reconciliation to rethink the transitional justice experiment of gaçaça schizoanalytically, in terms of a social ontology of immanent self-organizing processes.

Colonial and post-colonial Rwanda

Transcendental thought dissociated from the good sense and the common sense of immanent empirical consciousness and logical proposition is at risk of becoming-mad. Beginning in 1921, under a League of Nations mandate, Rwanda and Burundi, which was formerly part of German East Africa occupied by Belgian troops during-the first World War, came under Belgian rule. In 1931, Belgium inaugurated a social policy of issuing identity cards specifying, for the first time in Rwanda's and Burundi's individual and collective histories, the ethnic identity (Hutu or Tutsi) of the bearer. In 1946, Rwanda became a UN trust territory administered as a Belgian colony as a part of Congo. In 1959, the last prominent Tutsi king, Mutara Rudahigwa, died, and Hutu peasants massacred Tutsi, causing a mass exodus of hundreds of thousands of Tutsi to neighbouring Congo (then Zaïre), Uganda, Tanzania and Burundi. Then, in 1960, the Belgian Congo became independent, Rwanda became a republic, and in 1962, Rwandan independence was declared.

In concert with the colonizing missionary work of the French Catholic Church during Rwanda's colonial history, these conditions, in many important respects, set in place the sociocultural and political-economic conditions and forces responsible for Rwanda's violent post-colonial history. The colonial powers marked Rwandans as Hutu and Tutsi, as qualitatively different kinds of humans, and then magnified those fabricated differences by favouring the Tutsi, largely because the Germans, Belgians and Catholics found the Tutsi more European in appearance, giving them preferential treatment administratively, professionally, educationally, religiously and socially. To inscribe the preferential status difference more markedly, Belgium required all Rwandans to carry identity cards denoting their bearers as either Hutu or Tutsi, thereby transforming a previously inclusive disjunctive sociocultural synthesis into an exclusive one. Rwandans speak Kinyarwanda (the native language of farmers) and Kinyarwandan French, and belong to French Catholic and Pentecostal faith communities. Colonial policies created different kinds of Rwandan humans in large measure by institutionalizing racist ethnicity policies and practices at the level of state governance, effectively dissociating the ontological genesis of good sense and the logical genesis of common sense from immanent empirical consciousness, and set in motion a regression to the chaos of a primary order of corporeal/material schizoid depths of collective madness, meaningless violence and interpenetrations of partial-bodies and part-objects.

This is not to argue that virtual agonism inevitably actualizes as empirical antagonism, nor is it to argue that virtual antagonism inevitably leads to actual violence, terrorism, warfare, massacre and genocide. It is to argue from the Event of the 1994 Rwandan genocide that transcendental sense, when dissociated from the good sense and common sense of empirical consciousness, risks dissolution and regression to a pre-predicative, pre-individual primary order of schizoid violence. History provides countless examples of the horrific consequences of dissociating from empirical consciousness in a delusional dream that antagonism can restore agonism, that war can produce peace, that violence can produce non-violence and that truth reconciles trauma.

In January of 2002, The Third Republic was proclaimed in Rwanda, effectively consolidating the regime of President Paul Kagame. Since 1988, Kagame had been the commander and strongman of the Rwandan Patriotic Front (RPF), an assemblage of Tutsi militias operating out of Tanzania, Uganda, Burundi and Zaïre, after having fled Rwanda as long ago as 1963 (1 year after Rwandan independence was proclaimed) to escape the Rwandan army massacres of Tutsi. In 1990, this assemblage of Tutsi militias returned to Rwanda as the newly constituted RPF war machine and was victorious against Hutu extremist militias, called *interahamwe* (initially more a war machine than the 'pure' killing machine it became) that had been organized by the clan of Juvénal Habyarimana, the Hutu President of Rwanda elected in 1978. In 1993, a peace agreement was signed in Arusha, Tanzania (the Arusha Accords), between Habyarimana's Hutu regime and Kagame's Tutsi RPF forces. On 6 April 1994, President Habyarimana was assassinated when his plane was shot down by a missile on its landing approach to the Kigali Airport. The identity of those responsible for the assassination has never been determined. The next morning, 7 April 1994, Hutu extremist assassinations began, targeting political personnel, predominantly Hutu moderates, that had not fully supported Habyarimana's dictatorship.

For the next 100 days – from 6 April 1994 until 4 July 1994 – approximately 1 million Tutsi were slaughtered by extremist Hutu *interahamwe* and Hutu farmers, peasants and villagers, organized and led by the *interahamwe*. On 4 July 1994, Kigali centre fell to the RPF, a new government with a Hutu president was installed, General Paul Kagame became the minister of defence and the RPF war machine was incorporated into the regular Rwandan army. On 3 October of that year, the United Nations Security Council endorsed a report that described the Rwandan massacres as 'genocide'. In November 1996, Congolese rebel forces opposing President Mobutu Sese Seko's regime, supported by Rwandan forces, invaded eastern Congo, killing tens of thousands of Hutu refugees, and as many as 2 million Hutu refugees fled Congo and returned to Rwanda. Most *interahamwe* were killed by the RPF offensive or returned to Rwanda, surrendering to the Rwandan government, but many still live in Congo as mercenaries on the border in the Kivu region. In May of 1997, the Rwandan army invaded Congo, overthrowing Mobutu and bringing Laurent-Désiré Kabila to power. In August 2002, the gaçaça courts began operating in Nyamata.[1] Since assuming the Rwandan presidency in January 2002, the controversial post-genocide regime of Paul Kagame continues in its efforts to synthesize the ideology of democracy and axiomatic capitalism, resulting in impressive if controversial socioeconomic growth.[2]

The forms and substances of Rwanda's becoming-democracy are theorized here as a social-production experiment in managing agonistic and antagonistic post-genocide conflicts in ways designed to discourage escalation into violent antagonism and a return to genocide. The problems Paul Kagame's quasi-democratic governmental machines are busy processing – not unlike the problems bedevilling all contemporary quasi-democratic political regimes articulated to axiomatic capitalism – have to do with inventing ways of responding to the agonistic and antagonistic conflicts generated by attempts to synthesize ideological elements of democracy and axiomatic elements of capitalism. Democratic ideologies address the paradoxical relations and singular conditions perpetually generated by the dialectical tensions of individual liberty on the one hand and collective equality on the other. As territorial assemblages, democratic forms and substances of governance vary considerably; their common element, however, is their wholesale investment in axiomatic capitalism, which we will take up shortly. As for democratic ideology, it consists in collective assemblages of enunciation and the discourse formations that manage the inherently unstable political, military, legal, economic and religious relations between conservative traditions and forces (with their core values of individual liberty and individual human rights) and liberal traditions and forces (with their core values of collective equality and popular sovereignty).[3] They are, more precisely, three-fold experiments that attempt to synthesize qualitative differences in kind between matter and spirit, material content and affective expression, that is, between ideological substance and axiomatic form.

The first of these three synthesizing experiments entails connecting flows of desiring-production (e.g. connecting liberal and conservative desiring-production). The second synthesis is conjunctive (e.g. conjoining democratic ideology and axiomatic capitalism). The third synthesis is disjunctive (e.g. the conjunctive synthesis always fails, so the best that can be managed is an inclusive disjunction); such disjunctive syntheses also fail sooner or later. When disjunctive syntheses fail, they leave marks as signs signifying other signifiers of absence that practices and processes of governance are intended to address, normalize and legitimize inclusively. The failed disjunctive syntheses create differences as divisions, exclusive disjunctions, which constitute the preconditions of and for social conflict. The three passive syntheses are unpacked in greater detail in Chapter 4.[4] For the moment, connecting, disjoining and conjoining are thought of as different ways of synthesizing desiring-production and social-production. Flows of desiring-production connect and conjoin, and the sites of their failed disjunctive syntheses record themselves during these moments of anti-production, marking actual sites of conflict and their virtual sense.

Conflicts produced by unsuccessful attempts to synthesize the dialectic of neoliberal liberty and post-colonial equality are most apparent in the contrasts between Locke-inspired models of democracy (in which individual human rights, individual property rights and the rule of law are foregrounded) and Rousseau-inspired models of democracy (in which political liberties are distributed equally and the rights of public life are collectively shared).[5] Individual liberty consists in a collection of largely negative rights (i.e. freedom *from* the interventions of government in the affairs of individuals), whereas collective equality consists in positive rights (i.e. freedom *to* access opportunities equally). As structures of governance designed to manage unstable conflicts between neoliberal traditions and forces (with their core values of individual liberty and individual human rights), and democratic traditions and forces (with their core values of collective equality and popular sovereignty), they are perpetually in process and at risk. Given a becoming-democratic regime that reflexively comprehends its constitutive paradox as an irreconcilable schism dividing and setting the forces of liberty and equality forever against one another – as is the case for Rwanda's controversial regime – the radical indeterminacy of globalization makes any guarantee of liberty and equality impossible. It is by means of registering and recording (i.e. recognizing, acknowledging and engaging) the corporeal/material contents of conflicts between and within bodies (e.g. Hutu *interahamwe* and Tutsi *inkotanyi*), and by expressing the contents of those conflicts in and through (i.e. by means of) collective assemblages of enunciation, that temporary arrangements, accords and settlements are cobbled together.[6]

Agonistics, antagonistics and the democratic paradox

John Rawls claims, in *A Theory of Justice*, that 'justice is the first virtue of social institutions; truth is the first virtue of systems of thought' (Rawls 1972, p. 3). Most efforts to reconcile justice and truth are unsuccessful inasmuch as the difference between them is a difference in kind (i.e. quality), not simply a difference in degree (i.e. quantity). Consider that regimes of signs are conflict's forms of expression and that personal relationships, social relations, organizational hierarchies, institutional logics and cultural formations are the substances of conflict's expression. The actions and passions of bodies constitute the substances and forms of the content of conflict. When desiring-production overflows the constraints of social-production, contestatory, competitive, polemical and ideological relations become the preconditions for violent conflict. Protagonists and antagonists become mortal enemies; hostility, rage and violence fuelled by *ressentiment* and bad conscience consume the polemics of contestation and consummate a will to purge, annihilate and purify. Violent social conflict threatens the integrity and coherence of good sense and common sense that subtend immanent empirical consciousness and the logic of propositions (Hughes 2008, pp. 3–47). Deleuze underscores the precarious fragility of the transcendental surface of sense, which Hughes refers to as the secondary organization of the genesis of representation. This secondary organization of transcendental thought, when ruptured, dissolves into a primary order of meaningless corporeal/material depths, collisions and violent interpenetrations of bodies-without-organs, that is, collective schizophrenia and the bloodlust of genocide.

As the asymmetry of state-sponsored violence becomes increasingly evident to external witnesses, so do efforts to make sense of multiple events as an Event (i.e. as 'a' massacre or 'a' genocide), reframing *ressentiment* and bad conscience in moral rather than ethical terms. Reductively rational-transcendent moral accounts of good and evil effectively masquerade as good sense and common sense subtending logical propositions and empirical consciousness. Shame, humiliation and rage are the forms and substances of the contents of *ressentiment* and bad conscience expressed violently, now framed as narratives of victims, villains and heroes. The practical and conceptual problems facing conflict resolution studies, trauma studies and transitional justice studies alike have to do with creating qualitatively different narratives, different ways of thinking, conversing, negotiating and mediating the collective trauma of asymmetrical violent conflict. Intuiting quantitative and qualitative differences within and between agonistic and antagonistic conflicts is of critical importance in the ongoing work of challenging the transcendental physical illusions that threaten to overwhelm individual and collective life.

As the transcendental surface of thought becomes overwhelmed by the actions and passions of a primary order, the libidinality of desiring-production radically reconfigures good sense (i.e. that which is denoted) and common sense (i.e. that which is manifested and signified), reproducing a primary order of corporeal/material sensations without sense and without meaning on the tertiary order of empirical consciousness and logical propositions. This is not to claim that it is preferable or even possible to refrain from violence. It is to argue that actions and passions of violent social conflict emerge from the schizoid depths of a primary order of chaos and sensation that are capable of becoming denoted, manifested and signified. One of the several problems to be formulated in thought and expressed in language involves rethinking *ressentiment* and bad conscience, that is, shame, hatred, rage, lust, vengeance and violence. Addressing those problems requires a much different philosophy of polemics, hegemony and verbal representation. And *that* is why it is crucial to reimagine discourse formations as collective assemblages of enunciation, caught up in regimes of signs in ways that make good sense and common sense of genocide in the actual reality of its production.

Chantal Mouffe's critique of contemporary democratic theory and practice is that political theories and political parties, in the process of inventing ways to resolve conflicts deliberatively, are moving towards a pallid consensual centrist politics, a third-way politics lacking in combative vitality necessary for political validity (Mouffe 2000, pp. 108–40).

She stands against these consensual strategies, arguing against the position that consensus rests on the assumption that the axial paradoxes of democracy (i.e. liberty/equality) can and should be reconciled. Her conclusion, however, is not a necessary entailment of third-way deliberative political strategies, even though her critical concerns are on the mark for the most part.[7] For contemporary conflict resolution studies, the dream of resolution and reconciliation is that communication is capable of transcending conflict and ultimately synthesizing democratic ideology and axiomatic capitalism. It is the same dream that animates the forces of a conventional centrist politics of liberty and equality, of which Mouffe is so critical.[8] If a politics of consensus were the only virtually real resolution imaginable, Mouffe's critique would be compelling; after all, the dream of resolving and reconciling conflicts into relatively stable centrist resolutions remains a dream on a transcendental plane of disembodied thought, but a dream to the extent that it is dissociated from immanent empirical consciousness and experienced as an exclusive disjunction – 'either/or'. But failed disjunctive syntheses also produce inclusive disjunctions – 'either/or . . . or . . . or. . .' – series of independent virtual realities that Rancière theorizes as alternative frames of dissensus.

Instead of antagonistic relations between enemies who share no symbolic space as a necessary expression of the democratic paradox as she conceives it, Mouffe argues for the possibility of agonistic relations between adversaries who share a symbolic space, but who struggle to organize that space (i.e. the territorial assemblage) differently. Agonistic, and even antagonistic adversarial relations, are admittedly paradoxical; they are, in effect, relations of adversarial friends. For Mouffe, the concept of an agonistic/antagonistic adversary is the key to imagining a modern pluralist quasi-democratic politics capable of intervening into the relatively unchallenged neoliberal hegemony of dialogic democracy, a democracy of emotions, a deliberative democracy and a consensual politics of the centre (Mouffe 2000, pp. 80–107). Her default position is that no amount of conversing, debating, negotiating and mediating will ever persuade a ruling class to share, much less relinquish power, an argument which is difficult to refute.

Conflicting discourses contend and struggle with one another in the process of expressing actual realities, that is, the truths and traumas of desiring-bodies. Two or more competing discourses battle one another with claims to foundational truths and universal rights, which rather quickly morph into claims of moral superiority and ontological exclusivity. Libidinality and morality actualize as embodied affective intensities and disembodied transcendent representations. Desiring-production becomes rationalized, and what cannot be represented propositionally, that is, the virtual of transcendental thought, is repressed, denied, projected, or otherwise avoided. But discursive formations are always already incapable of representing virtuality, libidinality, desiring-production and the variable intensities of affect. Poetic discourse is capable of signifying some of those properties, but not of representing them in any complete and explicit sense. Even at that, however, discursive formations of collective assemblages of enunciation are capable only of partial and approximate denotation, manifestation and signification of the sense of the virtual.

Limitless desiring-production, the virtuality of transcendental thought and the immanence of empirical consciousness constitute a promise that virtual and actual conditions can always be otherwise. The pragmatic task of engaging conflict and escalating or de-escalating it is to engage the potentiality of that promise without dissociating from the immanence of empirical consciousness. Both immanent libidinal intensities and transcendent rationalities are enfolded in conflict. Rather than thinking of transcendent, epistemological and individualist concepts, think instead of immanent, ontological and collectivist concepts. 'Positions', 'interests', 'needs', 'risks', 'costs' and 'benefits' are libidinal concepts that become rationalized in the process of conversing, negotiating and mediating. 'Affectivities', 'intensities', 'imaginations', 'wills', 'resistances' and 'resolutions' are libidinal forces of desiring-production that correspond only approximately to rational interests, logical propositions, needs, risks, costs and benefits. The immanence of conflict is a production of the ways in which affect moves, the ways by which affects articulate to bodies and the forms and substances of the expressions of those articulations. The questions political science, international relations, comparative government, cultural studies, communication studies and media studies could address productively can be asked of individual, interpersonal, familial, local, organizational and institutional relations as well (DeLanda 2006, pp. 47–140). Local relations, after all, are where global relations work themselves out in the quotidian social-production of daily life. A persistent problem for conflict-resolving efforts is that their discourses are not capable of accounting for the ways in which local relations are implicated in global dynamics; they do not adequately account for the ways by which concrete historical, political, spiritual and economic resource determinations are made globally and locally. Thinking immanently is a transcendental-empirical method of inquiry that opens up potential for living.[9]

Mouffe fears that the exclusive practices and processes of neoliberal third-way political dynamics threaten the relative stability of the already precarious balance of liberty/equality. Conflating paradoxical tensions and political identities into faux stabilities and forced compliances in the interest of maintaining an exclusive transcendent consensus, and thereby avoiding antagonism, is not an inevitable consequence of articulating deliberative democracy to axiomatic capitalism. Thinking of tensions between liberty and equality as multiplicities of partial and transitory identifications rather than as closed oppositional identities makes sense of intuiting virtual conditions for creating newly emergent and unconventional relations to address singular conditions.[10] Such ontological thought experimentation virtually allows for and actually conditions libidinal identifications (i.e. affective intensities, spiritual passions, rights convictions, collective traumas and truth-effects) for articulation to logically propositional representations of empirical consciousness. This is not to argue that democratic regimes routinely manage conflicts agonistically. In point of historical fact, their management strategies and tactics are violently antagonistic. 'The United States is arguably one of the most aggressively violent, late-modern, Neoliberal, market-driven, first-world democracies on the planet' (Hopkins 2000).[11] In many respects, violent antagonisms are indications of the unwillingness (not the inability) of quasi-democratic regimes to recognize, acknowledge and respect agonistic differences both in degree and in kind, conjoining and disjoining the forces of liberty and equality.

Axiomatic capitalism

Of course, contemporary political life is considerably more chaotic and complex than any single dialectic could express. Enormously wealthy special interest groups and PACs of nameless and faceless power brokers, that is, conspicuous manifestations of the increasingly uneven distribution of capital wealth, are transforming democratic pluralities into neoliberal dichotomies and thereby rearticulating binary oppositions as common sense. Third-way political strategies for managing precarious sociocultural and nationalist political identities are ideological attempts to produce agonistic, deliberative forms and substances of democratic practice while axiomatically redistributing concentrated capital. However, '[t]he specificity of modern democracy lies in the recognition and the legitimation of conflict and the refusal to suppress it through the imposition of an authoritarian order' (Mouffe 2000, p. 113). The syntheses of connection, conjunction and disjunction are instrumental in the production and anti-production of conflict. To suppress conflict is to delegitimize the three passive syntheses that condition the emergence of empirical consciousness from the virtuality of transcendental thought. Mouffe's preference is clear; the democratic system she imagines is a system of civil political adversaries, a politics that does not become permanently dominated either by the forces of democracy or by the forces of liberty. Social conflict is to be worked: worked with, worked on and worked through. Democracy cannot be suppressed or denied in the name of stability and peace without simultaneously distorting and delegitimizing it as a territorial assemblage.

Insofar as quasi-democratic regimes differ constitutionally, economically, politically, culturally and historically, each is a singularity and each is expressed in and through characteristic formations of discourse.[12] Discursive formations of collective assemblages of enunciation articulate to machinic assemblages of desiring-bodies conversingly in the process of arguing, debating, negotiating and mediating immanent, empirically conscious life. Such technical communicative machines cannot resolve conflicts in any ultimate sense, but then nothing can. Nevertheless, there is no 'ultimate sense' in large part because sense as itself cannot be represented; sense remains virtual and transcendental. There are conversations capable of creating virtual and actual conditions for thinking otherwise and for producing reality-effects that condition workable agreements, settlements, alliances and coalitions. Attempts to put in place ultimate (i.e. final) solutions actually create resistances and exacerbate tensions, creating fissures – some of which break open – exposing paradoxes and problematics previously camouflaged ideologically, and often producing violence and genocide.

We are concerned with articulations of machinic assemblages of desiring-bodies (i.e. crowds, bands, packs, pairs and individuals of all kinds) and collective assemblages of enunciation (e.g., series and sequences of indirect and free-indirect discourse).[13] The pragmatic significance of the relations of conversational turn-taking and the eternal return of difference extends beyond the discursive to the extra-discursive forms and substances of expression. Manual DeLanda differentiates forms of expressions (regimes of signs) from substances of expression (social institutions effectuating incorporeal transformations) and he considers paralinguistic features of the expression of language (e.g. facial expressions and vocal intonations) to be substances rather than forms of expression (DeLanda 2006, p. 53). For the purposes of rethinking conflict resolution and trauma reconciliation, however, paralinguistic features of face-to-face conversation (DeLanda's paradigmatic example of the expression of collective assemblages of enunciation) are integral to and indistinguishable from regimes of signs as expressions of content. Regimes of signs and collective assemblages of enunciation remain virtually transcendental until singular expressions articulate to singular bodies, producing singular utterances in turns of actual conversation. Articulations of contents and expressions may be discursive or extra-discursive, but all such articulations are communicative, the significance of which will be taken up in greater detail in Chapter 4.

Now we turn to the concept of 'axiomatic capitalism'. For Deleuze and Guattari, the concept 'axiomatic' is pivotal for an understanding of capitalism and science. An axiom, in the philosophy of science and in mathematics, is an unprovable statement that defines relations between unprovable elements of a formal system, that is, an 'axiomatic', consisting in axioms that define the meanings of primitive elements, plus a set of inference rules for deriving additional statements or 'theorems' from said axioms or other theorems. Axiomatic systems demonstrate four properties: (1) independence, that is, no element can be defined by another element and no axiom can be derived from another axiom; (2) consistency, that is, axioms cannot contradict one another; (3) completeness, that is, truths of the axiomatized theory must be axioms or derivable as theorems; and (4) effectiveness, that is, the inference rules allow theorems to be enumerated. But as Mark Bonta and John Protevi point out, any robust axiomatic system cannot be complete and consistent; any powerful axiomatic contains at least one undecidable statement, that is, one that cannot be either proved or disproved in the system (Bonta and Protevi 2004, pp. 55–6).

In *TP*, Deleuze and Guattari explicate their political-economic, their epistemological and their ontological theorizing in terms of axiomatics; our concern here is with their treatment of political economy in terms of axiomatics. In the 'Axiomatics and the presentday situation' section in *TP*, Deleuze and Guattari address three aspects of the political economy of axiomatic capitalism – operationality, flexibility and multiple realizability (Deleuze and Guattari 1987, pp. 460–73). To claim that axiomatic capitalism is operational is to claim that it is a formal system in the sense that it has no bearing on truth and truth value. Rather, the truth of an operationally formal system is realized in a model; that is, the meaning of axioms is denoted, manifested and signified only when a model is realized. Deleuze and Guattari differentiate an 'axiomatic' from a 'code' by characterizing the political economies of three qualitatively different kinds of societies – 'savage', 'barbarian' and 'capitalist'. For 'savage' (coding) tribes, there is inherent meaning in the relation of bodily signs (e.g. tattoos, scars and so forth) to a territory; for 'barbarian' (overcoding) empires, meaning inheres in the relation of signifiers to other signifiers in a signifying chain (e.g. mythic systems, legal systems and so forth); and for 'Capitalist' (axiomatics), there is no meaning; an axiomatic is an operational mode of the regulation of flows that are realized in variable domains (Deleuze and Guattari 1987, p. 454). Bonta and Protevi summarize Deleuze and Guattari's discussion of the political economy of axiomatic capitalism as follows:

> In other words, capitalism, by means of credit markets, labor regulations, and other 'modes of realization' overseen by the State, brings together decoded flows of wealth (now known as 'capital') and human energy (now known as 'labor power')

> as 'purely functional elements' (that is, elements with no predetermined use, no marked qualities, but open to any use, as opposed to societies in which productive elements are coded or overcoded and hence limited in their range of potential uses). (Bonta and Protevi 2004, p. 57)

To claim that axiomatic capitalism is flexible means that it can add axioms indefinitely, always already capable of expanding its limits and creating new subject positions and formations. There are no inherent limits to capitalism; anything that can be reified and commoditized can be circulated. The opposite is true of capitalism as well; axiomatic capitalism can subtract axioms. In addition to being operational (i.e. formal and without meaning) and flexible (i.e. indefinitely additive and subtractive), capitalism is multiply realizable; the functions of capital and labour can be realized in extremely varied and variable territorial assemblages. Bonta and Protevi provide several instructive examples: English capitalism operating in Jamaican colony slave plantations and in Manchester factories, even though England had outlawed slavery; neoliberal capitalism in the USA and the UK; social-democratic capitalism in Tito's Yugoslavia; totalitarian capitalism in Stalinist USSR; and the anarcho-capitalism of Pinochet's Chile (Bonta and Protevi 2004, p. 58). Importantly for making sense of post-genocide Rwanda, Deleuze and Guattari contend that there is only one world capitalism market that accounts for all of these and other models of capitalist axiomatics – East and West, North and South. Bonta and Protevi conclude their synopsis of the political economy of capitalist axiomatics by pointing out that the post-Thatcher and Reagan neoliberal models were attempts to restrict the multiple realizability of capitalism by subtracting and limiting its axioms, creating a single model rather than enabling multiple models (Bonta and Protevi 2004, p. 58).

As productive as Deleuze and Guattari's explication of axiomatic capitalism is for political economy, their epistemological and ontological formulations of axiomatics are equally valuable for our study of post-genocide Rwandan transitional justice. They contrast 'axiomatics' and 'problematics;' the former is a formalization of basic principles (e.g. Royal Science), whereas the latter is the emergence of a new field of study prior to its axiomatization (e.g. a new field of science). With respect to conflict resolution studies, genocide studies, trauma studies and transitional justice studies, formalization of axioms has yet to be realized, hence the importance of 'problematics'. With respect to their discussion of axiomatics and ontology, Deleuze and Guattari oppose 'axiomatics' to 'diagrammatics'. Bonta and Protevi draw the contrast as follows: An axiomatic is a program of a stratum; a diagrammatic is an abstract machine for an assemblage (Bonta and Protevi 2004, p. 58). In our rethinking of Rwanda, an example of a diagram of an abstract machine would be the transcendental Idea of transitional justice; an example of a program of an axiomatic would be gaçaça courts. Subsequent chapters develop the political, economic, ontological and epistemological problematics that conflict resolution, transitional justice and trauma reconciliation face prior to their potential axiomatization. The most pressing questions to be formulated at this juncture, however, have to do with how best to theorize rationality and libidinality in terms of post-colonial Rwandan genocide and post-genocide transitional justice. Thinking of conflict resolution, transitional justice and trauma reconciliation without theorizing the libidinal genesis of representation from a primary order of corporeal/material depths to a secondary organization of nomadic/transcendental thought may produce comfortable rational models, but there is ample historical evidence that demonstrates the inability of those models to plumb the depths and to fathom the latitudinal and longitudinal parameters, both spatial and durational, of the problematic correctly stated.

Rationality and libidinality

Given the objective of rethinking social conflict theory in the philosophical tradition of transcendental empiricism, that is, as the search for the genetic conditions of social conflict, it is necessary to keep in mind that transcendental empiricism is the investigation of immanence, not transcendence. Transcendence is the condition of being above, over, beyond and removed relative to something else; immanence assumes that the criteria necessary for understanding something are immanent to and emerge from the empirical conditions of the thing itself. The criteria for understanding the emergence of social conflict, then, are immanent to its emergence, not above, over, beyond or removed from it, and not imposed from a transcendent (i.e. dissociated) outside. Importantly for our study of social conflict, Deleuze's transcendental empiricism is an attempt to rediscover a transcendental unconscious, what Hughes referred to earlier as the pre-predicative, pre-personal, pre-individual primary order of corporeal/material depths of chaos and schizoid violence. The transcendental unconscious is defined by the immanence of its criteria; the method of searching for those criteria Deleuze and Guattari refer to as 'schizoanalysis'.[14] The genesis of social conflict is the transcendental unconscious of the primary order rupturing the secondary organization, and to understand social conflict, particularly in the asymmetrically violent form of genocide, requires an understanding made possible by explicating its immanent criteria.

The task at hand is to invent intuitive schizoanalytic methods capable of imagining and engaging identity-based, rights-based and values-based conflicts that border on and pass over into violent asymmetrical antagonism. Such conflicts are notoriously resistant to rational models of transcendence, that is, models predicated on what Deleuze calls in *DR* the 'transcendental physical illusion' (Deleuze 1994, p. 278). This phrase refers to the doctrine that the order and organization of material systems is created and produced by an external agent that projects a pre-existing form on passive and otherwise chaotic matter (Bonta and Protevi 2004, p. 97). Existing work on such rationally driven methods of interest-based conflict resolution has pushed itself to its theoretical and practical limits. In realizing some of its lofty objectives of technically resolving conflict and crafting temporary settlements, rational models have fallen far short of proving themselves capable of comprehending the corporeal/material depths of the violence and chaos of a transcendental unconscious from which organized and systematic genocide emerges. The sublimation and symbolization of libidinality onto the surface of transcendental thought and virtual sense as it escapes the primary order of corporeal/material sensation and the realization of the libidinality of violence as the 'good sense' and 'common sense' of empirical consciousness have yet to be theorized.

An important ontological blind spot of rational models is that without adequate theorization of libidinality, models of conflict engagement and resolution, as well as models of trauma production and reconciliation, are not capable of making ethical sense of the widespread violence of war, terrorism, genocide and the systematic and organized rape of girls and women by male mercenaries and soldiers, a practice overlooked as a weapon of war, and only recently considered a war crime. Desiring productivities, ethnic identities, human rights and affective intensities, when given over to violent antagonism, inevitably overwhelm rationality. To naively imagine social conflict, even violent conflict, as simply a consequence of failed rationality, is to remain ethically culpable. Think instead of libidinally fuelled, pluralistically affective and massively violent forms and substances of contents and expressions of madness, and of collective psychoses that schizoanalysis is designed to fathom. The correctly stated problematic far exceeds the limits of rationality and the neuroses for which psychoanalytic methods were designed.

Nevertheless, much of the conventional macro-political work in conflict resolution and peacebuilding actually lives the dream of transcendence, a dream of transcendental physical illusion, a dream of 'as soon as . . .', that is, 'as soon as the rhizomatic complexities and the violence of immanent conflict can be overcome (i.e. transcended), then . . .' the transcendent dream of rational resolution and reconciliation can be realized. But quasi-democratic regimes of axiomatic capitalism consist in immanent practices and processes of conversing, debating, negotiating and mediating agonistic differences, antagonistic conflicts, corporeal/material and psychic/spiritual violence generated by the clashes of at least two contesting and incommensurable logics. Expressions of 'as soon as . . .' are delusional attempts to transcend the immanence of the content of conflict in the process of overcoding it and then representing those overcodings as 'planning', 'vision' and 'leadership', resulting in dissociation rather than resolution. The expression of delusion does not transcend the content of conflict.

Living in the three dynamic syntheses (i.e. connective, conjunctive and disjunctive) between sensations of the corporeal/material primary order and the virtual sense of secondary organization is to live in empty time (Aion). The virtual time of transcendental thought (i.e. Aion) is a time that perpetually divides into the immediate past and the imminent future. The point at which that division into past and present occurs, Deleuze refers to as the nomadic subject of transcendental thought. Left unanswered, however, are questions of *how* the primary order overwhelms the fragile surface of transcendental thought such that good sense of the denoted and common sense of the signified and the manifested are overtaken by reactive genocidal forces of anti-production. Ethically as important as the conditioning of *ressentiment* and bad conscience are questions of *how* life-affirming active forces of desiring-production can engage and defeat life-destroying reactive genocidal forces of anti-production.

Dissociative transcendence takes place when the sense, the denoted, the manifested and the signified (i.e. the four elements of representation) all remain at the secondary organization of the transcendental unconscious. Virtual sense becomes overwhelmed by reactive forces that arrest the ontological genesis of good sense and common sense subtending empirical consciousness and the logical proposition, that is, the tertiary order. The consequence is that virtual sense remains undifferentiated from the denoted, the manifested and the signified; they remain conflated, incomplete and badly formed. The static ontological genesis of good sense and common sense do not emerge as empirical consciousness of the logical proposition, remaining instead as the sense, the denoted, the signified and the manifested of the transcendental unconscious. Divisions and distinctions are badly analysed and solutions to the wrong questions are arrived at and performed as the tertiary order of empirical consciousness, but the genesis of representation returns to a primary order of chaos, corporeal/material meaninglessness and violence.

One consequence of reimagining the relations between the libidinality of desiring-production and the rationality of social-production as immanent to empirical consciousness rather than as a dissociated rational-transcendent consciousness is that discourse comes to be understood as immanent multiplicity, that is, (1) as a cause of conflict, (2) as the represented content of conflict, (3) as a medium of expression for conflict, (4) as a resource to conflict and (5) as a surface on which to engage with and work through conflict. As the medium through which conflict is materially, semiotically and psychically manifested, discursive practices are variably nomadic and sedentary; they traverse the surface of immanence as they configure it. Sedentary discursive practices stake out claims; nomadic practices modify those claims, expanding and contracting them and moving them spatially and temporally. And immanent surfaces constitute the conditions of potentiality for conflicts born of sedentary claims that at times are invested with enormous value, and at other times are contested to violence and death. In effect, discursive practices transform both the content (i.e. the substance and form of machinic assemblages of bodies) and the expression (i.e. the substance and form of collective assemblages of enunciation) of reality-effects, realizing actuality from virtuality.

Discursive practices, as articulations of content and expression, denote, manifest and signify subjects and objects in space and time, that is, 'us' and 'them', 'here' and 'there', 'now' and 'then'; yet these distinctions cannot be reduced to simple binary oppositions. 'Them' is not the opposite of 'us'; it is rather the signifier of what renders impossible any universal 'us'. The agonistics of undecidability politicizes the differences between 'us' and 'them', and revalues 'them' as either 'adversaries' or 'enemies'.[15] Individual and collective identifications can be transformed from the agonistic relations of adversarial identifications into the antagonistic relations of enemy identities. Reversing the direction of this revaluing process, that is, transforming antagonistic identities of 'enemies' into agonistic identifications of 'adversaries', entails deterritorializing sedentary claims of representation and reterritorializing resolution and reconciliation. By the same token, however, such reversals constitute a risk of dissolving virtual sense into corporeal/material 'communication' of a primary order of meaningless violence. In other words, divisions are enormously productive to the extent that the us/them division is not the only form that the adversary/enemy dialectic can assume; the method of intuition holds open the potential for correctly distinguishing between differences in kind from differences in degree, as will be developed in Chapter 3. Deleuze's ontological thought is not metaphorical at all! This is a fitting diagram of the Rwandan genocide; to appreciate the fit, it is necessary to look more closely at the ways in which conflict resolution and trauma reconciliation are currently thought of.

Generic theory, rational conflict and universal needs

Conflict resolution studies is a domain of theory and practice comprised of academic, professional, practitioner, activist, therapeutic, military, diplomatic, economic and legal discourses that, at this juncture of development as an academic discipline, have produced relatively sedentary, formulaic, normative ways of thinking and modelling social conflict. There are no transcendental–empirical diagrams that account for the genesis of social conflict and collective trauma; most of the research on conflict and trauma has been generated by the social and behavioural sciences, and the knowledge claims they have established are decidedly objective, rational, quantitative and normative. The irony is that there is relatively little that is either objective or rational about social conflict and collective trauma. When rational-objective models of conflict and trauma are mapped onto the libidinal-psychic dynamics of desiring-production, the results are approximate at best. Offering up quantitative answers and solutions to qualitative questions and problems rationalizes and objectifies desiring-production, making rational sense of chaotic, violent and schizoid (i.e. psychotic) corporeal/material conditions of empirical consciousness, as was true of colonial and post-colonial events in Rwanda.

Rational-objective accounts of social-production can never adequately trace, much less map, the forces of libidinally driven desiring-production. Yet rational-objective models of social conflict are founded on the assumption that quantitative research methods are not only superior to qualitative methods, but that quantitative methods are also capable of identifying significant qualitative differences.[16] Rational-objective knowledge is assumed to be generically if not universally valid. Social science research reifies active and reactive social and psychic forces by positioning itself outside of conflict, rendering it a transcendent object of study rather than immanent to empirical cosciousness.[17] Consequently, the rational, objective, transcendent epistemological commitments of the social and behavioural sciences have determined much of the research agenda, shaped much of the pedagogy and prescribed many of the practices for conflict resolution studies and trauma reconciliation studies. Much of this research was, and continues to be, produced at the intersections of sociology, social psychology, cultural anthropology, communication, social work, political science, international relations, regional studies, policy studies and political economics, accounting for most of the theory and practice of bargaining, negotiating, mediating and dialogue.

For many of these discourses, however, conflict resolution remains an unstable and troubled concept, implying as it does that (1) conflict is a bounded if not discrete problem or set of problems within a more or less rational quasi-democratic system of governance; (2) problems cause the system to malfunction in one or more ways; and (3) this malfunctioning can be fixed by solving and re-solving the problems. In many instances, what counts as problematic are the effects of contingent conditions for which solutions crafted earlier are no longer effective. In many instances, however, problems are badly stated, which dooms the solutions crafted for them from the outset. The libidinality of desiring-production is always already in tension with, and usually overwhelms the rationality of, the social-production of solutions designed for problems created as attempts to transcend desiring-production by means of rationalizing and objectifying libidinality. Ironically enough, once a problem is solved, it is assumed to be dissolved, that is, changed if not fixed, at least temporarily; solving, dissolving, resolving and transcending become conflated. Resolving refers to 'settling' conflict by means of transcending the complexities immanent to it, complexities that supposedly animate its instability and mobility. Resolution assumes that the conditions of 'as soon as . . .' will have been satisfied once transcendence has been achieved. But desiring-production cannot be foreclosed or held in place for long by the constraints of representational practices before escaping along lines of flight on planes of immanence where qualitative affects and quantitative intensities intersect and are denoted, manifested and signified once again.

Rational-objective models assume that conflict results when human needs are not met; those needs are assumed to be generic and universal, valid across cultural, social, historical, economic and religious differences. Given that the cause of so much conflict is assumed to be the result of unfulfilled needs and unevenly distributed resources, the ontological foundation on which those knowledge claims rest is worth considering here in some detail. Whether explicit or implicit, the founding assumption is that human needs manifest in the absence of generic resources. Social conflict is generated in the process of acquiring resources needed to transform scarcity into sufficiency, even if not abundance. What follows is a synopsis of nine commonly invoked human needs for which transcendent universal rationality and objectivity are claimed (Burton 1990, pp. 25–48). The first of these is a universal need for consistency, a patterned predictability of response to conditions in a probabilistic world; consistency in such a world is a precondition for the possibility of sociality. And at the same time, there is also a contravening universal human need for intensity, without which there would be no life, no movement, no thought, no change and no *élan vital*. A third universal need is for security in an insecure and at times overstimulating world. Security is needed, so goes the argument, to reduce the anxieties and dangers of living in a probabilistic world of no guarantees and no absolute determinations. In tension with a generic need for security is a universal need for recognition, which is a precondition for identity and stability in an unstable world. To be recognized as an identity, however, requires standing out from, even if not against, contingent instability and thereby becoming vulnerable in and to such a world.

These and other dilemmas inevitably create agonistic and antagonistic conditions productive of conflict and the need for distributive justice – transitional or not. To solve the problems of scarce resources and to resolve the disputes and conflicts that scarcity produces, resources need to be distributed more equitably among bodies of an unjust and inequitable world; and accomplishing more equitable distributions of resources depends on at least the appearance of rationality. John Burton distinguishes between a 'need for rationality' and a 'need to appear rational'. The implication is that the appearance of rationality suffices insofar as rationality's actualization may not be possible, or if it is possible, producing it may not be worth the effort. The appearance of rationality suffices. Rationality and logical propositions comprised of denotation, manifestation and signification are closely aligned. There is a universal need for meaning and for meaningful responses, and meaning is located in consistent patterns of response to the intensities of a probabilistic world in which recognition is a product of achievement, hence distributive justice must at least take on the appearance of rationality.

It comes as no surprise, then, that a need for a sense of control is posited as a generic universal human need as well. As we saw above with regard to the 'appearance' of rationality, control itself is not a universal human need; its facsimile will suffice. A 'sense' of control will make do, often in the same fashion as does the 'appearance' of rationality. Finally, rational-objective models posit psychological self-defence as an ultimate universal need. It is important to note here that it is not identity itself that is being defended, but rather a role, supposedly one of several that may be taken up, to properly suit co-evolving circumstances. For Burton, role defence consists in (1) resistance (primarily resistance by means of modern technology) to authorities without legitimate power; (2) individual and collective struggles for identity; (3) personal security, recognition and acknowledgement; and (4) distributive justice capable of eliding the illegitimate power of non-responsive institutions and authorities. Absence of control, lack of direction, systemic failure and impending change give rise to a fear of change and the escalating costs that change often extracts. And fear produces hostile bodies for those whose immediate needs, interests and positions are threatened; resistance is how those who are threatened defend their roles in reactive response.

As do most other objective-rationalists, Burton claims generic universal status for his theory of conflict resolution and *pro*vention; in doing so, he posits the nine universal human needs discussed above and the motivations to which they give rise. By 'generic theory', Burton not only means that it is a universal theory in its range of applicability at all levels of sociality – from intrapersonal to transnational – but also that it is capable of transcending differences of race, ethnicity, class, gender, sexual orientation and physical, emotional and intellectual ability. He claims to have laid the foundation for a paradigm shift by steering clear of Rousseau-inspired models of social systems while at the same time keeping a safe distance from Hobbes-inspired models. The former are models of social systems held together by shared values; the latter are systems whose coherence depends on the coercive exercise of power by the few over the many. Given their suspicions of models resting on human values rather than on human needs, negotiating the worlds of Rousseau and of Hobbes is important for Burton and other objective-rationalist thinkers. That suspicion motivates critiques of Rousseau and avoids models that supplant the primacy of the individual with social systems and their institutions, structures, norms and laws. And that is what feeds the suspicion of Hobbes. Interests derive from values, which, in turn, are derivatives of *a priori* universal human needs.

The prominent critique of generic claims of universality is a formal one; Burton's ninth universal human need (i.e. the need for role defence) undercuts the universality of the preceding eight. If the eight supposedly universal human needs are indeed universal (i.e. each of equal significance and each equally necessary), why is it necessary to guarantee the universality of what *is*? Why do we need a meta-need? Burton's theoretical strategy, in effect, opens the door to the possibility of adding as many purportedly universal human needs as is necessary to maintain the theory's integrity, as long as the final universal human need is the one that guarantees once more the universality of each of its already guaranteed universal human needs. The existence of the need for role defence suggests that the list of needs preceding it may not be universal and could be of indefinite length – a multiplicity.[18] Whether there are any human needs that are universal in their reach and relevance, however, is not really the point. The question that remains on point is how positing the existence of universal human needs provides any pragmatic purchase on how to work more productively with corporeal and material conjunctures that condition needs and with the conflicts those variable conditions create. To the extent that both scarce and abundant resources are inherent features of corporeal/material worlds, how does theorizing conflict in terms of scarcity and universal human needs assist in resolving conflicts that scarcity guarantees? How do they facilitate working relationships and political alliances that resonate with immanent circumstances? And how do they assist in designing practices better suited to negotiate their perpetual fluctuations?

One of the difficulties of constructing theories and practices for resolving conflicts predicated on assumptions of universal, unevenly distributed scarcity is that scarcity, once posited, can never produce abundance. By definition, there can never be enough resources in a world of scarcity; the problems always already resemble zero-sum games. On the other hand, beginning with assumptions of abundance holds out the material and virtual potentiality of transforming particular forms and substances of abundance (e.g. the abundance of poverty) into other forms and substances of abundance (e.g. the abundance of micro banking and micro lending) rather than holding out the always present and ever receding dream of transcending the contents and expressions of scarcity (i.e. poverty, in this example). The impulse to posit universality and to privilege consistency invests intensity, security, recognition, justice, rationality, meaning, control and defence with desiring-production that can make sense as a dream of transcending conflict and its libidinal economy of desiring-production. Rational-objective thought transcends incommensurable differences and intractable conflicts by fleeing the libidinal intensities and complexities of the transcendental unconscious, immanent desiring-production and self-reflexive empirical consciousness.

'As soon as. . .' all factions do what they *should*, *must*, *have to*, *need to*, *ought to* do (i.e. accept the obligations [to us] of [*our*] morality), 'then' the fear of desire and irrationality (or, more aptly, a-rationality and accountability for mortality) can be avoided. 'As soon as' rational, civil, respectful and tolerant discourses and actions are restored to their proper places (the places of [*our*] best interests), 'then' we can return to civility and normalcy (i.e. to the ways [*we*] already know how to be in the [*our*] world. 'As soon as' something happens that is not happening now (i.e. the conflicting factions come to their [*our*] senses and realize their [*our*] best interests), 'then' conflict will be resolved. Dangerously overlooked in such transcendent-rationalist thinking, however, is the immanence of the performatively challenging, singularly complex, enormously time consuming and imaginatively intuitive work that 'as soon as . . .' thinking manages to ignore in the process of sidestepping it. That formula holds promise only as long as one pins one's ontological hopes on transcendence. The actual work of engaging and resolving conflict is a function of the immanence of meticulous discursive and non-discursive labour practices (i.e. the labour of articulating bodies to/with discourses) in singular circumstances of the moment.

Schizoanalysis and collective assemblages of enunciation

Conflict resolution and trauma reconciliation, thought of schizoanalytically rather than universally and rationally, articulate abstract machines and their diagrammatic functions to machinic assemblages of desiring-bodies. The formal distinctions are between expression and content of communication. Given utterances as statements of propositions, and given their tracings of mixed semiotics and maps of the regimes of signs, the pertinent question becomes: What diagrams and abstract machines emerge via schizoanalysis, and what new collective assemblages of enunciation take shape along these lines? Deleuze and Guattari insist that these questions apply as much to destratification, that is, to the production of smooth spaces and planes of consistency (i.e. transitional justice and trauma reconciliation), as they do to the stratifications of institutions (i.e. post-genocide state-reformation). They conclude: 'there are no syntactically, semantically, or logically definable propositions that transcend or loom above statements' (Deleuze and Guattari 1987, p. 148). Regimes of signs are not founded on language; rather it is the other way about – language is founded on regimes of signs, abstract machines, diagrammatic functions and machinic assemblages extending beyond semiology, linguistics or logic. It is with this sense that Deleuze and Guattari conclude their plateau 'On Several Regimes of Signs', asserting that pragmatics (i.e. schizoanalysis) is the fundamental element upon which logic, syntax and semantics depend (Deleuze and Guattari 1987, p. 148).

Language, as a medium of representation, is inherently problematic. Deleuze and Guattari teach us that language is not oriented to representation, but to experimentation, that is, to practical effect. The elementary unit of language, he insists, is the order-word which functions by triggering incorporeal transformations. Order-words, which we take up in Chapter 5, are elements of regimes of signs that intervene in bodies and direct content in an assemblage. Language, they insist, is the medium for transmitting order-words; transmitting content is at best only a secondary function of language. As interventions in contents, order-words do not so much represent contents as anticipate them, move them backwards and forwards, slow them down and speed them up, separate and combine them and delimit them in different ways (Deleuze and Guattari 1987, p. 86). In effect, order-words are capable of expanding and contracting the interval between excitation and execution, between cerebral registration of percepts and the affective response of the bodily core – between body and spirit. And as we shall come to appreciate, potential resolution of social conflict and reconciliation of collective trauma take place durationally in the immanence of intervals. This is why intuiting attunement to durations, which is the focus of Chapter 3, is so vitally important to both conflict resolution and trauma reconciliation.

Variable registers of minor communication machines articulate bodies to regimes of signs in different ways and produce incorporeal transformations pivotal to both transitional justice and collective reconciliation. Language, by itself and by definition, is problematic insofar as it is pressed into service as a tool for representation; communication, on the other hand, thought of as the legitimate synthesis of language pressed into service as a tool for expression and incorporeal transformation, is instrumental in producing transitional justice, collective reconciliation and any other incorporeal transformations its order-words are capable of triggering. To the extent that representational language is conflated with experimental communication, that is, to the extent that language is pressed into service primarily for purposes of representation rather than experimentation, language creates the confusion of badly formulated problems and conflicted relations of confusing composites (our experience) resulting in illegitimate (i.e. conflictual) interior relations.

Consider as an example the utterance of a proposition addressed to the other, 'You murdered my husband.' Deleuze tells us that the one who begins to speak is the one who manifests; what one talks about is the denotatum; what one says are the significations (Deleuze and Guattari 1977, p. 181). Such utterances are propositions insofar as they are syntactically, semantically and pragmatically defined verbal aggregates. An initial task of schizoanalysis (i.e. pragmatics) is to determine to which statement an articulation of content and expression corresponds; a proposition's statement can be embedded in entirely different utterances, that is, articulations of content and expression. The first determination to be made has to do with which regime of signs an utterance takes up as a proposition. This was the problem at issue in the trial of the Rwandan print and radio journalists eventually found guilty of inciting genocide. In which regime of signs was it possible to 'call for' extermination of Tutsi? 'What nonlinguistic elements or variables of enunciation give it consistency' (Deleuze and Guattari 1987, p. 117)? How is the membrane of the virtual sustained in/with consistency?

For Deleuze, schizoanalysis involves working with and across presignifying, countersignifying, centre of signifiance and postsignifying elements of propositions. A *presignifying* 'You murdered my husband' might be uttered at a gathering of villagers awaiting the arrival of elected elders to convene gaçaça. Contrast that to a *countersignifying* 'You murdered my husband' that works distributively as a polemical utterance during gaçaça having to do with genocide, massacre and relations of pogrom. There is a 'You murdered my husband' that is addressed to *the center of signifiance* of gaçaça 'using interpretation to make a whole series of signifieds that correspond to the signifying chain' (Deleuze and Guattari 1987, p. 117). And there is a *postsignifying* 'You murdered my husband' that constitutes 'a proceeding beginning from a point of subjectification, then another, and yet another' (Deleuze and Guattari 1987, p. 117). 'You murdered my husband' in a countersignifying paranoid regime of signifiance is not the same utterance as 'You murdered my husband' uttered in a postsignifying regime of subjectification.

A second determination looks into the possibilities not only of which proposition an utterance corresponds to at a given 'moment', but also looks into the possibilities of mixtures, translations and transformations of utterances into propositions of other regimes of signs. The incorporeal transformation of forgiving or of retraumatizing are examples of such mixtures, translations of utterances and of corresponding incorporeal transformations. Which utterances remain irreducible, nomadically schizophrenic and dissociated from empirical consciousness, and which flow representationally producing the passing time of Chronos of the proposition? A third determination is to create novel, unprecedented utterances of a singular proposition, 'even if the result were a patois of sensual delight, physical and semiotic systems in shreds, asubjective affects, signs without signifiance where syntax, semantics, and logic are in collapse'

(Deleuze and Guattari 1987, p. 118). Schizoanalysis traces mixed semiotics across experiential mixtures, mapping regimes of signs, diagramming abstract machines, and programming for performative, distributive, integrative and transformative pragmatics.

We also make use of what Deleuze and Guattari refer to as Pragmatics, or schizoanalysis, consisting in *generative pragmatics*, *transformational pragmatics*, *diagrammatic pragmatics* and *machinic pragmatics* (Deleuze and Guattari 1987, pp. 145–6). *Generative pragmatics* studies the internal structure of an actual regime of signs, which creates a tracing from the act of representing. The generative pragmatics of gaçaça processes consists in the study of the discourse of gaçaça court proceedings, that is, procedural instructions, questions asked by the elected elders who presided in each sector of each town, accounts of those accused of crimes of genocide, narratives of assembled villagers participating in the process, verdicts handed down by the nine presiding elders and conversations among all those attending prior to the formal start of the gaçaça proceedings and following the close of the official process. *Transformational pragmatics* studies the ways regimes of signs can and do change from one regime to another, and the ways they mix and create new regimes, which create a map in the form of the multidimensional circuitry of rhizomatic assemblages that can be plugged into at any point and are connectable via their lines of flight to other assemblages. The transformational pragmatics of gaçaça transitional justice consists in the study of the ways by which the endogenous, complex synthesized concept of gaçaça was created as a dynamic experiment designed specifically to meet the singular conditions of post-genocide Rwanda in both its state-run and extra-official (i.e. more nomadic) forms.

Diagrammatic pragmatics studies the relation of unformed matter and non-formal functions in the abstract machine subtending regimes of signs – relations that create a diagram, that is, relations that return to immanence, to the plane of consistency. A diagram outlines the traits of expression of an abstract machine. The abstract machine subtending the gaçaça transitional justice experiment in Rwanda is reciprocity in the form of conversing, or more appropriately, 'itinerate conversing' (Deleuze and Guattari 1987, pp. 372–4). Designed to deterritorialize vast residues of post-genocide, post-conflict trauma, gaçaça courts were also created to reterritorialize Rwanda's sociocultural order and stability. As social machines, gaçaça courts constituted 'holey spaces' that were hoped to function as third spaces for tunnelling into and through pre-genocide striated spaces, stratified systems and post-genocide collective trauma (Deleuze and Guattari 1987, pp. 414–5). Following the cacophony and horror of genocide and against the striations of post-genocide conditions, the abstract machine of reciprocity created a diagram of conversing, negotiating, mediating and dialoguing for reterritorializing Rwanda to stratifications of relative steady-state stability.

Machinic pragmatics studies the effectuation of the abstract machine of a regime of signs in machinic assemblages of bodies, which creates a program. A gaçaça program was thought of as a coordinated sociocultural process across all of Rwanda for an indefinite duration. Such a program specifically designs court forms and substances of contents and expressions to fit singular conditions of individual villages, individual genocide suspects (of which there were approximately 120,000) and individual victims and survivors (of which there were hundreds of thousands) (Clark 2010, p. 51).

A program of gaçaça courts effectuating the abstract machine of a regime of signs in this territorial assemblage is pivotal to a nuanced implementation of the pragmatic forces of transitional justice processes. Consider that during the 1994 Rwandan genocide, an estimated 500,000 women were raped and at least 250,000 women were impregnated due to rape during those 100 days. Very little research has been done on these women victims. Towards the end of 2007, separate gaçaça courts were created for women victims of sexual crimes of genocide, particularly rape. Prior to 2007, when women victims of genocidal rape appeared before gaçaça courts and asked to tell their stories, they were not represented by lawyers, they were subjected to obscene cross examination and they received no witness protection. Only a handful of these women came forward to testify at gaçaça. Currently, research is being conducted to map the experience of those women genocidal rape victims who have come forward since 2007 to testify in women's gaçaça courts (Morris 2011).

Schizoanalysis and machinic assemblages of trauma

Schizoanalysis thinks of the body as an assemblage of 'organs', all parts of the body, not just sex organs and sensory organs. The concept 'body-without-organs' problematizes rather than presupposes the organ-ization of the body, which is crucial to the task of thinking the individual and collective bodies of traumatized subjects. For Deleuze and Guattari, the concept of 'schizophrenia' designates a body with no pre-established or fixed organ-ization; the 'body-without-organs' is the synthesizing ego of the primary order in their theory of the genesis of representation. Certainly rape is the most unreported and under-reported traumatizing war crime of the Rwandan genocide. This trauma is exacerbated by the fact that so many women survive their rapes to learn they are pregnant and infected with HIV. Recall that Deleuze insists the surface of transcendental thought is extremely fragile, easily overwhelmed by the violence and meaninglessness of the corporeal/material depths of the primary order. Traumatized bodies are catapulted back into that primary order of timeless psychic violence, remaining there, ontologically stranded in the dissolution of the body and the dissociation of the mind/spirit, that is, between a failed conjunctive synthesis and a failing disjunctive synthesis, sublimated onto a transcendental surface of thought, traversing a Hieronymus Bosch landscape of perverted good sense and common sense. Recorded on the surfaces of the traumatized bodies are marks as signs of conjunctive syntheses that have been violently disjoined, making inclusive disjunctive syntheses all but impossible, and shattering the remnants of the boundaries of exclusive disjunctive syntheses. Their bodies bear the marks of collective psychosis; they bear its collective trauma.

The interval between body and spirit, between event and sense, collapses, imprisoning affect, recollection-memory and contraction-memory. There is a difference in kind between the (psychological) present of perpetual becoming and the (ontological) past of present being. For Bergson, the time of the present is 'pure becoming' inasmuch as the present *acts*, but it *is not* in the sense of being a positive extensive presence. In this sense, the present *is* 'outside' itself. The time of this transcendental time is Aion, that is, the time of no present tense. On the other hand, and unlike the present of Aion, the past no longer *acts* in the sense of doing anything. The past *is* the past in the sense that it does not cease to be, unlike the present which, in perpetually becoming, always already ceases to be. Because the past does not act, but *is*, the past is impassive and inactive, and in that sense the past *is*, not *was*. In this manner, the ordinary sense of time is turned upside down, or reversed; at every instant the present 'was' and the past 'is' eternal (p. 55). It is a mistake to believe that the past must first be present to become past, and to believe that the past becomes somehow reconstituted by the new present whose past it now *is* and is remembered.

These mistakes lead to the conclusion that there is only a difference in degree between recollection and perception. In fact, recollection and perception are different in kind, that is, perception corresponds to the body, and memory corresponds to the mind. The past and the present are constituted at the same time; 'the past is contemporaneous with the present that it has been' (Deleuze 1991, p. 58). The present is thought of as a psychological pure becoming that does not cease to pass and the past is thought of as an ontological pure being through which all presents pass. Each present goes back to itself as past. Actualization, then, involves the adaptation of the past to the present in five moments or movements. The first moment of actualization is a point of contact between the ontological past and the psychological present as the past moves towards the present. The second moment is an interpolation and expansion of the past in the present, distinguishing the past from the present. A third moment is an attitude of the body that reorients the first two moments, extending them. A fourth moment in the process of actualization is the physical movement of the body performing in the present. Finally, there is a displacement; the past is embodied, but now only in terms of a present that is different from that which had been, constituting an interval. In the instance of trauma, the ontological domain of the past makes contact with the psychological domain of the present, but in the second moment of actualization, the ontological past overwhelms the psychological present, triggering the perpetual ongoing repetition of the first two moments. The third moment is not the body's reorientation of the first two moments, but a mistaking of the ontological for the psychological – re-experiencing the trauma as the psychological present. They fuse and in the process ontological time transposes itself as psychological time – the time of Chronos of the proposition is mistaken for Aion of transcendental thought. The psychologically traumatizing event(s) do not pass.

Crucial to our comprehension of the production of social conflict and transitional justice and the reconciliation of collective trauma is Bergson's conception and analysis of language; he thinks of language in ways that are identical to the ways in which he thinks of recollection-memory and contraction-memory. We do not somehow stand outside of language and then make sense of the sounds we hear and the images we associate with those sounds. Rather, we leap from a primary order of corporeal/material sensation into transcendental sense. For Bergson, this is a true leap of Being. Once in the secondary organization of transcendental sense and verbal representation, a body becomes actualized in the process of psychologically perceiving sounds and images. Importantly for our comprehension of social conflict, violent or otherwise, this secondary organization of transcendental sense is the ontological foundation of language. And it is in this sense that for Deleuze's Bergson, only the present is psychological; the past is pure ontology; pure recollection and contraction have ontological, not psychological, significance. Bergson summarizes his theory of memory by noting that when we search out a recollection that at the moment escapes us, we detach ourselves from the present, which is the psychological, and locate ourselves in time, that is, in the past, which is the virtuality of transcendental sense, the ontological realm of recollection-memory and contraction-memory.

The ontological 'problem of fit' is for a desiring-body-becoming-subject 'to fit' into the regimes of signs of a historical system of representation. Eugene Holland reminds us that for Deleuze and Guattari, the body-without-organs (the plane of consistency, the plane of immanence on which signs are recorded disjunctively) is produced as a tabula rasa; it is produced from the primary order of mechanical repetition, instinctual determinations and the fixations of neurosis. The body-without-organs is produced, in effect, by the transformation of energies of connections into energies of recording (Holland 1999, p. 31). The syntax of the transformative operation of the disjunctive synthesis of recording consists in the open-ended series: 'either . . . or . . . or . . .' continuing indefinitely. And in similar fashion to the ways in which productive connective energy can become frozen and fixated, anti-productive disjunctive energy can result in permanent breakdown. The genesis of empirical consciousness and of representation, emerging as it does from a primary order of the corporeal depths of chaos and schizophrenia, is not predetermined.

The conjunctive synthesis of consumption-consummation generates a range of subjective forms of content (i.e. of actions and passions) for a variety of substances of content (i.e. bodies). Laid out as a continuum, the extreme form of instinctual determination – the production of production (i.e. the connective synthesis) – anchors one end, and the extreme form of catatonic breakdown – the production of recording (i.e. the disjunctive synthesis) – anchors the other end (Holland 1999, pp. 28–30). The conjunctive synthesis of consumption-consummation operates between these two extremes to produce variable forms of subjectivity. It is crucial to underscore here, once again, that a subject is produced as a by-product (i.e. as an after-effect) of the selections and investments desire makes from among the disjunctive syntheses recorded on the surface of immanence, that is, the body-without-organs. Subjects and their subjectivities are the results of the contestation and interplay of productive and anti-productive forces that constitute desiring bodies. In other words, the productions and anti-productions of desire precede the appearance of a subject and subjectivity. Moments of conjunctive consummation – these retrospective identifications – are derived from and at the same time generated by prior connective and disjunctive syntheses. The syntax of conjunctive synthesis is of the order: 'So, that's what it was,' 'So that's what was going on,' 'So that's what felt so intense,' and crucially, 'Oh, so that was me.' Whereas some of the energy of a connective synthesis (i.e. the production of production) was transformed into the energy of a disjunctive synthesis (i.e. the production of recording), some of that energy is transformed into a conjunctive synthesis (i.e. the production of consumption-consummation).

A subject is produced in a process of consummating recognition (i.e. 'Oh, so that was me') accompanied at the same moment by consuming appropriation (i.e. 'So that's mine, that belongs to me'). Desiring-machines, produced elsewhere at an earlier time and having produced a subject off to the side as a by-product of conjunctive synthesis, produces the illusion of sovereign subjectivity (Holland 1999, p. 33). As a consequence, a conjunctively constituted subject of subjectivity experiences its subjective identity as the cause of the very forces of the desiring-machines that produced it. In short, desiring-production, when attracted connectively to the psyche (i.e. the body-without-organs), is recorded disjunctively on its surface, which then appears conjunctively as the source (i.e. the subject) of that which gets recognized as the intensities of its consuming and consummate experience. The connective synthesis of production generates continual series (i.e. 'and . . . and then . . . and then . . .') and the disjunctive synthesis of recording generates open-ended series ('or . . . or . . . or . . .'). The conjunctive synthesis of consumption-consummation generates networks of relations as states of intense experience that are recognized consummatively and appropriated consumptively by a subject (as its own) as it passes through those networks of relations of intensity. It is in this sense that a subject both consumes and consummates networks of relations through which it passes, and with each conjunctively synthetic experience, a subject is created/born again. Identity, then, is that which a subject experiences as the relative constant entity or container of and for these series of conjunctive experiences (Holland 1999, pp. 33–6).

The connective flow of desiring-production can and does disjoin, get interrupted, disconnected and broken, in effect punctuating analogue flows producing digital signs, interrupting, and even temporarily blocking desiring-production and social-production, resulting in temporary anti-production. But neither desiring-production nor social-production can be permanently halted by anti-production and reduced to identities and dialectical relations. Sites of disjunctive syntheses of anti-production are marked, registered and recorded as striating signs on surfaces. Contents of machinic assemblages of bodies articulate to marks as signs of disjunctive syntheses that constitute collective assemblages of enunciation. Desiring-production invests the content of machinic assemblages of bodies with their actions and passions, which articulate to collective assemblages of enunciation as forms and substances of expression. Bodies – as the material substance of the contents of machinic assemblages of desiring bodies, and actions and passions as the form of the contents of machinic assemblages of desiring bodies – articulate to forms of expression recorded disjunctively as regimes of signs whose substances of expression are the institutions of social-production that effectuate incorporeal transformations. Bodies of desiring-production articulate to forms and substances of social-production, that is, to regimes of signs and their social institutions, becoming-subjects *of* and *for* those institutions and their semiotic expressions.

Articulation is more than an intransitive linking and connecting; it is a creatively transitive process of becoming and doing, which has important affective implications for conversing, negotiating, mediating and dialoguing. Yet to be imagined, however, is an adequate theory of engaging, even if not resolving violent conflicts and reconciling collective traumas. As a processual method of and for connecting, disjoining and conjoining bodies and discourses, articulation is less a matter of knowing and claiming, and more a matter of becoming and performing via 'abduction'.[19] Articulations are not predicated on transcendent foundations; they are constituted in and through the immanence of contingent circumstances. There are no spaces of immanence-out-of-time, or times of immanence-out-of-space. The spaces and times of conversing, negotiating, mediating and dialoguing active and reactive forces, shifting interests, rhizomatic relations and incommensurable commitments cannot escape immanence. Articulations may perpetuate relations of dominance as readily as they disarticulate them, deterritorializing them and articulating radically different relations.

For embodied subjects of territorial assemblages, the political objective of their actions and passions often is to destabilize and deterritorialize stratified conditions of a relatively stable material-semiotic system. How substantive contents of a territorial assemblage are engaged depends upon the intensive affects of the formative contents of machinic assemblages of bodies – that is, its actions, passions, desire, will, imagination, resistance and resolve – as much or more than it does on the striated relations of economic rationality, psychological interests, formal logic, linear time and dominant discourse. Bodies of machinic assemblages articulated to collective assemblages of enunciation and their regimes of signs are capable of forging relatively sedentary subjective identities from relatively nomadic identifications, and identities with passionate attachments to subject positions become notoriously resistant to disarticulation and deterritorialization. The reactive forces of affect, in this case the reactive and passionate attachments of desiring bodies to transcendent, sedentary and totalized identities of discursive subject positions (i.e. Tutsi or Hutu), are capable of overwhelming the active forces of affect (i.e. nomadic, multiple, partial, immanent and schizoid identifications), collapsing them into one-dimensional, totalized, sedentary and paranoid identities.

Deleuze and Guattari distinguish 'affect' from 'affection'. Affect refers to intensities or bodily states that enhance or diminish a body's power to act and to be acted upon, which they call 'latitude'; affection refers to relations of extensive parts of a body, which they call 'longitude'. Affection resulting from an extensive encounter is distinguished from affects as intensive capacities of a body to act and to be acted upon in an assemblage. Affects are thought of as capacities to produce intensive emergent effects in assemblages, that is, as 'becomings'.[20] Affections are thought of as modifications of extensive relations from an encounter. Bodies of immanent nomadic identifications have greater latitude and longitude than bodies of transcendent sedentary identities. Both intensities (i.e. bodily states, latitude) that enhance and diminish a body's power, and extensities (i.e. parts of a body, longitude) of modifications of relations of an encounter are greater, with respect to the virtual potentialities and actual possibilities for bodies of nomadic identifications, than they are for bodies of sedentary identities. Flows of desiring-production carry along bodies with variable capacities to articulate to different discursive formations constituting collective assemblages of enunciation, at times producing paranoid subjects of resistance, at other times producing vulnerable, schizoid subjects of willingness.

Imagined along these lines, conversing, negotiating, mediating and dialoguing articulate 'the production of identity on top of differences, of unities out of fragments, of structures across practices. Articulation links this practice to that effect, this text to that meaning, this meaning to that reality, and this experience to those politics. And these are themselves articulated into larger structures, etc' (Grossberg 1992, p. 54).

The task at hand is to think of conversing, negotiating, mediating and dialoguing as processes of and for punctuating affect so as to create practical ways of disarticulating and rearticulating identities on top of differences, unities out of fragments and structures out of chaos. Transcriptions of conversing, negotiating, mediating and dialoguing (as recordings of punctuated discursive processes of collective assemblages of enunciation articulated to territorial assemblages of desiring bodies) can be read as traces of affects and articulations. An agreement, settlement, resolution or reconciliation is a transcribed record of a conjunctive synthesis consisting in the articulation of particular elements that strengthen certain affective relations of force and compromise others. The schizoanalytic question is how such articulations of affect are produced.

Stuart Hall reminds us that '[t]he unity formed by this combination of articulation is always, necessarily, a "complex structure": a structure in which things are related, as much through their differences as through their similarities. This requires that the mechanisms which connect dissimilar features must be shown – since no "necessary correspondence" or expressive homology can be assumed as given. It also means – since the combination is a structure (an articulated combination) and not a random association – that there will be structured relations between its parts, i.e. relations of dominance and subordination.'[21] As is true of violent conflict and collective trauma, any resolution or reconciliation is a highly unstable structure consisting in combinations of articulations and affects that remain only temporarily invariant durationally. As resolutions and reconciliations articulate and disarticulate, virtual potentiality transforms as well, informing narratives and performing conversation, negotiation, mediation and dialogue in the shifting ruptures and gaps of affects and actions.

Desiring-production of relations among bodies of machinic assemblages that recognize in and through consumption (i.e. 'Oh, so that's me') and appropriate by means of consummation (i.e. 'So that's mine') are conjunctively produced as identities; bodies not consumed and consummated are not recognized, appropriated and identified as subjects of and for discourse; they remain objects and partial objects. The void that inaudibility and invisibility produce threatens to collapse the variable and multiple identifications of nomadic subjectivity into an essentialized sedentary identity of objectivity cut off from collective assemblages of enunciation. A passionate, embodied, affective response to the invisibility and inaudibility of mute non-recognition, and the abject impotence of non-appropriation, is reactive rage born of nihilistic terror, a response that risks symmetrical escalation from agonism to antagonism, from dispute to conflict to violence to massacre to genocide.

Ironically, a transcendent escalation of conflict actually produces a descent into the nihilism of the schizophrenic primary order it so violently is trying to escape via the purification and destruction of transcendence.[22] The libidinality of vengeance triggers a threat of the loss of identity and the unfathomable horrors of chaos and schizophrenia, of disarticulation and deterritorialization, of vanishing identity. The more bodies of a machinic assemblage of desire react rather than act, that is, the more desiring bodies retaliate in vengeance and a rage of ontological panic in desperate attempts to assert identity and to erase the Other, the more other desiring bodies react in kind, refusing to recognize (i.e. consummate) and to appropriate (i.e. consume multiple), and thereby to validate and legitimate partial nomadic identifications. 'It becomes a never-ending race to catch up with myself. As soon as I attempt to eliminate the Other as a way of being certain of my own essence, I start to endanger my own identity.'[23]

Collapsing multiple identifications of bodies of machinic assemblages into identities of impure, reviled and non-human identities, then attempting purification of the territorial assemblage by purging and subtracting those reviled, non-human, objectified identities – which in itself is evidence of a will to dissociate and transcend the materiality of immanence – produces the very conditions of possibility for systematic slaughter and collective trauma, not at all the virtual and actual conditions of purity and vitality. Subtracting bodies from machinic assemblages of desiring-production does indeed destroy material bodies; but such a dramatic disjunctive synthesis registers collective trauma and records collective memories on the desiring bodies of the survivors. Surviving bodies of machinic assemblages of desire count as potential occupants of discursive subject positions in formations of collective assemblages of enunciation.

3

Intuiting Attunement to Conflict Duration

Chapter overview

The focus of this chapter is on the expressive processes of conflict production, conflict resolution and trauma reconciliation rather than on the substantive and formal differences in content conventionally taken into account in its rational analysis. If conflicts are thought of as the shrinking or collapsing of counter-actualizing intervals separating event and response, then resolving conflicts has more to do with methods of intuition and duration than with rationality and causal analysis. This chapter brings Deleuze's reading of Bergson's method of intuition to the immanence of social conflict, rethinks collective trauma reconciliation in terms of attunement to duration and redraws the lines along which 'solutions' are imagined. The double objective is to resolve conflict and to reconcile trauma without dissociating from empirical consciousness, remaining immanent by mapping Deleuze's reading of Bergson's method of intuition onto the genesis of representation.

Intuition and badly stated questions of conflict

The 'problematic' of the Rwandan genocide is to make sense of a seemingly incomprehensible Event and to take the measure of experiments in transitional justice as methods of resolving injustices and reconciling trauma in post-genocide Rwanda. The immanent ethical work of re-imagining and coming to terms with asymmetrical violent social conflict is intuitive, that is, knowing in the sense of intuiting virtual reality regarding when and how to intervene, in what sorts of matters and coming to terms with the devolution and dissolution into the collective psychosis that was the 1994 Rwandan genocide. The controversial model of and for post-genocide transitional justice efforts in Rwanda began with a traditional dispute resolution process and ended with something different; it has yet to be determined whether the difference is in degree or in kind. Post-genocide gaçaça courts, arguably, were the best solution, given the decimated legal infrastructure and the depletion of lawyers and judges. Reconciliation of collective trauma was never discussed in those terms and in that register, and no accommodations were made until 2004 for the more than 500,000 Tutsi girls and women who were raped, many by HIV positive Hutu *interahamwe* rapists.[1] Little to no attention was paid to rape, either as a war crime or as a civil crime, nor was much thought given to reconciling collective trauma, other than President Paul Kagame's insistence on the enforcement of his Rwandan Unity policies making it a crime to talk about the Event of genocide or of referring to Rwandans as Hutu and Tutsi in contexts other than gaçaça court proceedings.

The questions traditionally animating conflict resolution studies have to do with: (1) How can conflict best be managed, if not resolved? And (2) How can resolution of conflict (whatever forms and substances it takes) best be achieved and sustained? Until relatively recently, collective trauma as a by-product of asymmetrically violent social conflict has not been taken up in conflict resolution studies. This chapter argues that, as phrased, those two questions pose false problems; false not in the sense that conflicting forces do not present problems, but false in the sense that the questions are badly stated. They are not the most foundational questions to be addressed. They presuppose a consensus definition of 'conflict', they presuppose 'conflict' to be a relatively uniform category of actions and passions. Presumably, as discussed in Chapter 2, conflict is a consequence of scarce resources, the effects of which are compounded by their inequitable distributions of whatever sorts of resources are in contention. When conflicts are formulated as problems and quantitative solutions are devised, problem/solution and conflict/resolution become conflated; the actions and passions of conflict resolving become the reasons and logics of problem solving. The desiring-production of libidinality and trauma drop out of the equation as rationality and technique become the equation's solution.

Resources for and factions of overtly conflicting assemblages are distributed unevenly, and their uneven quantities are taken to be causes of problems that advantage some and disadvantage others. Those conditions and circumstances are judged by some to be unjust and unfair; by others as the natural order of things. As disadvantaged factions press claims of discrimination, contestatory agonism bends towards combative and violent antagonism. At some point, contesting oppressive conditions and circumstances seems pointless, even dangerously naïve. Antagonistic sociocultural and political-economic conditions become reified and represented as 'a' singular conflict (i.e. an Event) of varying degrees of intensity. Violence is assumed to 'break out' when disagreements, arguments and disputes 'break down', that is, when violence forecloses discourse, and sedentary forces of any current regime, as a matter of course, resist nomadic forces of change. The signifier 'conflict' comes to be thought of as signified, a signifier that signifies an approximately bounded and relatively autonomous configuration of antagonistic relations. As such, the nomadic, emergent and dynamic pattern of variables at work, and the intricate complexities of their manifold relations, become arrested in time and reduced in thought to a sedentary, if temporary, state of affairs referred to as 'a' conflict – an intransitive noun/verb, but not a gerund – not 'conflicting'.

For purposes of conflict analysis and resolution, the variably fluid durational dynamics and the networks of intricate exterior relations constituting conflict assemblages are named and thought of primarily as a spatial 'problem' (e.g. 'the Rwandan genocide', 'the Middle-East conflict', 'the war in Afghanistan') in need of a materially practical 'solution', or more to the point, in need of a 'resolution' insofar as the current antagonistic and/or violent conditions and circumstances are consequences of prior solutions now standing in need of resolving. Intuitively, however, we know (i.e. we sense virtually) that conflict is not an autonomous, limited and bounded phenomenon. As formulated, the questions of how best to think of conflict and how to sustain resolution in several important respects set up the wrong problem to be addressed. It assumes that the categories 'conflict' and 'resolution' are self-evident and self-explanatory; it assumes that conflict *ought* to be resolved as a *moral* imperative and that conflict is capable of being resolved. Further, it assumes that conflicts differ from one another quantitatively (i.e. conflicts differ spatially in scope and in degrees of extensity), thereby obscuring qualitative difference; that is, conflicts that differ durationally, in terms of kind – dispute, fight, resistance, rebellion and war on the one hand, and assault, ambush, massacre, pogrom and genocide on the other – become conflated.

Deleuze and Bergson on the method of intuition

How, then, are we to make sense of the Rwandan genocide as an Event, as a molecular segmentarity becoming molar segments of binary oppositions descending into a presignifying regime of violence, rigidified by state endorsement? How is the effect of the creation and deployment of the gaçaça process in post-genocide Rwanda to be made sense of? This will not be a discussion of morality, human nature or the nature of evil. Nor will it engage the debates focusing on international criminal law. Rather, I propose to rethink asymmetrically violent social conflict largely in terms of Deleuze's *Logic of Sense* and *Difference and Repetition*, and with Felix Guattari, *Anti-Oedipus*, *A Thousand Plateaus* and *Kafka*, and with Claire Parnet, *Dialogues* and *Dialogues II*. But it is *Bergsonism* and Deleuze's reading of Bergson's method of intuition and the concepts 'duration', 'memory' and 'virtual coexistence' that I turn to at this point for thought-forms with which to rethink conversational, negotiational, mediational and dialogical processes, that is, minor communication machines (to be taken up in Chapter 4) for engaging and transforming the virtual and the actual, the transcendental and the empirical.

For Bergson, intuition is a method capable of immanently experiencing durational worlds as wholes in which we are immersed. His work in effect explicates intuition conceptually as it demonstrates it pragmatically; that is, Bergson claims and demonstrates that his method establishes philosophy as a 'precise' discipline (Deleuze 1991, p. 20). Intuition as a method of philosophy is a way of thinking otherwise, a way of thinking *qualitatively different* problems. How are we to think and to understand the relations between body and spirit, between excitation and execution, between cerebrally registering percepts and the affective responses of the core, that is, the body? How are we to understand the pre-predicative, pre-individual, impersonal and pre-representational genesis of representation? How are we to imagine the infants' presignifying experience of a corporeal/material world? And importantly, why is it necessary to do so in order to come to terms with asymmetrical violence of genocidal proportions? Because remaining on the plane of psychology and rational analysis cripples our thinking; we are incapable of imagining anything beyond neuroses and the psychoanalytic formulations of the unconscious. The Rwandan genocide, however, cannot be fathomed in terms of psychoanalytic concepts of the unconscious on the plane of psychology. Deleuze's transcendental empiricism posits a plane of the transcendental unconscious as that from which representation and empirical consciousness emerge. The Deleuzean transcendental unconscious is capable of accounting for much of the collective psychosis that was/is the Event of the Rwandan genocide; it was a collective regression of a territorial assemblage of desiring-bodies misidentifying the desiring-production of the primary order from which transcendental thought emerges as empirical consciousness resulting in social-production itself. In short, Deleuze's thought is indispensable to the difficult but ontologically necessary work of more ethically fathoming asymmetrical violence and collective trauma.

The immanence of Bergson's concept of immersion is open-ended; its virtualities transform in concert with unfolding actualities. I propose to think of 'conflict' and 'resolution', 'trauma' and 'reconciliation', as composites of experience immanent to the genesis of representation, from a primary order of corporeal/material depths of sensations, through a secondary organization of transcendental thought, verbal representation and the virtual, to a tertiary order of empirical consciousness and logical propositions. Bergson's philosophical method of intuition is crucial in rethinking and restating the problems of conflict resolution and trauma reconciliation in terms of duration and sound, rhythm and tempo, pacing and scale. Events denoted and signified as conflicts become manifest as good sense and common sense, conversing, negotiating, mediating and dialoguing between the secondary organization of verbal representation/transcendental thought of virtual sense and the tertiary order of empirical consciousness/logical proposition.

For Deleuze's Bergson, three distinctly different acts determine the rules of the intuitive method of philosophy; the first act concerns stating (i.e. inventing) true problems; focusing on the adequacy of the stated problem rather than on the veridicality of an announced answer. The second act concerns the discovery of genuine difference in kind via the intuitive method, and not confusing differences in kind with differences in degree and intensity. The third act concerns the apprehension of real time. Consider each act in turn. The first rule reads: 'Apply the test of true and false *to problems* themselves. Condemn false problems and reconcile truth and creation at the level of problems' (Deleuze 1991, p. 14). Stating the problem correctly is the work of inventing, not discovering; invention gives being to what did not exist in actuality. For this first rule there is a complementary rule: 'False problems are of two sorts, "nonexistent problems," defined as problems whose very terms confuse the "more" and the "less", and "badly stated" questions – their terms represent badly analyzed composites' (Deleuze 1991, p. 17). To return to our earlier examples, how are distinctions made between asymmetrical violence such as 'massacre', 'terrorism', 'pogrom' and 'genocide' on the one side, and symmetrical bilateral violence such as 'resistance', 'rebellion', 'revolution' and 'war' on the other? How do differences in degree (i.e. differences in quantity and intensity) differ from differences in kind (i.e. differences in quality and duration)? More importantly, why do answers matter?

'Being', 'order' and the 'existent', for Deleuze, are truth itself; 'Life is essentially determined in the act of avoiding obstacles, stating and solving a problem' (Deleuze

1991, p. 20). The problem for both Bergson and Deleuze is that we tend to see nothing but differences in degree and differences in intensity where there are profound differences in kind, that is, qualitative differences between, say, war and genocide. The qualitative difference between war, which is a violent, bilateral and symmetrical conflict, and 'terrorism', which is a violent unilateral asymmetrical conflict, provides contrast. This difference between quantity and quality is crucial to rethinking conflict, and to reconfiguring attempts to converse, negotiate and mediate their resolutions and reconcile their traumas. Mistaking differences in degree for difference in kind is a dangerous and usually egregious mistake, an unnecessary one to make even as it presents itself as inevitable. Deleuze proposes that we react to this anti-intellectual tendency by bringing to life in intelligence another tendency, one which is critical. A critical intuition rediscovers differences in kind beneath the differences in degree, and importantly, makes available upon critical analysis the criteria that enable it to distinguish between true and false problems (Deleuze 1991, pp. 19–20).

The Second Rule reads: 'Struggle against illusion; rediscover the true differences in kind or articulations of the real' (Deleuze 1991, p. 20). As stated, the rule determines acts leading to the discovery of genuine differences in kind that appear in experience as composites, as differences in degree and intensity. For Deleuze's Bergson, experience is a composite, a mixture of matter and spirit that must be divided. Not doing so, for him, is the source of the false problems and illusions that overwhelm us. False problems and illusions overwhelm us, as well, when the converse is the case, that is, when differences in degree and intensity are misrecognized as differences in kind and extensity. The consequences can become devastating; in Rwanda, Hutu transformed Tutsi into 'vermin' and 'cockroaches' to be eliminated in the paranoiac transcendent interests of purification and beginning anew.[2] The Complementary Rule to the Second Rule states that the real is not only that which is 'cut out' according to natural articulations (or differences in kind); the real is also that which 'intersects again' along paths converging towards the same virtual point. The function of this complementary rule is to show how a problem, when properly stated, tends to resolve itself. Bergson claims, however, that we no longer know how to distinguish in the representation of experience the two component elements, which differ in kind. *That* confusion is productive of false problems and overwhelming illusions.

Keep Bergson's dualisms in mind here – that is, duration–space; quality–quantity; heterogeneous–homogenous; continuous–discontinuous; the two multiplicities; memory–matter; recollection–perception; contraction–relaxation; instinct–intelligence; the two sources; etc. For Bergson, only tendencies differ in kind; given that, composites (i.e. experience) are to be divided on a line between qualitative and qualified tendencies. Intuition is a method of philosophy that identifies and articulates those tendencies, along natural divisions of matter (i.e. extensity) and spirit (duration).[3] His method of philosophical intuition is an enormously productive method for reimagining social conflict resolution experiments as durational enterprises. In effect, it is a method of reasking ontological questions and restating ontological problems, which is the focus of Chapter 5. The effects of differences in degree being misidentified as differences in kind can be devastating; for many post-colonial Rwandan Hutu, Tutsi were different in kind, not degree. They were recognized as always having been 'cockroaches', 'vermin' and 'snakes'. Once that move was made – of misidentifying differences in degree for differences in kind – and the wrong turn taken, a primary order of corporeal/material schizoid depths manifested as chaotic, terrifying intensity. Machinic assemblages of bodies dissociated from collective assemblages of enunciation become overwhelmed by the ramifying consequences of dissolving into partial-bodies and part-objects in what Deleuze refers to as 'Chronos of the depths', that is, time that does not pass in representation because representation has dissolved into the immanence of a primary order.

Deleuze explicates crucial symmetries of Bergson's method of intuition by drawing two diverging/converging lines. The first is a line of the interval consisting in perception, object and matter; the second is a line of subjectivity. Deleuze reminds us that there is no difference in kind between the corporeality of the brain, which registers excitation, and the reflex and response functions of the core, that is, the body. Bergson refers to the division between perception and execution or response as an interval.[4] For Deleuze's Bergson, the brain does not manufacture representation in the moment of the percept; rather, the brain complicates (i.e. mediates) the interval, separating (i.e. cutting out) the perception of movement (i.e. duration) and matter (i.e. extensity) on the one hand from a subsequent corporeally embodied response on the other. The second line is that of subjectivity, which addresses that which fills in the interval between corporeal cerebral perception and material embodied response. Three elements take advantage of this interval and fill it in, thereby constituting subjectivity: affectivity, recollection-memory and contraction-memory. Affectivity is that which assumes that the material body is something more than a mathematical point in time, and more than extensity of matter in space (i.e. spirit). Affectivity is inclusive of emotionality, libidinality and rationality, but affectivity cannot be reduced to any one of them. The second element filling in the interval is recollection-memory, which articulates instants to each other in the process of interpolating the past into the present. The third element constituting the line of subjectivity is contraction-memory, which contracts matter and makes quality appear. For Bergson and Deleuze, it is recollection-memory and contraction-memory that invest duration in the body and that provide it with its substantive qualities. Together, affectivity, recollection-memory and contraction-memory come to fill in a line of subjectivity that traverses the myriad intervals dividing material perception from corporeal body. These elements of memory and the unconscious are taken up again in a later section of this chapter.

For Deleuze's Bergson, representation attempts to bridge the division separating perception (which puts us immanently in matter) and memory (which puts us immanently in mind). Matter and mind divide as perception and memory. The two lines – of matter and of memory, of perception and of subjectivity – intersect and mix, and the resulting mixtures and composites of mind and matter constitute our experience. For Deleuze's Bergson, our experience is representation itself. Bergson is insistent that, 'All of our false problems derive from the fact that we do not know how to go beyond experience toward the conditions of experience, toward the articulations of the real, and rediscover what differs in kind in the composites that are given to us and on which we live' (Deleuze 1991, p. 26). Perception and recollection, matter and memory 'always interpenetrate each other, are always exchanging something of their substance'. It is the method of intuition that leads us to go beyond the immanent corporeal conditions of experience, a method for opening up to the inhuman and the superhuman, for opening up to durations that are superior and inferior to human duration, and for going beyond human conditions in the important work of learning critical lessons from Rwanda's genocide Event, and from its post-genocide transitional justice experiment with the gaçaça process. We will return to this feature of the method in a subsequent section of this chapter.

Going beyond human conditions and opening up to the inhuman and the superhuman, for Deleuze, is the meaning of philosophy, which is necessary insofar as Bergson is correct in assuming that the process of becoming-human actually conditions us to live in badly analysed experience, and as a consequence to become badly analysed composites ourselves (Deleuze 1991, pp. 27–8). It can be argued compellingly on a very different plane of analysis that what comes to be called 'genocide' is a self-organizing and self-ordering durationally compounding consequence of 'badly analysed' composites 'badly analysing' themselves and their conditions – it is the production process of madness and collective psychosis. Intuition, as Bergson and Deleuze insist, goes beyond the turn in experience. I put that method to work here mapping the projections of partial-bodies and part-objects escaping the meaningless and timeless violence of the primary order, becoming synthesized and projected onto a transcendental surface of thought, now unconstrained by the corporeal/material forces of a primary order. And intuition goes beyond transcendental thought; experience becomes configured in accord with good sense and common sense onto a plane of empirical consciousness and logical proposition constituting a tertiary order, that is, the actual.

Finally, the Third Rule determining the method of intuition reads: 'State problems and solve them in terms of time rather than of space' (Deleuze 1991, p. 31). For Deleuze, this third rule is the 'fundamental meaning' of intuition; it presupposes durations; he focuses on this principal Bergsonian division. All other divisions derive from differences between 'duration' and 'extensity'. For Bergson, differences in kind are durational differences, not spatial ones; differences in degree and intensity are spatial differences. The intervals of the line of subjectivity are 'filled in' with affect, recollection-memory and contraction-memory while traversing and mediating the differences in kind between percept and subject. There is a difference in degree, not a difference in kind, between Hutu and Tutsi in Rwanda. Yet state-official, public-unofficial, and vernacular (i.e. minor) discourses came to deterritorialize the ontological concept Tutsi into the chaotic primary order of 'vermin', 'insect' and 'reptile' part-objects and inhuman partial-bodies. I attend later to the particular order-words transmitted by state-sponsored pre-genocide and genocide radio broadcasts and directives inciting the extermination of the Tutsi.

Intuition presupposes duration; it entails thinking 'experience' in terms of duration. This move represents a shift in how we think and imagine 'social conflict', efforts to resolve it, and ways to reconcile collective trauma. Intuition unfolds durationally; it is a process *of* time, a process that consumes time as it consummates becoming. Remember the principal Bergsonian division between duration and space; all other divisions derive from it, or they result in it. The division occurs between duration, which tends to take on or bear all differences in kind insofar as duration is capable of qualitatively varying with itself, and space, which is quantitative homogeneity that never presents anything but differences of degree. Deleuze cites Bergson's example of a dissolving sugar cube, which has duration and ways of being in time that constitute its actual process of dissolving. Although not inorganic, conflict can be thought of as a haecceity that resolves and in some senses dissolves durationally. Conflict differs in kind not only from other conflicts, but also, more importantly, from itself durationally; a social conflict differs from itself through time. In the machinic (as opposed to the organic or inorganic) sense, social conflict can be thought of as territorial assemblages deterritorializing and reterritorializing – they do not dissolve, returning to their constitutive 'pre-conflict' forms and substances. It is a badly stated question to ask how conflict dissolves, as though in doing so, a conflict melts away and returns to prior conditions.[5]

Trauma's production along with attempts to reconcile it, however, can be thought of in terms of dissolution. A dissolving trauma is a becoming-memory; a dissolving human subject is a becoming-body-without-organs. Trauma resolves as memory. What we apprehend when we experience trauma is duration; until it begins to dissolve, trauma is not available as memory. When we think of trauma as duration, what is dissolving in time is the content and expression of the way 'things' have been. What is emerging from dissolving trauma is the intensity of relatively smooth spaces in the process of things becoming-otherwise, becoming-memory. *Intuition* is the methodical movement by which we emerge from our own duration of trauma, becoming empirically conscious of different durations figured as ways of being and becoming in time. Those ways of being and becoming are manifested in and through time, the two types of which – Chronos and Aion – we take up momentarily. Conflict assemblages and collective trauma manifest durationally; Deleuze at one point says that one's own duration, and how one chooses to live it, reveals qualitatively different durations from one's own. In short, duration is the location and the environment of qualitative differences in kind, in this case between memory and trauma.[6]

Conflict, representation and time

For Deleuze's Bergson, there are two kinds of time: Chronos and Aion. However, in reading Deleuze's account of the genesis of representation, Joe Hughes identifies two kinds of Chronos. Chronos of the depths is a timeless time of primary order consisting in movement of material part-objects in unmediated communication with one another, movement productive of sensations, 'movement of bodies which penetrate one another' (Hughes 2008, pp. 25–7). A primary ontological order is a corporeality/materiality of depths, a schizoid domain of violent and unmediated forces. There are as yet no surfaces, no bodies, no sense, no designation, no signification and no manifestation; there is corporeal sensation of material movement. It is a timeless order inasmuch as it is 'the always limited present that measures the action and passion of bodies as causes, and the state of their mixture in depth', (Hughes 2008, p. 26) which serves as a nuanced if incomplete characterization of genocide, or at least certain aspects of its description.

This is the time of bodies and mixtures in the schizophrenic depths of corporeal/material sensations without meaning (Deleuze 1990, p. 162). Deleuze imagines it as primary order, immersed in an unmediated physical present which does not pass; it is timeless present that traces (it is not a mapping process) the immediate actions and passions of bodies. In contradistinction to Chronos of the depths, Aion is immaterial time, freed from the movement of bodies but not independent of bodies. Dissociation is transcendent thought and virtual reality experienced as independent of body, a return of sorts to a primary order. Aion is, as Deleuze says, 'the empty form, of time', time with no present; it infinitely divides at an aleatory point – a point of nomadic subjectivity – the present into past and future (Deleuze 1990, p. 165). Just as Chronos corresponds to a primary order of depths, Aion corresponds to secondary organization and to the sublimated and symbolized events which populate the transcendental field of the surface of thought. Deleuze describes Aion as 'the time of event-effects' and 'the locus of incorporeal events' (Deleuze 1990, pp. 162, 165).

Deleuze refers to Aion – a second form of time – as the 'essential' or 'original' time. Whereas Chronos of the depths is a time with an indefinite present, Aion is a time with no present, only a nomadic and timeless aleatory point, a nomadic subject, separating an immediate past from an imminent future. Aion is not a time of present progressive tense; it is, rather, a time of that which has just happened and that which is just now about to happen, a time of impersonal thought that makes mobile, that is, nomadic, connections between memories and expectations.[7] It is in this sense that Aion is an immaterial time freed from the movements and constraints of bodies, an 'empty form of time' (Deleuze 1990, p. 165). Whereas Chronos of the depths is a primary order of timeless corporeal/material schizophrenic immediacy and meaningless, violent interpenetrations and sensations, Aion is a time of secondary organization of sense and the virtual reality of events of thought projected (i.e. sublimated) and ordered (i.e. symbolized) onto the surface of transcendental thought and verbal representation. Nomadic thought is in the process of making sense of incorporeal disembodied events being projected onto, and ordered on the surface of sense, all the while communicating with one another.

Recall from Chapter 2 that this transcendental surface founds a second, static ontological and logical genesis, which will, in turn, by means of good sense and common sense, produce a tertiary order of empirical consciousness and logical propositions. Chronos of the proposition, that is, the time of empirical consciousness and logical propositions, is a serialized time of logical propositions, a time of empirical consciousness and propositionality. Unlike Chronos of the depths, Chronos of the proposition, in and through logical representation, serializes the passing time of empirical consciousness. Deleuze posits that Chronos assumes two forms. Its first form is the present, understood as the unindividuated corporeal mixture of bodies: a primary order. A dynamic genesis emerges from this chaotic mixture of bodies, producing a transcendental surface. The genesis of the transcendental surface of thought in secondary organization is a surface that leaves materiality behind, becoming incorporeal. In leaving the movement of unindividuated bodies behind, this genesis produces a completely different kind of temporality – Aion. For this 'original' time there is no present; there is only an aleatory point – Deleuze also refers to this point as a 'nomadic subject' (Deleuze 1990, p. 162) – traversing the virtual topography of thought and imagination, always already separating the just past from the just about to happen. It is the time in which impersonal thought makes mobile connections between memories and expectations. The static ontological and logical genesis of representation returns us to Chronos, but now Chronos takes a completely different form. The static genesis returns to a present which has become, thanks to the work of genesis, 'a denotable state of affairs in view of a physical time characterized by succession' (Deleuze 1990, p. 184). And this succession passes in representation, unlike the Chronos of the depths of a timeless primary order. Chronos of the proposition and its denotable state of affairs is defined by succession and representation. In the return to matter from a transcendental field of thought, matter has become individuated. Chronos of depths is unindividuated and defined by the violence of bodies acting and reacting directly on one another; the Chronos of the proposition is individuated, successional, orderly and packed into the forms of language (Hughes 2008, p. 26).

To what extent is it productive to think of Rwanda's genocidal Event in terms of a descent to a primary order of corporeal/material depths of genocidal violence and collective psychosis, or alternatively as its eruption onto the transcendental surface of thought and virtual sense? To what extent can an order of pre-predicative reactive forces and part-objects, methodical movements and the murderous sensations of collisions and interpenetrations of part-objects and partial-bodies manifest, denote and signify empirical consciousness in ways that account for one-hundred days of systematic butchery? The other side of that question is how to make immanently ethical sense of post-genocide, post-pogrom, post-massacre experiments in the social-production of transitional justice and trauma reconciliation? Rwanda's deployment of the gaçaça process provides one such experiment, different in some important respects from truth and reconciliation commissions in other parts of the world, and different as well from the proceedings of International Criminal Tribunals, one of which was assembled for the Rwandan genocide (the ICTR). What follows is not a study of comparative justice systems; rather, it is a continuation of the thought experiment I have been developing, that is, mapping Rwanda's gaçaça process onto Deleuze's ontological account of the genesis of representation.

How does an ethnically marked, state-based, largely agrarian social formation, already troubled with a long history of postcolonial *ressentiment*, bad conscience and violence descend into a primary order of corporeal/material depths and collective psychosis, a 'becoming-genocide'? And, as importantly, how does an ethnically divided, severely fractured and collectively traumatized post-genocide Rwanda 'respond' to this 'Event'? What are the denoted, the signified and the manifested aspects of post-genocide truth and justice? How is the interpolation of truth and justice into that interval between the Event of genocide and the Event of justice to be balanced with and against the Event of collective trauma and the Event of collective reconciliation? Can machinic assemblages of bodies articulate to collective assemblages of enunciation in ways that produce approximations both of the truth of justice and of the reconciliation of trauma? The interval between violent asymmetrical social conflict and any singular response is an interval the parameters of which are negotiable within uncertain ethical limits. For Tamsin Lorraine, this interval between percept and affect, between event and response, between physics and metaphysics, between body and spirit is the precise location of the production of immanent ethics.[8]

An interval is a hesitation or a duration that permits a return from the transcendental field of sense to the primary order of genetic origins, corporeal materiality and the depths of schizophrenia. That return to genetic origins is the first aspect of Deleuze's reading of Nietzsche's eternal return. The second aspect of the eternal return is a return from the primary order, through the sublimation (i.e. projection) and symbolization (i.e. ordering) of events, onto the virtual surface of a transcendental field, to express the ways by which the events of thought communicate with or return to all the others in the form of the aleatory point or nomadic thought and verbal representation.[9] The work of eternal return in the interval between body and spirit entails shifting between the times of Chronos and Aion. The problems of resolving violent asymmetrical social conflict, producing transitional justice and reconciling collective trauma are more productively stated in terms of inventive 'interval work' separating action and reaction. In the Event of the Rwandan genocide, the slaughter of Tutsi and moderate Hutu, and the subsequent but less widely publicized slaughter of Hutu by Tutsi RPF forces were manifestations of a failure of the second aspect of the eternal return, a manifestation of having been seduced by the primary order of libidinal and genital violence.

The interval remains timeless, given the dissolution into part-objects and partial-bodies in violent conflicts and clashes. The chaos, violence and corporeal/material depths overwhelm the transcendental organization of thought, making schizophrenic sense rather than transcendental sense. The denoted (i.e. the Tutsi 'cockroaches'), the signified (i.e. the contamination, extermination and elimination) and the manifested (i.e. the systematic and organized slaughter) became the dominant good sense and common sense of genocidal empirical consciousness. Instead of returning through sublimation and symbolization to the surface of the transcendental field, part-objects violate and interpenetrate one another in an order devoid of meaning. Consequently, the first aspect of the eternal return gets lost in time, lost in the primary order of corporeal/material depths. The duration of the violence of the primary order becomes timeless; the present remains monolithically immanent.

When the primary order of the depths overwhelms the transcendental surface of sense, in turn overwhelming good sense and common sense in the genesis of the tertiary order of empirical consciousness and logical proposition, the two orders of time – Chronos of the depths and Aion – conflate, producing a transcendent timelessness, a mythic time of a timeless present. An important pragmatic consideration for both conflict resolution and trauma reconciliation concerns how to produce incorporeal transformations as well as durational shifts and movements of time, from Chronos of the depths, synthesizing through a virtual secondary organization via Aionic time, and then by means of good sense (i.e. the denoted) and common sense (i.e. the signified and the manifested) onto a tertiary order of empirical consciousness and logical proposition with its three essential relations – denotation, manifestation and signification. Sense, the fourth essential relation of the logical proposition, however, remains implicit and virtual on the surface of transcendental thought. Good sense, Deleuze says at different times, is agrarian work, the work of gathering and cordoning off extensity, territorializing nomadic thought denotatively as good sense.

Bergson calls into question the legitimacy of the order of needs, actions and society that sets us up to retain only that which interests us; general ideas tend to obscure difference in kind – recall the earlier discussion of universal human needs. Differences tend to dissolve into generalities, into the general order of ideas. 'We make differences in kind melt into the homogeneity of the space which subtends them' (Deleuze 1991, p. 33). Experience gives us mixtures and composites. Things tend to present to each other and to us only differences in degree. It makes more sense in this respect to think with terms that resolve conflicts (not egos, which currently attempt to solve badly stated problems and badly analysed composites of experience). Conflict becomes a term for durational differences of actions and passions invested in a conflict assemblage as a solution to a problem for which no other solution could be actualized. Conflicts are solutions to badly stated problems; it makes little sense to state the problem as though conflict were the problem rather than the solution to conditions and circumstances that are problematic.

Thought of in these ways, a conflict assemblage is working as a configuration of solutions responsive, albeit problematically, to current problems; solutions with considerable history, intensity, momentum, resolve and will are invested in them. After all, based on historical results, human beings have demonstrated a voracious appetite for and a practiced competence performing conflict in any stratified territorial assemblage. A more productive experiment, the one we are proposing here, is to think of conflict along ontological lines – assuming *a priori* difference and conflict – as agonistic and antagonistic forces that converge and diverge, often articulating as badly analysed self-reflexive experience by badly analysed composites trying to solve false or non-existent problems and trying to answer badly stated questions. The most pressing ontological question is how to deterritorialize conflicts; how to resolve them as viable solutions rather than 'trying' to solve them while simultaneously dissolving trauma.

For Bergson, duration is not reducible to psychological experience; instead, duration became for him a theme of a complex ontology. The absolute has two sides or aspects, each side sending out a line: spirit imbued with metaphysics, and matter known by science. The absolute is difference, but difference has two facets, that is, differences in degree and differences in kind.[10] Intuition forms a method of critique of false problems and the invention of genuine ones. In this sense, intuition is a method of finding problems, of problematizing conditions and of inventing new conditions. Those are the sorts of acts that determine the three rules of the method of intuition. One tendency of my critical scrutiny of post-genocide transitional justice, particularly gaçaça courts in post-genocide Rwanda, is precisely the confusion of degree (intensity) for kind (quality). A second critical tendency is a concern with badly analysed composites (i.e. experience).

Intuiting beyond the decisive turn

'Beyond the decisive turn' has two meanings. First, it denotes the moment when the two lines, that is, the line of the interval and the line of subjectivity, set out from an uncertain common point (e.g. a body in a violent conflict, or a traumatic event) of lived experience, and diverge according to their differences in kind. That phrase also denotes another moment when these lines of difference in kind, that is, the difference between body and spirit converge again giving us a virtual image of the common point – a resolution and/or reconciliation of body and spirit, of percept (i.e. interval) and affect, of recollection-memory and contraction-memory (i.e. that which fills in the interval) – for a people-yet-to-come. The task is to prolong the diverging lines of percept and affect to a point where they do indeed intersect again. For Deleuze's Bergson, this method of divergence/division and convergence/intersection is the only one that can bring about a decisive advance in metaphysics. The method of intuition – this way of thinking pre-predicative reality and its relations to representation – promises to bring about a decisive turn in conflict resolution studies and trauma reconciliation studies as well. Prolonging divergences and assisting convergences of body and spirit, moving artfully between virtual and actual reality, between transcendental thought and empirical consciousness, between interval and affect, recollection-memory and contraction-memory is a productive way of framing the artistic, scientific, libidinal and political work of social conflict resolution and collective trauma reconciliation.

Keep in mind that for Bergson, duration is memory; hence duration is consciousness, freedom (Deleuze 1991, p. 51). As we noted earlier, there are two forms of memory – recollection-memory and contraction-memory. Recall that the time of transcendental thought and verbal representation (i.e. Aion) divides time at each instant into two directions: recollection-memory is oriented and dilated towards the past; and contraction-memory is oriented and contracts towards the future. In demonstrating how duration becomes memory and how life becomes self-consciousness, Bergson, in *Matter and Memory*, posits five aspects of subjectivity: *need-subjectivity* is a moment of negation during which a body's need disrupts the continuity of sensate experience (this is *not* the conception of 'universal need' discussed in Chapter 1); *brain-subjectivity* is the moment of indetermination, the interval between the brain's perception of the disruption of continuity and the body's execution of a response; *affection-subjectivity* is the moment of embodied sensation, of the brain's conscious perception of the interval separating its excitation from the body's execution of a response; *recollection-subjectivity* is the recollecting of the affect that fills in an interval, the primary aspect of memory becoming embodied and actualized; and *contraction-memory* is the production of qualities from recollections of experienced events (Deleuze 1991, pp. 52–3).

These five aspects of subjectivity constitute the lines of objectivity and subjectivity; need-subjectivity and brain-subjectivity constitute the line of objectivity; recollection-subjectivity and contraction-memory constitute the line of subjectivity. Affection-subjectivity is the intersection of these two lines, that is, of perception and need on one line intersecting with recollection and quality on the other. By itself, affection does not constitute subjectivity; it is the body's perception of need intersecting with the mind's recollection of events and their qualities, constituting an interval of indetermination, that constitutes what Bergson refers to as 'pure subjectivity'. The brain and the body are different in kind – not in degree – from mind and memory; consequently, recollections, being on the line of subjectivity are not stored in the brain on the line of objectivity, but rather they are preserved in duration. It is in this sense that duration constitutes conscious life. In the case of trauma, whether individual or collective, recollections on the line of subjectivity become fused to and stored in the brain on the line of objectivity. Matter and memory become confused, as do present and past, but Bergson's thinking clarifies this in important ways.[11]

Bergson's theory of memory, introduced in Chapter 2, posits a difference in kind between matter and memory, perception and recollection, present and past, that is, between the line of objectivity and subjectivity. As discussed earlier for Bergson, the present is 'pure becoming'. The present *acts*, but it *is not*. In that sense, the present *is* outside itself; it is not present. This 'pure becoming' is the time of Aion, the time of transcendental thought, of verbal representation, the 'time of no present' in and of itself but rather an *acting* aleatory point or a nomadic subject dividing time into a dilating orientation of a past extending indefinitely and a contracting orientation of a future extending indefinitely. The past, unlike the present, no longer *acts*; the past in and of itself does not *do* anything – it *is* the impassive, inactive past. But just because the past does not do anything does not imply that it ceases to be. Bergson insists that the past is impassive and inactive, but *it is* – it is *not was*. In this sense, the past *is* present insofar as the past continues to be. So in this way it can be thought that the past is the form of being placing itself – as being in itself – outside itself as past into the present of *is*. This is the sense of Deleuze's Bergson insisting that the ordinary sense of time is reversed; that at every instant the present becoming-*was*, and the past being *is* eternally, for all time (Deleuze 1991, pp. 54–5).

In contrast to Freud, Bergson does not use the concept 'unconscious' to denote a psychological reality outside of consciousness. For Bergson, pure becoming (the time of Aion) is psychological; pure recollection (the time of Chronos) is ontological. Locating ourselves outside of pure becoming in search of (via the work of memory) recollections and contractions removes us from the psychological realm of becoming and locates us in the ontological realm of being. Nonetheless, the past *seems* to be situated between two presents; that is, the old present that the past once was and the actual present in relation to which the past is now the past. But this 'seeming' is a psychological image (as opposed to the ontological image) of reality that gives rise to two false beliefs about the past: (1) we mistakenly believe that the past is only constituted after having been present; (2) we also mistakenly believe that the past is somehow reconstituted by the new present whose past it now is and from which it is now remembered as being (Deleuze 1991, p. 58). These two false beliefs, however, lead us to assume that there is only a difference in degree between recollection and perception; and this, for Bergson, is a badly analysed composite (i.e. experience). There is, indeed, a profound qualitative difference in kind between psychological perception and ontological recollection.

For Bergson, the most profound paradox of memory is that the past would never be constituted as the past if it had not been constituted first of all at the same time it was present; the past is constituted at the same time it was (not is) present. So, in this sense, the past is 'contemporaneous with the present that it has been', (Deleuze 1991, p. 58) which is one way of thinking of trauma. If the past had to wait in order to be no longer present, it could never be *that* past. This seeming paradox dissolves when the past and the present are no longer thought of as two successive moments, as would be the case if the past and the present were differences in degree, but they are different in kind; they are two different elements (i.e. a psychological element and an ontological element) that coexist. The present is thought of as a psychological 'pure becoming that does not cease to pass' and the past is thought of as an ontological 'pure being through which all presents pass' (Deleuze 1991, p. 59). In this sense, each present returns to itself as past. *Trauma reverses this relation; each past returns to itself as present.* Recall from Chapter 2 Deleuze's explication of Bergson's theory of actualization; it involves the adaptation of the past to the present (what Bergson calls 'attention to life') and consists in five moments.

The first moment consists in *a point of contact* between the past, which is the present of 'pure being' (i.e. ontology), and the present, which is the past of 'pure becoming' (i.e. psychology). This contact is made possible by the past moving towards the present, that is, a contracting of the past (i.e. the ontological present of 'pure being') and the present (i.e. the psychological past of 'pure becoming') to a point of contact. The second moment consists in *a transposition, a translation, an expansion* of the past in the present, that is, a re-collection that restores the distinctions between past and present in virtue of both the contact and the expansion. The third moment is *a dynamic attitude* of the body to harmonize the first two moments, which in effect reorients the first two moments and extends them to their limits. The fourth moment of actualization consists in *the physical movement of the body* and its performance in the present. The fifth moment, then, is *a displacement* by which the past is embodied only in terms of a present different from that which it has been; this difference is *the interval* discussed earlier. For trauma, the present is the same as that which it has been – the eternal return of the same rather than the eternal return of difference.[12]

The psychological unconscious and the ontological unconscious can now be differentiated. The psychological unconscious represents the movement of recollection in the course of actualizing itself; the ontological unconscious represents pure recollection, virtual and impassive. Psychological recollections try to become embodied, originating as they do from the perpetually passing present; ontological 'attention to life', that is, the ontological unconscious, wards off dangerous and/or useless recollections. Trauma represents a failure of this 'attention to life'. Bergson argues that there is no contradiction between these two different kinds of unconsciousness – psychological and ontological. Given this line of thinking, trauma can be thought of as a conflation, that is, a con-fusion of the psychological and the ontological; the former is mistaken for the latter. Trauma is pure being overwhelming and taking over pure becoming; a con-fusion and contraction of the ontological and the psychological, an event becoming-unceasing psychological passing; in effect, a present becoming never ceasing to be.

Importantly for Deleuze, intuition and duration are not one and the same. 'Intuition is not duration itself. *Intuition is rather the movement by which we emerge from our own duration, by which we make use of our own duration to affirm and immediately recognize the existence of other durations, above or below us*' (Deleuze 1991, pp. 32–3, emphasis mine). Mediating conflict and trauma, reconciling and synthesizing the two, to the extent that is possible, requires openness of its subjects of enunciation, openness to affect, and to recollection-memory and contraction-memory, to becoming-affected by the immanence of experience of other subjects of enunciation. *Intuiting attunement to durational wholes of conflict and trauma, that is, of witnessing reality effects, is crucial to the process of creating virtual conditions and actual processes of and for dissolving and reconciling trauma.* It is not so much a matter of making space for mediating to take place, although that can be challenging at times, but more important is making time, both the time of empirical consciousness and logical propositions (i.e. Chronos of the proposition), and the time of the transcendental field of the virtual and verbal representation (i.e. Aion) to interpenetrate and interpolate empirical consciousness via good sense and common sense. Gaçaça court processes of minor communication machines (the focus of Chapter 4) is an experiment in making time take place for witnessing truth-effects.

Resolving violent social conflicts, reconciling collective traumas and producing transitional justice are different kinds of social-production processes, not simply different versions of a generic model, and any attempt to produce all three Reality-effects with essentially the same methods of social-production works at cross purposes to itself. Resolving conflicts without dissolving egos into a primary order of violence, reconciling trauma without dissociating transcendental thought from empirical consciousness and producing transitional justice without sacrificing truths are three different kinds of social-production problems involving three different kinds of social machines; each presupposes qualitatively different forms and substances of content and expression. Remember that for Deleuze and Guattari, in *A-O*, desire has two forms of psychoses at the extremes – paranoia at one pole and schizophrenia at the other. Paranoid-fascism insists on one-dimensional, obedient subjects with closed and fixed identities that are overtaken by overcodings and overwhelmed by relatively uncoded flows of desire. Schizophrenic anarchy allows nomadic subjectivities to be carried along and carried away by desiring-production, taking their bodies in qualitatively different durations to smoother spaces of far-from-equilibrium-conditions, that is, far-from-axiomatic good sense and common sense of empirical consciousness and the logical propositions of family, community and state formations.[13]

Territorial assemblages of violently conflicting interior and exterior relations among subjected and subjectivated bodies with relatively closed, one-dimensional identities rarely, if ever, are disputing 'the same' contents and expressions of 'the same' territorial assemblage. Territorial assemblages constitute networks of exterior relations of content and expression. Violently antagonistic desiring-bodies become open to the sublimation of violent thought events and corporeal/material excitations, confusing symbolization of genital sexuality and libidinal desire circulating on the surface of transcendental thought and verbal representation. The denoted of good sense, and the signified and manifested of common sense remain con-fused with transcendental sense, become actualized as a primitive territorial machine and/or a barbarian despotic machine, and not (despite all of its cruelties) a civilized capitalist machine. Desiring-bodies, forms and substances of content, and forms and substances of expression become distributed along vertical strata and across horizontal planes throughout a conflict assemblage such that even when partial resolutions are becoming-manifest, trauma persists long after violent asymmetrical social conflict may have been adjudicated, even if not resolved, and transitional justice may have been decided, even in the absence of fairness.

This is especially the case when collective trauma – which Adrian Parr defines straight-forwardly as 'an incommensurable experience or reality' (Parr 2008, p. 112) – involves internally and externally identified victims of violent asymmetrical social conflict with little or no power and with most of the shame, self-loathing, hatred and depression on the one hand, and internally and externally identified perpetrators who have most if not all of the resources as well as most of the guilt, blame, denial, *ressentiment*, bad conscience and self-pity on the other. Resolution and reconciliation processes bending towards transitional justice and collective reconciliation are thought of as both smoothing and striating forces deterritorializing and reterritorializing oppressive assemblages of differences, that is, articulating, binding and coordinating everyday ordinary durations and geographies of social-production with the everyday, ordinary, standard times of Chronos. But reconciliation processes bending towards transitional justice remain primarily affective libidinal processes of Aionic time, not propositional processes of Chronotopic time.

An ethic of truth-effects

Consider the discursive and psychic dynamics at work when trauma invades the subjective territory of temporality, exploding the spatiality of immanent experience. As an 'event', trauma ruptures ordinary time, space and knowledge, collapsing them into a void from which the realization of a truth may emerge. Not all ruptures, however, come to be named events, and not all named events are traumas. But traumatic events explode ordinary knowledges, structures of feeling and forms of expression, exposing voids that Alain Badiou calls exceptional realms of singular truths that emerge from voids of trauma by taking over the bodies of its subjects, and these truths of experience persist through the fidelity, discernment and restraint of choices and actions of embodied subjects to singular truths.[14] Bodies become subjects to truth, subjects who bear a truth revealed by the void of a traumatic event, as ethical adherents to a cause. In the absence of an emerging truth, the void of an 'event' functions as a hole into which an embodied subject plummets, losing its identity. In either case, an event leaves the marks of a void on an embodied subject's psyche. Extreme instances of lost souls and forgotten identities are the domain of therapeutic and religious interventions. All conflict, however traumatic, leaves its marks on embodied subjects as contemporary Reality-effects, and those marks inform conflicts, resolutions and reconciliations. Embodied subjects in conflict, however, are capable of choosing otherwise in an interval. The constraints on those choices, of course, vary from situation to situation, from one contingent moment to another. An embodied subject is held accountable by some agency or agencies for its choices and the consequences of those choices; it cannot avoid making choices, and choices always have consequences. Granted, choices are made under an extraordinarily wide range of conditions. An embodied subject has no determinate control over what happens prior to a moment of choice, that is, an event. In effect, an embodied subject cannot control what befalls it, but it can choose how to respond in the interval, however threatening and dangerous the choices may be.

This line of thinking opens onto different ways of imagining the ethics of conflict resolution and trauma reconciliation that lead to alternative ways of framing ethics in relation to truth and justice. Badiou's philosophical work is very much to the point here insofar as it stands as an affirmation of fidelity, discernment and restraint with respect to truth-procedures such as conversing, negotiating, mediating and dialoguing. Badiou is critical of what he refers to as 'the ethical ideology of the Other' and offers in its place 'an ethic of truths'. Instead of following a neoliberal path of ethical thought laid down by philosophers such as Martin Buber, Mikhail Bakhtin, Emanuel Levinas, Jacques Derrida and Gayatri Chakravorty Spivak, who predicate their thinking on a tolerance of, if not an unqualified reverence for, Otherness, Badiou instead follows a quite different path. He argues that mainstream ethical principles actually reinforce the dominance of the status quo and that negative human rights and tolerance of difference, for example, cannot inform and direct decisive interventions. Nor can such an ethical paradigm sharpen our contemporary understandings of evil and morality. In Hallward's words, our current ethical ideology is little more than 'a jumbled confusion of legalistic formalism, scandalized opinion, and theological mystification' (Hallward 2001, front cover). Badiou's 'ethic of truths' sustains and inspires a disciplined subjective adherence to four types of truth, each of which defines one of the four domains of philosophy – love, art, science and politics. These four domains of truth demarcate the possible subjectivities that a truth affirms and that a subject bears. Love pertains to individuals and politics to collectivities. Art and science combine individual bodies that, in turn, serve as collective vehicles for aesthetics and rationality. And these four domains of truth are also the domains of agonism and antagonism, of conflict and of possibilities for its resolution and reconciliation, as well as for post-conflict peacebuilding.

One might object that Badiou's ethical schema does not appear to include the domains of religion and identity, a critique, if true, that seriously compromises its intellectual and practical utility for reimagining conflicts fuelled by identity and value differences. But Badiou's project does not imagine ethics as being either framed by or as being dependent on religious and identitarian questions. Both religion and identity are derivatives of politics. Religion is nothing if not a collective affirmation of identity; and identity, for its part, is nothing if not an individual affirmation of politics. Religion, as an experience of having been found, identified, chosen and saved, (i.e. of having Truth) constitutes a collective identity. Having found one's universally True identity, one knows *the* way and *the* Truth. And that sense of Truth is experienced as a general universality in the sense of being held to be True for Others (i.e. everyone) and for all time, whether Others currently know it or not. Rather, Badiou is explicating an ethic of truths (lower case plural) for which a truth is *a* universal singularity rather than *the* universal generality. A universally singular (rather than generally universal) truth is true in its universal address, and singular (rather than universal) in its application. Such a truth is universally true for me, not necessarily for Others (i.e. everyone else). Nor should a universally singular truth be imposed on Others as though it were a general universality, and as though one had a moral obligation to impose a truth – as Truth – on Others. Making this crucial distinction between general universality and universal singularity installs a politics of truths. General universality of Truth struggles with universal singularity of truths. The former strives for hegemonic consent; the latter for ethical praxis. And for Badiou, love is construed broadly enough to embrace all matters of individual and collective desiring-production, including imagination-desire, subjection-experience, will-agency and resistance-resolve of religious phenomenologies, each addressed in detail in Chapter 5.

At first glance, Badiou's ethic of truths might look self-centred, elitist and uncompromising, at least by the standards of the general universality of the ethical ideology of the Other. But he advocates a disciplined, even militant (not to be confused with 'militaristic') subjective adherence to an affirmation of an ontological truth (or a cause). Such a truth is revealed by an event, a break in and from the realm of ordinary, common-sense knowledge and a rupture in the dominance of the supposedly seamless hegemony of the status quo. Events as breaks, ruptures and traumas produce the possibility of access to the realm of truth. Events – traumatic or otherwise – are situated at the edge of a void of incomprehensibility, a void around which is organized a relatively conventional, consensus-based status quo stratified in dominance in terms of the hegemony of common sense, conventional practices and traditional processes of daily living. An event is a sudden, wholly subjective, corporeal or incorporeal, non-discursive transformation, by which Badiou means that a radical and profound shift takes place in and on the body and the psyche of an embodied subject.[15] The material conditions constituting the world of that subject may or may not remain unchanged. In the radical disorientation brought on by an event, a consummating and consuming truth transforms a subject into its bearer, revealing itself with a profound clarity and without any rational bases. Different truths may become apparent to different bodies with respect to different domains of subjectivity, that is, love, art, politics and science. A truth thus revealed is neither good nor bad ethically, neither good nor evil morally. An ethic of truths becomes relevant for consideration and judgement in terms of what subjects of truth choose in the face of challenges to a truth. Gaçaça courts were intended to produce three qualitatively different truth-effects – legal truths, the production of which entails delivering evidence to prove a subject's guilt or innocence; therapeutic truths, the production of which involves the psychic healing of individuals; and restorative truths, the production of which entails shaping truths in order to rebuild post-genocide communal relationships.

Does a subject choose to affirm truth or to betray it? Does a subject discern a truth from its facsimiles? And does a subject refrain from imposing a universal singularity on Others, as though it were a general universality? It is in this domain of disciplined subjectivity that Badiou invokes the concept of fidelity to a truth. Fidelity to a truth entails the tireless work of not betraying or otherwise abandoning it. A truth, once taken on (i.e. assumed), requires an inordinate amount of passionately ethical discipline to not betray it, to not mistake it and to not impose it on others, particularly when its embodied subjects are in the grips of trauma, disillusionment, resistance and doubt. Fidelity to a truth may require militant adherence. Badiou distinguishes between the militaristic imposition of the Truth on Others supposedly for their own good, and a militant adherence to an affirmation of a truth that overtakes an embodied subject's mere mortality. Truth imposed on others is no longer *a* truth; it has become *the* Truth, an ethical ideology of the Other, an ideology whose hegemonic force supposedly increases as the number of its adherents increase, that is, a subjected group. Badiou appeals to an immortal value beyond such negative rights and mortal privileges. It is by means of being captured by a truth that mortals become caught up in the immortality that a truth and its ethic make possible. Discernment avoids mistaking a truth for its approximation or its resemblance, a mistake that when made produces delusion. Whereas fidelity remains faithful to a truth, and to a commitment not to betray it, discernment distinguishes delusion from the immortality of a truth. To betray a truth when exhaustion and fear become unbearable is understandable, even if not excusable. And a universally singular truth can have an indefinite number of zones of singular application, but each such application requires the subtlety and discipline to make finely tuned distinctions and discernments.

In company with the ethical challenges of fidelity and discernment, restraint is the third challenge to an ethic of truths. The experience of a truth revealed in an event can easily become a desire for homogeneity, a desire to 'share' (i.e. impose) that truth totally and unqualifiedly 'with' (i.e. on) Others, a desire for supremacy that produces terror from truth, and evil from good. Badiou's claim is that evil comes from good, not the other way round. The tragic mistake is assuming that a partisan and singular truth that is universal in its *address* is universal and uniform in its *application*. A singular truth of immortal and universal address is mistaken for *the* received Truth that ought to be (i.e. that morally deserves to be) uniformly and universally applied, and that obligates its adherents to do so. However, in the immortality of a truth, restraint is crucial. To apply, impose or otherwise force a truth, as *the* Truth, on Others is to betray truth by embracing the universally transcendent delusions of authoritarianism, imperialism, colonialism, totalitarianism, fascism and terrorism to force its adoption, thereby producing evil from intended Good. Betrayal, delusion and imposition produce evil on individual, familial, communal, organizational, institutional, regional, sub-national, national, international and global planes. Unlike consensus thinking regarding the ethical ideology of the Other, which assumes an evil world and deploys ethics to counteract evil in the interests of imposing good on evil, Badiou turns this assumption on its head. He argues that all evil is produced in the process of doing 'good' in accord with the ethical ideology of the Other. Rather than tasking ethics with the job of respecting difference by practising tolerance, Badiou begins with the assumption, as does Deleuze, that difference is the natural state of the world. Difference constitutes the banal conditions of life. As such, difference in and of itself is not particularly interesting. Of much greater interest is the difficult and ethically challenging task of *recognizing the Same* (i.e. that which is not yet, that which will become indifferent to difference, which for Deleuze entails the eternal return of difference). Difference matters, but it is not the focus of primary interest or ongoing concern once the coming of the Same becomes virtually imaginable and actually possible. It is the Same that renders difference irrelevant by traversing it, sliding across it and pervading it by means of flowing through it without erasing it.

Badiou's ontology assumes that there is no One, no Whole, no Totality – only multiples without One. The law of being, then, is unbounded multiplicity, and its only stopping point is the void, which is the vortex of any organized form of life, the void around which languages, cultures and worldviews are organized. Badiou relies on Pascal for the insight that the infinite is the banal reality rather than the predicate of transcendence of every situation (Badiou 2001, p. 25). Every situation is composed of infinite elements, and each element is itself a multiple. Whereas the ethical ideology of the Other holds that an embodied subject transcends the banal particulars to reach infinity (i.e. the One), an ethic of truths assumes that the banal particulars of difference are infinite and that recognizing the Same, which is not yet, is to be realized in the infinite elements of a situation by means of a truth-procedure. A truth-procedure entails perseverance – keeping going – in terms of fidelity, discernment and restraint. For an event to have transformational consequences for trauma, some embodied subject must recognize and name the break as an event of a situation. This recognizing and naming of an event is what Badiou refers to as an intervention, which is the first moment of a process of fundamental change. The UN General Assembly did not intervene to declare Rwanda a genocide state until several months later. An intervention, as the initial moment of a process of fundamental change (i.e. a transformation), inaugurates a generic truth-procedure, a series of enquiries that ask into and map out the implications of the disruptive and deterritorializing consequences of an event. Those enquiries are what open up and unfold prior singularities as new multiples 'stripped bare of any predicates, any identity' (Badiou 2005, p. 21). Badiou refers to those who recognize and name an event and enquire into an event's situation and its pragmatic entailments as militants, that is, those who act in fidelity to an event by enquiring about it in the interests of the discernment of and the restraint of a truth. 'The object of these enquiries is to work out how to transform the situation in line with what is revealed by the event's belonging to the situation' (Badiou 2001, p. 25).

What then is the status of the Other, of difference and of the coming of the Same? Any experience whatsoever is the expression of infinite differences. A body's experience of subjectivity is not evidence of unity, but rather of a labyrinthine system of differentiations. There are as many differences between any two bodies on the planet as there are elements of a singular body; as many, but neither more nor fewer: 'The animals of the species *Homo sapiens* are ordinary multiplicities' (Badiou 2001, p. 50). The difficulty lies not on the side of difference but on the side of 'the Same'. It is not as if differences do not exist; quite obviously they do – *ad infinitum*. And that is Badiou's point. They are of little interest, however, insofar as differences constitute the multiplicities of immanence. The principle to be affirmed is that since difference is quite simply what *is* (i.e. it is the entering condition) and since every truth is a coming to be of what is not yet, differences are precisely what truth-procedures depose and render insignificant. A truth is that to which the advent of 'the Same' comes to be. It is in this sense that a truth is indifferent to differences (pp. 25–7).

Reconciling trauma durationally

Intuition, unlike representation, leads us beyond the state of experience, towards the conditions of experience, and these conditions are no broader than that which is conditioned. They are the singular conditions of actual experience. Intuition opens us up to the inhuman and the superhuman, that is, durations which are inferior or superior to our own, leading us beyond the human condition, beyond the decisive turn of experience. This, Deleuze claims, is the meaning of philosophy. The conditions of experience are determined largely in pure percepts. When we have followed each of the 'lines' – the objective line of intervals and the affective line of subjectivity – beyond the turn in experience, we must also rediscover the point at which object and subject intersect again, where the lines cross and the different kinds of tendencies link back together, giving rise to the Event as we know it. Percept and affect, object and subject, body and spirit, physics and metaphysics articulate again at a virtual point, at a virtual image (i.e. Event) of the point of departure, which is itself located beyond the turn in experience (i.e. event), and which finally gives us the sufficient reason (i.e. it makes sense) of the thing. In this instance, the composite trauma is the sufficient reason, the sense we make of the Event; that is, the point of traumatic departure. The divergence of percept and affect converge; the logical and the ontological come together; composite experience makes sense to us.

Coming to ethical terms with the Rwandan genocide requires never losing sight of the fact that in many profound ways the genocide is not over; body and spirit have yet to converge. Not only do Hutu *genocidaires* continue intermittently executing Tutsi survivors and Hutu moderates well into the twenty-first century, but the Tutsi and Hutu moderate survivors continue to live in close proximity with the extremist Hutu *genocidaires* who slaughtered their extended family members and who raped and infected grandmothers, mothers, wives and daughters with HIV. In so many ways it sounds hopelessly naïve for Rwandans to think in terms of *post*-conflict and *post*-genocide. Survivors continue a living death, both living with death, and living with the dead who have an unshakable hold over them. Lauren Wolfe observes that to even begin to comprehend the concept of reconciling collective trauma under these conditions requires coming to terms with the dead. In her interview with Richard Neugebauer, a professor of clinical epidemiology in psychiatry at Columbia University, he observes: 'if Rwandans can resume their lives in the world, many of them must first renegotiate their ties with the deceased' (Lauren Wolfe, *Atlantic*, p. 3). The question of ethical immanence is how to go about such renegotiating work; is it even possible?

Consider the scale of the collective trauma and the scope and duration of collective reconciliation: (1) As of 2014, nearly everyone over the age of 20 has recollection-memories and contraction-memories of an entire country witnessing friends, acquaintances and loved ones hacked to death, raped and maimed; (2) 15 percent of Rwandans who were children during the genocide actually hid under dead bodies to survive; (3) 90 percent of the surviving children believed they would die; (4) in order to produce 1,170, 000 corpses in 100 days, seven unarmed men, women, children and infants (not counting foetuses) were hunted down and killed every minute. The individual accounts of both survivors and *genocidaires* are numerous and breathtaking to read.[16] Keep in mind that this rate of the production of anti-production was accomplished with low-technology hand tools – machetes, clubs and spears. 'The dead of Rwanda accumulated at nearly three times the rate of Jewish dead during the Holocaust. It was the most efficient mass killing since the atomic bombings of Hiroshima and Nagasaki' (Gourevitch 1998, p. 3).

Several other sociocultural forces are important to factor into our study. First, as Consolee Nishimwe, a Tutsi woman who was 14 during the 100-day massacre and was repeatedly raped by Hutu *interahamwe* boys and men and infected with HIV, tells

Lauren Wolfe in an interview, 'In our culture, we don't talk a lot about experiences' (Wolfe, 4/14/2014, p. 1). That virtual tendency is compounded currently in Rwanda by a government programme called 'Vision 2020', inaugurated by President Paul Kagame, to transform 'post-genocide' Rwanda into a thriving, 'healthy' state with a quasi-democratic regime of signs articulated to an axiomatic capitalist economy (Wolfe, p. 2). Currently, Rwanda is experiencing impressive economic growth driven by Western capital investment and booming construction, particularly in Kigali, the capital of Rwanda. In interviews, President Kagame has expressed his intention to model Rwanda after Singapore, an economically successful authoritarian democracy. For him and his RPF government, it is of vital importance for Rwanda to 'move on' from the 'tragedy' and to 'never lose control again'. To that end, he has forbidden discussion of the genocide, except during the state-sponsored proceedings of gaçaça courts. Otherwise, referring to Rwandans as Hutu and Tutsi is strictly forbidden. There is a 'script' of Rwandan Unity that is referred to by Rwandans today when interviewed by journalists and when doing business with US and Western European capitalists currently investing heavily in Rwanda's future.

Agonistic and antagonistic discourses are confusions of ontological and psychological composites (experience), of conflated Chronos and Aion, a time both now and not-now in space that is both here and not-here. Affect remains long after percept fades. Conflict and reconciliation discourses are vernacular insofar as they are local, and vehicular insofar as the 'over there' of the other is the vernacular for each, which it rarely is. The respective discourses are contents and expressions of radically different historicized places and spatialized times, which ensures the inexhaustible immanent inevitability of conflicting traumatized discourses grappling with the pragmatics of how to proceed and what to say, if anything, without a map, with only the vaguest of instructions, and with no guarantees. As mixtures and composites of material and psychic forces, as composites of brain and mind, body and spirit, experience continues to leave all sorts of marks on the surfaces of bodies and spirits. Acknowledging and thereby implicitly affirming their signifiance is a precondition for transforming from Aion to Chronos, from transcendent dissociated depths of a primary order beyond the reach of language to transcendental virtual sense, verbal representation, good sense, common sense and immanent empirical consciousness; that is the focus of Chapter 5.

In a number of important respects, coming to immanent ethical terms with the scale, speed and barbarity of the Event of the Rwandan genocide requires concepts that Deleuze, and Deleuze with Guattari, create for their transcendental-empirical philosophy. It is not uncommon in journalistic and historical accounts of the Rwandan genocide to invoke the phrase 'killing machine', at times to refer to the entire Event, at other times to refer to the 'work' of the *interahamwe*. In *A-O*, Deleuze and Guattari refer to the concept 'machine' as any connection of organs linking flows in networks of desiring-production; in *ATP*, they refer to 'machine' variously as any assemblage functioning as the 'cutting edges of deterritorialization', (Deleuze and Guattari 1987, p. 333) and as any functional structure under the command of a higher unity (Deleuze and Guattari 1987, p. 457). More precisely for our purposes, the concept 'machinic assemblage' (Deleuze and Guattari 1987, p. 71) refers to an actualized abstract machine maintaining consistency, the teamwork of heterogeneous elements. The contents of the territorial assemblage of post-colonial, pre-genocidal, genocidal and post-genocidal Rwanda are referred to as a 'machinic assemblage of bodies' (Deleuze and Guattari 1987, p. 88) and its expressions are referred to as a 'collective assemblage of enunciation', that is, a collection of order-words that produce or effect incorporeal transformations of the bodies comprising machinic assemblages.[17]

The concept 'order-word', which is taken up in greater detail in Chapter 4, refers to 'the elementary unit of language' (Deleuze and Guattari 1987, p. 76) and a 'trigger for incorporeal transformation' (Deleuze and Guattari 1987, p. 79). Deleuze and Guattari insist that language is oriented to experimentation, not to representation, which is the conventional communication studies understanding of language, that is, that language represents 'things', thereby giving them their 'meanings'. Oriented to experimentation, however, language is thought of as a resource for producing practical effects. Order-words are assembled in regimes of signs; they intervene in bodies as expressions directing content in an assemblage. Expressions are articulated to desiring-bodies and interpolated into content as interventions, not to represent contents but to do things to and with contents, that is, to anticipate and to move them, to slow them down or speed them up, to separate and combine them, and to delimit them in a variety of ways.[18] Chapters 4 and 5 examine order-words and phrases that triggered incorporeal transformations of machinic assemblages of Hutu boys and men, transforming them into *interahamwe*, and then transforming *interahamwe* into a functional killing machine under the command of the Hutu government (Clark 2010, pp. 24–5).

In many important respects, the *interahamwe* constituted a 'war machine', which Deleuze and Guattari refer to as a machinic assemblage that effectuates the abstract machine of creativity in the world by forming a smooth space which maintains social formations in a far-from-equilibrium or 'intensive crisis' condition (Deleuze and Guattari 1987, p. 457). A 'war machine', then, is a smoothing counterforce to the state's stratification machine, which forms hierarchical, centralized and overcoded social formations. A war machine is that which effectuates 'non-organic life' (Deleuze and Guattari 1987, p. 411). Deleuze and Guattari emphasize the creative capacity of war machines as counterforces to state stratification, so when a war machine is captured by the state and becomes an apparatus of the state (e.g. as a standing police force and/or an army) capable only of destruction and war, it fails as a war machine. Although it can take the form and substance of a violent fighting force, the creativity of a war machine cannot be denied. But to the extent that the *interahamwe* became a machinic assemblage under the command of the Rwandan government prior to and during the genocide, it failed as a creative and productive war machine (e.g. nomadic guerilla forces, terrorist cells, covert and clandestine operations) as it was becoming a killing machine. It was never a legitimate war machine insofar as the *interahamwe*, from its inception, was always already complicit with the state, implicitly at first and explicitly after President Habyarimana's assassination.

During his International Criminal Tribunal for Rwanda (ICTR) trial in Arusha following the genocide, the then former prime minister of the interim government, Jean Kambanda, provided a detailed account of the five-level command structure that had driven the 1994 genocide from 7 April to 4 July. At the top was the army's crisis committee with a 'phantom structure' which included the unnamed mastermind of the genocide, Colonel Théoneste Bagosora; the second tier was the official military hierarchy, followed by the political leaders under the influence of, even if not under the direct command of, the military; the bottom two tiers were the interim government and the civilian self-defence programme, respectively.[19] In many ways, Grégoire Kayibanda, as the first president of the post-colonial Rwandan Republic, fostered a sense of impunity with respect to violence against the Tutsi population, who by this time had become scapegoats. But this sense of impunity was more than benign tolerance; the Hutu regime gradually (and not so gradually) encouraged violence against Tutsi. Following the formation of *interahamwe* militias, they operated with total impunity, and in the last years of Habyarimana's presidency, Tutsi were openly massacred with no threat of arrest and/or prosecution. In this way, Rwanda was becoming a murderous state long before the Rwandan genocide Event; the pogrom had been taking place for quite some time. Once immanent to the state bureaucracy, the reactive forces of impunity took on a life of their own, gaining resiliency and momentum. In fact, extremist Hutu planning of Tutsi massacres was well under way prior to President Habyarimana's assassination on 6 April 1994.[20]

Gaçaça courts as partial war machines

Witnessing (in the doubled-sense of 'observing' and 'testifying to') the marks of trauma during the process of gaçaça proceedings recognizes and acknowledges the signs of both the content and the expression of the actions and passions of bodies. Witnessing, in effect, actualizes the articulation of the content of the unspeakable to the expression of the disembodied. Witnessing is necessary durational work in the course of 'coming to terms', never satisfactorily, with experience now interpolated, as contraction-memory consumes recollection-memory. In short, the marks of experience must be witnessed, that is, recognized, acknowledged and imagined in order to reconcile truth and creation at the level of the problem becoming-resolved, and it is necessary to shift from the virtual, the time of Aion and transcendent mythic verbal representation to another time and another discursive register. Given the immanence of empirical consciousness and the transcendental surface of thought, how is it possible to 'shift time' from Aion to Chronos, from a time of transcendental nomadic thought to the time of empirical consciousness, a serial present that passes in representation and is understood in terms of logical propositions?

The extent to which conversing, negotiating and mediating-machines conjure a transcendental mythic past (Aion) is the extent to which their discourses actually consummate and consume the immanent present (Chronos); stepping outside of our human durations is necessary to become aware of the durational contours and rhythms of other subjects and objects. The articulation of bodies to discourses opens onto two kinds of time – Chronos and Aion. Machinic assemblages of bodies bring the corporeality/materiality of content (i.e. its substance and form) to the substance and form of expression afforded by the discursive registers (i.e. the communication machines) of collective assemblages of enunciation – the extensity of bodies articulate to the durationality of expression. Bear in mind that the time of verbal representation, of virtual sense, of transcendental thought, of Aion is never present – it has only just occurred, and is only about to happen; it is empty time. It is nomadic thought unencumbered by the immensity and immediacy of corporeal/material forces of the primary order of the schizoid depths. Transcendental thought may remain transcendent, that is, virtual, cut off from the ontological genesis of the denoted of good sense and the logical genesis of the manifested and the signified of common sense.

Escalation to violent antagonistic social conflict is all but inevitable to the extent that conflict's sense remains transcendental, con-fused with good sense and common sense, and thereby dissociated from empirical consciousness and logical propositions. Escalation to violent social conflict is a seemingly inevitable by-product of transcendental verbal representation disconnected from the good sense and common sense founding empirical consciousness of the tertiary order in Deleuze's genesis of representation. The immanence of 'here' and 'now' (i.e. the present of Chronos of the proposition) is present time in and through which resolving conflict and reconciling trauma actually take place durationally. They become actually (i.e. empirically) immanent and virtually real. Keep in mind that the generative, transformational, diagrammatic and machinic components of regimes of signs (to be taken up in Chapter 4) only partially account for the myriad and variable ways in which duration (differences in kind) is experienced as composites (differences in degree). Conversing, negotiating, mediating and dialoguing, as communication machines, constitute different registers of expression for regimes of signs, each regime capable of transforming into another, articulating utterances of expression by extracting from them unformalized signs. Those extracted regimes of unformalized signs constitute unformed traits that combine with one another, producing utterances.

The discursive registers of conversing, mediating, negotiating and dialoguing are double-articulation machines, drawing forms of content from flows of matter and energy, and forms of expression from collective assemblages of enunciation. As articulations of content and expression, articulations may or may not be addressed to a second-body; implicitly, they are addressed to a third-body. Mikhail Bakhtin claims that each utterance has three audiences: the addresser is the body manifesting as the speaker of the enunciation; the addressee is the body or bodies manifesting as the intended listener(s) of the enunciation; and the superaddressee is an implied witness who may or may not be explicitly addressed. Bakhtin contends that when the superaddressee is ignored and/or forgotten the ethical lapses can be horrendous. We know what it looks like and sounds like when these ontological lapses take place; differences in degree are distorted and collapsed into the bloodlust of sacred and absolute purification. Most certainly discourse that represents conflict, that is, discourse 'about' conflict, is different in kind from discourse 'of' conflict and 'of' resolution and reconciliation. The discourse 'of' conflict is constitutive; it is that which, along with material assemblages of bodies, embodies the conflict's unfolding. It is discourse of verbal representation remaining transcendent with no present, discourse that fails to articulate good sense and common sense to the propositional logic of empirical consciousness. Said another way, it sounds and looks like discourse with little or no reflexivity, that is, discourse that ignores or forgets its superaddressee and unfolds without witness and with little or no articulation of transcendental sense to logical propositions of empirical consciousness.

At that juncture, language becomes incomprehensible sounds of partial-bodies and part-objects colliding and interpenetrating, the sounds of the sensations of the primary order of schizoid depths. Intuiting attunement to a superaddressee of immanent ethics of the interval is one line of flight to empirical consciousness with a present time that passes in representation.

For Deleuze, the concept 'machine' refers to any connection of organs linking together flows in networks of desiring-production. More specifically, 'social machines' are assemblages linking together bodies and regimes of signs; 'technical machines' (Bonta and Protevi 2004, p. 107) can only be used when linked with bodies to form parts of social machines. The connections man-bow-horse is a *technical machine*; for our purposes, as assemblages linking bodies and regimes of signs, *social machines* such as conversing, negotiating, mediating and dialoguing link bodies and regimes of signs. Gaçaça courts are technical machines; they are machines that can only be used when linked with bodies to form *parts of social machines*. Gaçaça courts, then, are technical machines (i.e. linking state support-elected elders-*genocidaires*-survivors-community-members) with social machines (i.e. conversing-arguing-negotiating-mediating-dialoguing) insofar as gaçaça courts operate as technical parts of social machines that, in turn, function as part of post-genocide territorial assemblages. The social machines of conversing, arguing, negotiating and mediating consist in registers of minor or vernacular communication, which is the focus of the next chapter. Such registers are minoritarian not in the numerical sense of being determined by smaller numbers and by diminished significance, but minoritarian in the sense of being vernacular and local rather than dominant and official.

Forces of transitional justice conjured by gaçaça court processes and practices can be thought of as a kind of 'war machine' as well, although it is an unlikely name for a concept referring to a social machine designed to produce transitional justice. Once again, a war machine is a machinic assemblage that effects and produces (i.e. effectuates) an abstract machine of creativity (i.e. transitional justice) smoothing the striations (i.e. the unimaginably deep wounds) that the affect of recollection-memory and contraction-memory fill in the interval between embodied trauma and psychic spirit. Gaçaça courts, thought of as a war machinic counter-force to Rwanda's stratified post-genocidal bureaucratic administration of governance, were designed to go beyond the experience of genocide to the conditions of experience in order to decode the overcoded social formations that had produced the genocide. Deleuze and Guattari characterize the state as always already attempting to incorporate 'war machines' into the state apparatus, military or otherwise. But the moment the state captures a nomadic war machine (such as gaçaça, or the *interahamwe*), and/or when violence erupts and war actually 'breaks out' and 'takes place' is the moment the 'war machine' fails in its creative capacity. In this respect, gaçaça courts functioned more productively as war machines than did the *interahamwe*. However, the dialectic of nomadic war machines and state-organized militaries remains a self-organizing assemblage of internal and external relations.

Unlike state-sponsored military forces, war machines actually tap into, connect with and articulate to the powers of self-organizing, self-governing, self-sustaining forces and tendencies. In the twelfth plateau of *ATP* – '1227: Treatise on Nomadology:–

The War Machine', Deleuze and Guattari state quite directly, 'in other words, the war machine is that which effectuates "Non-organic life"' (p. 411). Some of those far-from-equilibrium conditions of intense crisis and relatively smooth spaces become rather quickly reterritorialized and restratified, actualizing as variable proportions of paranoid-fascistic desire or schizoid-anarchistic desire. Keep in mind that for Deleuze and Guattari, all interconnected operations of abstract machines (of what they refer to as the 'Mechanosphere') perform three primary functions: creation, stratification and capture. Mark Bonta and John Protevi synopsize these three functions of abstract machines as 'life (i.e. creation) and that which captures life to stratify it, to set life against itself so as to limit itself (i.e. stratification and capture)' (Bonta and Protevi 2004, pp. 47–9).

Gaçaça courts, thought of as instrumental technical machines of transitional justice in Rwanda's post-genocide territorial assemblage, were state-sponsored but locally administered, leaving room for conditioning gaçaça processes to local circumstances, that is, allowing local conditions to actually condition the creations that were set up against life to limit it. It would have been impossible for Paul Kagame to ignore the Event of genocide and to proceed with governance as though no pogrom had taken place, and no trauma had been produced, although Kagame has refused to acknowledge Tutsi RPF retaliatory massacres of Hutu subsequent to 4 July 1994. No Tutsi have appeared as defendants in gaçaça courts. Another conceivable response to the events of the Event of genocide would have been to invite an International Criminal Tribunal to Rwanda to try as many individual cases as possible. Insurmountable problems remain: How much weight should be given to truth and justice, how much to creation and reconciliation? What is fair and just in each case? What is true and right, given the decimated judicial infrastructure, the available evidence, the willingness of survivors to testify, and importantly, the duration of such an undertaking? The two lines of the method of intuition, that is, the line of the interval and the line of subjectivity (i.e. the line of justice and the line of reconciliation), began as one and became separated. Colonialism left indelible scars from cutting differences in kind where only differences in degree had existed, making the work of producing transitional justice and collective reconciliation all but impossible, at least in any imaginable duration. Intuition projects the convergence of body and spirit beyond the turn of experience; the question without an answer at this juncture is the duration prior to convergence. How might such convergence be facilitated, if it is even immanently ethical to pose such a question, for people-yet-to-come during times-yet-to-come? Nelson Mandela may have been an example of 'the fullness of time' – that is, a duration of convergence in South Africa. He intuited a convergence during a time-yet-to-come; he intuited an eventual articulation of what is fair and just, what is true and right. Presently, Paul Kagame and most Rwandans (Hutu and Tutsi) are wrestling with those paradoxical questions in Rwanda.

When resolutions and reconciliations actualize as social-productions of gaçaça courts, they do so primarily in and through affect and will, that is, the line of subjectivity, in the sense of will (i.e. willingness) to go beyond experience. Willingness can be conjured subjectively and discursively and expressed as open-ended vulnerability. Resolution and reconciliation have much more to do with vulnerability and becoming-willing than they do with logical propositionality. Becoming-willing relaxes paranoia in the intervals between percept and affect, body and spirit. Intervals, Deleuze's Bergson reminds us, are the hesitations and gaps between excitation and execution, between when the brain perceives and when the body core responds. This is one of the many work sites where conflict resolution can be revitalized, rethought along Deleuzian and in some important instances, Deleuzian-feminist lines.[21] The pivotal question, really, is how to convoke vulnerability and conjure willingness; how to 'create' and negotiate and mediate willingness, however it manifests.

Turns to and returns from the meaninglessness and madness, the schizoid depths of violence, the corporeality/materiality of partial-bodies and part-objects (i.e. the hacked and bleeding bodies, severed limbs, object-rape and genital-rape, the machetes, clubs and spears, the marijuana, banana beer and adrenalin, the cultural history of German and Belgian colonialism, the *ressentiment* and bad conscience colonialism breeds, the discourse of hatred, the exhibition of superiority and the authorization of murder with impunity) overwhelm transcendental thought and verbal representation of secondary organization of the genesis of representation. The affective dynamics of a primary order of chaos and violence become sublimated onto and symbolized on the transcendental surface of thought, overwhelming virtual sense, overtaking good sense and common sense, and in the process primary order, secondary organization and tertiary order collapse into one another. The denoted, the signified, the manifested and transcendental sense – now conflated transcendentally on a surface of thought overwhelmed by the chaos, schizo-madness and the corporeality/materiality of partial-bodies and part-objects of a primary order – become empirical consciousness and logical propositionality. The witness of a superaddressee is forgotten.

The three stages of the genesis of representation collapse into one another in a timeless time of a mythic Aion, a becoming-collective madness with impunity passing as good sense and common sense that found a genocidal empirical consciousness and logical propositionality. Badly analysed composites (i.e. experience) incrementally 'fill in' the line of intervals between event and response, between body and spirit, collapsing the interval and conflating affect, recollection-memory and contraction-memory into unreflexive consciousness configured as a transcendental unconscious. The turning and returning of the eternal return becomes a return of the same rather than the return of difference; certainly not a coming of the Same. The affect/percept dynamics of a primary order spread incrementally and imperceptibly, as if by silent, unspoken contagion, becoming-sublimated and symbolized and at the same time becoming-common sense and good sense, actualizing collective madness, an incremental psychosis with no perceptible 'break'. How are we to 'make different and more adequate sense' of the truths of such asymmetrical social violence and its failure of exemption from immanent ethics? What sense does it make to imagine a justice of genocide, and a reconciling of unspeakable trauma, even if trauma reconciliation may never be actualized?

4

Minor Communication, Regimes of Signs and Conversing Machines

Chapter overview

To create spaces for victims and survivors to speak of unspeakable violence and to witness the affect of unimaginable trauma in a sustained effort to converse, negotiate and mediate transitional justice, and to reconcile collective trauma – that was arguably the most daunting ontological and ethical problem for Rwanda in the wake of the 1994 genocide. To actualize transitional justice without crippling Rwanda's uneasy post-genocide stability, the Paul Kagame-led government adapted the traditional Rwandan form and substance for resolving disputes among family members and within villages. Although a controversial solution to the problems for which it was intended, gaçaça courts had the potential of becoming spaces where 'smoothing' and 'striating' forces could negotiate double articulations from which coherent transitional justice and collective reconciliation might emerge. Although gaçaça courts were state-sponsored, and in that sense they were stratified state structures, gaçaça courts were also locally administered by elected elders and attended by villagers, victims and survivors, and in that sense they were smooth spaces conditioned by local circumstances. In effect, gaçaça courts constituted the conditions of possibility for actions and passions of desiring-bodies to articulate to regimes of signs and social institutions, thereby producing an 'uneasy peace'.[1]

Rwanda as a territorial assemblage

The stratifications of Rwanda's sociocultural order are the historical products of German and Belgian political colonization and of Catholic religious colonization. Pre-colonial Munyarwanda cultural identity and cultural memory consisted in a tripolar conception of the universe; relationships were established in terms of family members (i.e. *umuryango)* and friends, in terms of enemies (i.e. *abanzi)*, and in terms of the third party (i.e. *rubanda*). The durational effects of colonial religious, social and propagandist discourses transformed the Munyarwanda tripolar cultural identity and memory into a bipolar conception of the universe, consisting in *bakristu* (i.e. Christian) and *bapagani-bashenzi* (i.e. pagan). The third term dropped out of this colonialist conception of Munyarwanda cultural identity and memory: the category *bakristu* was introduced and equated to Hamite (i.e. children of Ham, son of Noah), becoming-Hutu; the category *bapagani* was *bakristu's* oppositional other and equated to Bantu, becoming-Tutsi. In effect, a bipolar cultural identity and memory displaced a dynamically balanced tripolar ontological universe. Twa, which equated to pygmy, effectively disappeared.[2] Agonistic relations and tensions between Hutu, living predominantly as pastoralists, and Tutsi, living predominantly as herders, became increasingly antagonistic, even though relations between them had persisted in states of uneasy peace prior to German, Belgian and Catholic colonialism.[3]

Stratification processes for Deleuze are the products of double articulations, as elaborated in the preceding chapter, that is, processes of extracting material from a milieu and organizing that material semiotically, producing relatively stable material-semiotic structures (Deleuze and Guattari 1987, pp. 40–1). The first articulation is territorialization, a selection of a substance of content from a flow of material or matter in an assemblage, and coding, a selection of form of content for ordering the substance of content. German, Belgian and Catholic colonialists selected Gatutsi substance from the Munyarwanda flow of material, and ordered the Gatutsi hierarchically as superior to and privileged over Gahutu substance (Semujanga 2003, pp. 78–90). The second articulation is overcoding (i.e. a form of expression that is the creation of new linkages) and sedimentation or cementation (i.e. a substance of expression that creates new entities with emergent properties). German and Belgian colonialists overcoded Gatutsi, Gahutu and Gatwa as Hamite and Bantu; Catholic missionaries/colonialists overcoded *bakristu* (Christian) Hamite as Tutsi and *bapagani-bashenzi* (pagan) as Hutu. Double articulation of stratification results in relatively stable structures of state institutions; to that end, the Belgians instituted mandatory identity cards. Post-colonial Rwanda experienced escalating violence fuelled by intensive hatred and resentment born in large measure of these colonial practices of double articulation: the 1959–60 revolution; a tumultuous declaration of independence in July of 1962; ongoing massacres of Tutsi throughout the 1960s (the best known of these was in Gikongoro in January 1964 resulting in between 7,000 and 10,000 deaths); the *coup d'état* of Juvénal Habyarimana in January 1974 inaugurating The Second Republic; and catastrophic poverty during the early 1990s leading up to the 1994 assassination of Habyarimana and the onset of the genocide in April of 1994 (Semelin 2007, pp. 66–8).

Following the 1994 Rwandan genocide, violent conflict continued to spread throughout the Great Lakes region, particularly intensively in the DRC, with widespread implications for the Rwandan territorial assemblage. The first Congo war of 1996–97 erupted in the former Zaire when the Rwandan Patriotic Front (RPF) post-genocide government forces, in conjunction with Ugandan and Burundian forces, supported Zairian rebels led by Laurent Desirée Kabila to overthrow Mobutu Sese Seko, then the president of Zaire. In a reactive response, Mobutu allied with Angolan, Namibian and Zimbabwean forces, creating a pan-African territorial assemblage. Zaire deterritorialized into a fluid space of intensive smoothing processes, a battlefield for foreign interests and reactive forces competing for the abundant mineral and agricultural resources of the largest country in sub-Saharan Africa. Despite its geographical size, its rich farmlands and its abundant copper, diamonds, gold, coltan and enough hydropower to fuel the entire African continent, Zaire currently is one of the poorest and most hopeless nations on earth. Following the post-genocide RPF Tutsi retaliatory killing of suspected Hutu genocide suspects, an estimated 1.5 million Hutu refugees, including many of the architects of the genocide and members of the *interahamwe*, fled in advance of RPF forces into Zaire at the Goma border crossing. Ironically, and probably unwittingly, these refugee Hutu forces were fed and clothed by Western aid organizations, enabling them to train in the refugee camps and to make violent incursions into Rwanda in an effort to finish killing all the Rwandan Tutsi. In May of 1997, facing Kabila's superior forces, Mobutu went into exile, which among other effects scattered *interahamwe* forces and Mobutu militias throughout the eastern region of DRC.[4]

When Kabila's Alliance with Rwanda, Uganda and Burundi came apart in 1998, a second Congo war erupted and continued through 1999. Although the Alliance unravelled, it did not deterritorialize. Rwandan, Burundian and Ugandan forces did not leave the eastern region of DRC; they remained to pillage the region's gold, diamonds and coltan – a rare mineral used in the manufacture of mobile phones (Halvorsen 1999, p. 24). Most of this nomadic war machinic activity was accomplished via military proxies. For example, Rwanda supported and backed Rally for Congolese Democracy (RCD) forces, which were more of a state-sponsored militia than a nomadic war machine. In reactive response to these proxy military attacks, Kabila armed Rwandan Hutu *interahamwe* and local militias known as Mai Mai to drive foreign forces, their proxies and Congolese Tutsi out of DRC. Rwandan government forces reacted, in turn, by attacking the border-crossing city of Goma, and Bukavu and Uvira in North and South Kivu. Kabila, in his reactive turn, forged alliances once again with the governments of Angola and Zimbabwe, exchanging a share of the DRC's mining resources for their support in repelling Rwandan, Burundian and Ugandan forces. Hutu–Tutsi hatred, along with a desire for DRC's mineral wealth, fuelled this conflict from 1998 to 2000, killing nearly 2 million people as a result of violence, disease and deprivation, and systematic assaults on hundreds of thousands of women have earned Congo the label 'the rape capital of the world'.[5]

The most recent violence and trauma in the DRC is in the northeastern province of Ituri, between two local ethnic groups – the Hema and the Lendu. The Hema, like the Tutsi in Rwanda and Burundi, are nomad pastoralists and the Lendu, like the Hutu, are sedentary cultivators and farmers. In 1999, a conflict over land in Ituri ignited violence between Hema and Lendu. Ugandan forces had supported Hema as business allies, enabling Uganda to pillage Ituri's natural resource wealth. In 2002, Hema and Ugandan forces attacked and killed hundreds of Lendu militia and civilians. Lendu militias retaliated, escalating violence and trauma on both sides that human rights groups identified as genocide. Phil Clark concludes: 'The conflict in Ituri therefore follows the pattern of other recent conflicts in the DRC, involving rapidly changing alliances between rebel groups supported by regional governments, with ethnicity, greed and power the protagonists' primary motivation' (Clark 2010, p. 25). He insists that Rwanda's intense involvement in the violence of eastern Congo explains why, following the 1994 genocide, Rwanda remains such a heavily armed and militarized state. The Rwandan Tutsi RPF-based government remains hyper vigilant in its post-genocide preoccupation with containing Hutu rebels and *interahamwe* in DRC. 'The Rwandan government invokes the threat of a second genocide to justify its military presence in the DRC' (Clark 2010, p. 25).

Social-production is perpetual libidinal-economic production of virtual and actual reality. A paranoid, fascist subject, overtaken by the terror of chaos and schizoid motion, clings tenaciously to its conjunctively produced identity, whereas a schizoid nomadic subject is carried along by energy flows of desiring-production taking it beyond familiar territorializations of family, private property and the state. Given an entering assumption of scarcity, a capture mentality with an acquisitive logic and a rapacious libidinal- and political-economics, consummation and consumption are incapable of ever transforming scarcity into abundance. Scarcity can only reproduce itself reactively. Given the intensities of immanent smoothing forces, desiring-production only produces flows of uncoded desire and capital that deterritorialize overcoded stratifications of sedentary formations, flows that multiply, distribute and disperse partial identifications that, in turn, threaten sedentary identity. Schizoid flows of uncoded desire become coded and then overcoded paranoically and fascistically, and the abundance of schizoid, nomadic experimentation is not recognized and registered as virtual potentiality.

Sustaining paranoid scarcity produces subtractive forces moving centripetally towards an essentialized transcendence. By contrast, thinking of desire as centrifugal forces moving expansively and multiplicatively, desiring-production is thought of as becoming-abundance. Desire flows and overflows out along lines of flight, crossing borders and transgressing boundaries; it *needs* nothing at all. Desire is not an acquisition machine seeking to satisfy scarcity; it produces rather than consumes, adds and multiplies rather than subtracts and divides, and it affirms rather than negates. As centrifugal forces, desiring-production expands, and when blocked relationally and overcoded it becomes self-referential. It turns back on itself, becoming-centripetal, becoming an inward reactive force. When desire of machinic assemblages of bodies turns back on itself, prior to articulating to collective assemblages of enunciation, desire comes to desire itself, which is a centripetal reversal of desire's centrifugal expansiveness. A body's centripetal, self-referential and inward turning blocks flows of desiring-production; 'becoming-' is captured and contained by 'being', that is, an exclusive (rather than inclusive) disjunctive synthesis of anti-production.

War machines and killing machines

Rwandan Hutu, largely *interahamwe* militias of young men and boys, who most certainly constituted a killing machine, had been consuming PARMEHUTU (Hutu Power) propagandist discourse disseminated from a variety of sources, including a private radio and television network financed by the Mouvement Révolutionnaire National pour le Développement (MRND) *nomenklatura* and broadcast over the Radiotélevision libre des mille collines (RTLM), exhorting Hutu to exterminate the 'enemy within' and 'traitors' to the Republic. But the genocide arguably was not a *micro*-managed state military action executed through a hierarchical and disciplined chain of military command and executed by trained military personnel. It was, however, a centrally planned and organized genocide by centrally placed, high-ranking extremist Hutu government forces. Deleuze and Guattari insist that a state actually going to war, or otherwise executing violence to enforce its will, with an army capable of exercising untold violence, is actually the moment that a war machine disperses throughout social formations.[6]

Rwanda's post-genocide government did not incorporate the *interahamwe* nomadic killing machine into its state military apparatus; the RPF became the post-genocide state-sponsored military. The *interahamwe* were rounded up and incarcerated or they fled to DRC or to Uganda. The psychotic intensity of overt genocidal forces was largely suppressed as the Rwandan Patriotic Front began organizing and establishing its regime.[7] The genocide had decimated Rwanda's judicial infrastructure – there were few if any functioning courts, and many of the judges and lawyers either had been killed or had fled the country. As a creative war machine, gaçaça formed by connecting desiring flows and self-organizing forces of social-production. Their object was not to wage actual war; it was to draw creative lines of flight. In this regard, post-genocide Rwanda can be thought of as a territorial assemblage, that is, as intensive networks productive of emergent self-ordering forces of heterogeneous material. Those emergent self-ordering forces were productive of transitional justice, the contents of which were machinic assemblages of bodies (i.e. genocide suspects, survivors, victims, elected elders, villagers) and the expressions of which were collective assemblages of enunciation (i.e. the discourses of minor communication that constituted quasi-legal proceedings of gaçaça courts). Gaçaça courts were neither state-sponsored courts of law nor internationally sponsored criminal tribunals, nor were they truth commissions.[8] They were invented as transitional justice territorial assemblages whose intensive processes consist in minor communication, which will be taken up in detail in subsequent sections of this chapter and the next. They were social machines, that is, assemblages linking material bodies and regimes of signs to produce transitional justice and to converse, negotiate and mediate collective trauma, that is, to deterritorialize genocidal Rwanda, and to reterritorialize post-genocidal Rwanda.

Rwandan genocide, thought of as the massive failure of a war machine, ultimately failed in its production of a smooth space, that is, it failed in its attempt to erase an entire category of its population, to destratify and deterritorialize the striated geopolitical spaces that constituted colonial and post-colonial Rwanda. State-sponsored and supported Hutu *interahamwe* militia forces attempting to destratify Rwanda by means of erasing all Tutsi and Hutu moderates did not 'succeed' in installing the permanent order of collective psychosis. In what follows, post-genocide gaçaça courts are thought as social machines of territorial assemblages (i.e. machinic assemblages) articulating bodies to regimes of signs. As social machines of machinic assemblages, gaçaças actualized the abstract machines of transitional justice and collective reconciliation. In the process of stratification, gaçaças were the 'surface of stratification' (Deleuze and Guattari 1987, p. 40). Given the relative chaos of the territorial assemblages that constituted post-genocide Rwanda, the contents and expressions of gaçaça courts as social machines can be thought as collective assemblages of bodies (bodies of elected elders, genocide suspects, genocide survivors, interested villagers and government officials) that articulated to collective assemblages of enunciation (consisting in sets of order-words, among other discursive and extra-discursive registers) capable of incorporeally transforming bodies and institutions.

Remember that for Deleuze and Guattari, connections constitute machines, and machinic assemblages are connections whose relations are external to the nodes of connection. Gaçaça courts were partially state-captured and only approximately overcoded social machines that produced transitional (i.e. emergent) justice by striating the smooth (i.e. 'scorched earth') spaces of genocide's devastating aftermath. Gaçaça courts were accountable to the police and Rwanda's national legal system, which meant that genocide suspects were legally mandated to appear and to participate in gaçaça courts and their transitional justice processes. However, gaçaça courts constituted more than technical judicial machines that produced verdicts and judgements; they furnished 'the model of a form of content that is applicable to the whole social field, whereas the juridical statement furnishes the model for a form of expression applicable to any statement. . . . [M]achine, statement, and desire form part of one and the same assemblage. . .' (Deleuze and Guattari 1987, p. 83). Gaçaça courts functioned as a model for the form of content and the form of expression for empirical actualizations of a return to more near-equilibrium, steady-state stratifications and sociocultural order.

Minor communication

Minor communication functions communicatively much as minor literature does in Deleuze and Guattari's study of Franz Kafka's oeuvre. Minor communication, like minor literature, has three characteristics: the deterritorialization of language; the connection of the individual to a political immediacy; and the collective assemblage of enunciation. For Deleuze and Guattari, 'minor' no longer designates specific literatures, but the revolutionary conditions of every literature within the heart of what is called 'great literature' (Deleuze and Guattari 1986, pp. xiv–xvi, 16–28). In their reading, communication is the dissemination of representations and the circulation of indirect discourse, carrying forward contraction-memory from a past by extending it into the present and forecasting it as a possibility – certainly an apt characterization of late-consumer capitalist, mass-mediated discourse. Communication and information have become so conflated as to blur distinctions between marketing discourse and information, the primary function of which is to traffic in mundane conversations of daily living, creating the information/communication glut that Deleuze and Guattari hold in such contempt. In this chapter, I distinguish between molar or dominant discourse and molecular or minor communication, a distinction Deleuze and Guattari map by creating the concepts of minor and major literature and writing.

In the case of communication, 'minor' no longer designates specific genres or conventional formats of communication, but the revolutionary potential of all forms of communication within the heart of what is called Language-in-action; 'tensors' or 'intensives' are the internal tensions of a language (Deleuze and Guattari 1986, pp. 22–3).

Conversing, negotiating, mediating and dialoguing are minor communication machines not under the administration and regulation of a state apparatus; as such, they have the revolutionary potential of rogue semiotics. Rogue semiotics are regimes of signs not fully captured by nor incorporated into the dominant assemblages of enunciation of state stratification; they are semiotics that enable minor communication machines. Conversing, negotiating, mediating and dialoguing, as minor communication machines, are the cutting edge of deterritorialization of conflict and trauma. Of course, those same communication machines, when captured by and incorporated into the stratified semiotics of the state, become transcendent forces of stratification.

In *Kafka: Toward a Minor Literature*, Deleuze and Guattari refer to a tetralinguistic model of language that Henri Gobard created based on the research of Ferguson and Gumperz. *Vernacular language* is maternal or territorial language used in rural communities, or rural in its origins; *vehicular language* is urban, governmental, even worldwide language, a language of businesses, commercial exchange and bureaucratic transmission, a language of the first sort of deterritorialization. *Referential language* is a language of sense and of culture and cultural reterritorialization. *Mythic language* is on the horizon of cultures, caught up in a spiritual or religious reterritorialization. The spatiotemporal compass of these languages differ sharply: vernacular language is *here*, vehicular language is *everywhere*, referential language is *over there* and mythic language is *beyond* (Deleuze and Guattari 1986, pp. 23–4). Minor communication hybridizes regimes of signs and models of language, creating unconventional registers, that is, unformed content and non-formal expressions, within dominant conventions of usage and sense. Minor communication mixes vernacular, vehicular, referential and mythic languages and their respective spatiotemporal domains relative to conventional and normative conceptions of geographical spaces and temporal durations. In doing so, it creates, circulates and distributes positions and turns, one crucial implication of which is that creation and communication need not be thought of as mutually exclusive. Minor communication is populated by conceptual personae, which is Deleuze and Guattari's thought-figure for articulations that are beyond the scope of any particular personal self.[9] Rather than attempting to transcend collective trauma and violent conflict, conceptual personae articulate conflict's empirical immanence and record those articulations, producing nomadic subjectivations of multiple identifications rather than sedentary subjectifications of fixed identities. And this is one of the profound accomplishments of gaçaça transitional justice processes – uneven as they are – when they are affirmatively productive; minor communication accounts for the accomplishment of many of gaçaça's schizoanalytically pragmatic objectives.

Regimes of signs

The concept 'regime of signs' refers to any 'formalization of expression' considered as 'a semiotic system' (Deleuze and Guattari 1987, p. 111). A regime of signs can be isolated by abstracting the form of expression (which is another name for 'regime of signs') from the form of content and from the substance of expression that together accompany any regime of signs. A territorial assemblage is composed of substance and form of content and of substance and form of expression. The former is a machinic assemblage of bodies, the latter a collective assemblage of enunciation. Keep in mind that the substance and form of content (a machinic assemblage of bodies) and the substance and form of expression (a collective assemblage of enunciation) together constitute a territorial assemblage. The collective assemblage of enunciation is comprised of social institutions responsible for incorporeal transformations of the appropriate order-words that constitute the form of the regime of signs.[10]

Regimes of signs are signifying regimes, that is, signs that signify other signs, and this referencing is a limitless signifiance, which in effect deterritorializes the sign.[11] 'The (imperial) signifier reigns over every domestic squabble, and in every State apparatus' (Deleuze and Guattari 1987, p. 117). A second principle of signs is that they are always 'brought back by other signs'; they never fail to return, which Deleuze and Guattari refer to as the circularity of the deterritorialized sign. A third property or principle of signs is that 'the sign jumps from circle to circle and displaces the center at the same time it ties into it'. These signifying circles expand, which is the inevitable product of interpretations that mark signifiers as signifieds at the same time they redeploy signifiers, assuring endless interpretosis. An infinite set of signs 'refers to a supreme signifier that presents itself as both lack and excess', that is, as the despotic signifier. The form of this supreme signifier has a substance, that is, a body and Face, for example, Hitler, Stalin, Mao, Tito, Kagame – portraits of faces. A line of flight away from a regime of signs is a line of excommunication; a body is marked as unworthy, condemned and expelled, marked as a scapegoat. For extremist Hutu, the bodies of Tutsi and moderate Hutu were not only marked as scapegoats and excommunicated; Tutsi were signs of vermin to be completely exterminated. Finally for Deleuze and Guattari, a regime of signs is a universal deception, 'in its jumps, in the regulated circles, in the seer's regulation of interpretations, in the publicness of the facialized center, and in the treatment of the line of flight' (Deleuze and Guattari 1987, p. 117). The above can be read as a rather precise characterization of post-colonial, genocidal and post-genocide Rwanda.

For Deleuze and Guattari, there are an indefinite number of regimes of signs; they discuss four ideal types – ideal in the sense that every semiotic system is mixed, consisting in fragmentary signs of one or more other semiotic systems. In addition to the imperial signifying system discussed above, Deleuze and Guattari describe a presignifying semiotic, which does not indicate that this semiotic system comes first or that it somehow precedes the others. This primitive or presignifying semiotic refers to relatively natural codings that operate without signs. Signifiers are not reduced to faciality and there is no subtraction of form from content. Instead, there is a plurality of forms of content, for example, rhythm, dance, gesture, ceremony and vocality. Signifiers constitute a multidimensional, pluralinear semiotic that resists circularity. In its linear segmentarity, it avoids universal abstractions, imperial signifiers, circular statements, state apparatuses, priests and castes, and scapegoats, all of which are properties of an imperial signifying regime. For a presignifying regime of signs, there is no point of subjectification, as there will be with the postsignifying semiotic regime. In many respects, from what can be known with any confidence of early pre-colonial Rwanda, its mythic-cultural history was a mixed, but predominantly, presignifying semiotic.

Certainly multidimensional and pluralinear in form, it was a system with three chiefs and a mwami, none of whom functioned as a despotic centring signifier. Statements were pluralinear and multidimensional, not circular. Filial relations were collections and combinations of relatives rather than distributions of individuals, and villages and property were figured as totals rather than as arrangements and accumulations. Priests were chiefs, not white Christians; there were tribes, not castes; and lines of flight constituted hunters and travellers, not excommunicated scapegoats. All of that came later, with German, Belgian and Catholic colonialism.

Deleuze and Guattari refer to the countersignifying semiotic as 'the fearsome, warlike, and animal-raising nomads, as opposed to hunter nomads, who belong to the previous semiotic', (Deleuze and Guattari 1987, p. 118) as did the animal-raising Tutsi of the presignifying semiotic. The countersignifying semiotic operates more in accord with arithmetic and numeration than with segmentarity. Numerical signs institute systems of marking mobile, plural distributions (rather than collections) and arrangements (rather than totals) that determine functions and relations and operate by breaks, transitions, migration and accumulation (rather than by combination). '[A] sign of this kind would appear to belong to the semiotic of a nomad war machine directed against the State apparatus' (Deleuze and Guattari 1987, p. 118). This characterizes Hutu during the colonial period, discriminated against as they were by the German and Belgian colonialists. The line of flight for the countersignifying regime of signs is a nomadic turning back against an imperial empire, cutting through or conquering them, unlike the imperial signifying regime whose line of flight is a scapegoat, a victim, an excommunicated body, as were the Hutu during the colonial period. With European colonialism, particularly the Belgian institutionalization of a system of mandatory identity cards identifying the favoured Tutsi and oppressed Hutu, scapegoats became victims, respective populations were enumerated and recorded, distributions were noted, as were breaks, transitions, migrations and accumulations. During Belgian colonialism, there was widespread preferential treatment of Tutsi and oppression of Hutu, subsequent Hutu violence and oppression of Tutsi during the last years and months of Belgian colonialism and throughout the post-colonial years, and nomadic counter strikes and retaliations by Tutsi militia against post-colonial Hutu oppression and violence.

The postsignifying regime of signs is defined by a procedure of 'subjectification'. Deleuze and Guattari characterize a postsignifying semiotic system as having been defined by a 'decisive external occurrence, by a relation with an outside that is expressed more as an emotion than an idea, and more as effort or action than as imagination (i.e. more as "active delusion than as ideational delusion")' (Deleuze and Guattari 1987, p. 124). The assassination of President Habyarimana on 6 April 1994, the event triggering the Event of the genocide, was such a decisive external occurrence, expressed as emotion and action rather than as idea or imagination. A postsignifying regime of signs 'operates *by the linear and temporal succession of finite proceedings, rather than by the simultaneity of circles in unlimited expansion*' (Deleuze and Guattari 1987, p. 120 emphasis mind). Deleuze and Guattari are drawing a distinction between on the one hand a paranoid, signifying, ideationally delusional regime of signs organized infinitely in circular fashion around a despotic signifier, and on the other hand a subjective, actively delusional, authoritarian postsignifying regime, one that is organized as '*a sign or packet of signs [that] detaches from the irradiating circular network* and sets to work on its own account, starts running a straight line, as though swept into a narrow, open passage' (Deleuze and Guattari 1987, p. 121, my emphasis). This is certainly an apt characterization of the Rwandan genocide Event.

The point at which a sign or a packet of signs detach from a regime of signs is the point of subjectification, that is, the point at which a passional subject emerges and differentiates itself from paranoid, ideationally delusional signs, that is, from paranoid authoritarianism. Passional subjectification of postsignifying regimes differs from despotic countersignifying and authoritarian signifying regimes insofar as the line of flight for the signifying regime is negative and requires some sort of negative disciplining. The line of flight for the subjective regime, that is, the postsignifying regime, is positive because the sign breaks its relations of signifiance with other signs as it moves at variable speeds along its line of flight towards absolute deterritorialization. It is difficult to characterize the passional subjectification of the genocidal postsignifying regime as positive in any sense other than that there was no negative disciplining. On the contrary, the genocide ran unchecked and undisciplined in a negative sense for 100 days of positively disciplined 'productivity'. The line of flight for a sign of a signifying regime, by contrast, continues to refer to other signs and as a set to the signifier itself; as a result, its deterritorialization is relative rather than absolute, as is the case for the sign-become-subject of the subjective regime.

The line of flight of a postsignifying regime is determined by a turning away from a centring signifier (President Habyarimana) that itself had turned away (from international law); the point of detachment is a double turning away that inaugurates the line of flight of subjectification (genocidal slaughter), the double turning away is the detachment from which the subjective emerges as it detaches from the semiotic (of previous forms of governance). Deleuze and Guattari summarize the passional postsignifying regime of subjectification as follows. First, such a regime has no centre of signifiance connected to indefinitely expanding circles or spirals, as was the case with signifying and countersignifying regimes of signs. Instead of a centre of signifiance, there is a point of subjectification (killing all Tutsi and Hutu moderates), which is a point of departure for the line of flight of genocide. Second, the signifier–signified relation disappears; taking its place is a subject of enunciation that emerges from the point of subjectification (radio broadcasts explicitly calling for the extermination of Tutsi and Hutu sympathizers), and there is a subject of the statement that stands in a determinable relation to the subject of enunciation (Hutu Power and cockroaches). Finally, there is no longer any sign-to-sign circularity; in its place is a linear proceeding into which the sign is swept along by subjects (Deleuze and Guattari 1987, p. 127). Deleuze and Guattari insist that they are not identifying regimes of signs or semiotic systems with historical moments; there are complex mixtures of presignifying, countersignifying and postsignifying elements in any active signifying regime. Their object is not to write history or to trace evolutionary trajectories, but rather to make maps of regimes of signs. And that is my object here as well.

Post-genocide Rwanda, as is true of any semiotic system, consists in relatively dominant and relatively latent regimes of signs in complex mixtures and combinations that are the objects of study for what Deleuze and Guattari call Pragmatics, or schizoanalysis. In fact, all semiotics are mixed; they function as concrete semiotic systems only to the extent that they are mixed and to the extent that they capture fragments of other semiotic systems.[12] But semiotic systems are also capable of transforming from one abstract or pure semiotic into another by means of language's capacity for overcoding. Transformations of semiotics into the presignifying regime Deleuze and Guattari refer to as *analogical transformations*; those taking semiotics into a signifying regime are *symbolic*; transformations taking semiotics into countersignifying regimes are *polemical or strategic*; transformations of semiotics into postsignifying regimes they refer to as *consciousness-related or mimetic*; and transformations that 'blow apart' semiotic systems or regimes of signs on the plane of immanence are called *diagrammatic* (Deleuze and Guattari 1987, p. 136).

Conversing machines

Reciprocity, on any scale of analysis, can be understood as self-organizing, turn-taking, itinerative conversing machines that produce interdependencies and presuppositions of recognition and identification – even if not always the consummation and consumption of identities.[13] As discursive reciprocity, conversing can be thought of as itinerate primordial logic articulating desiring-production to social-production. As conversing unfolds, bodies of machinic assemblages of desire take turns occupying discursive subject positions that collective assemblages of enunciation make available. In the reciprocity of turn-taking that social-production presupposes, a series of turns become a conversation, that is, 'simply the outline of a becoming' (Deleuze and Parnet 1987/2002, p. 2). As such, conversing embodies, that is, it turns and animates body and mind. Turns perform, distribute, integrate and transform articulations of desiring-production and social-production, and conversing is machinic insofar as it 'connects organs linking together flows in networks of desiring-production' (Deleuze and Guattari 1987, pp. 333, 457). Taking turns operationalizes reciprocity, not necessarily familiarity or intimacy; taking turns actualizes conversing in a potentially endless rhizomatic process, that is, itineration. Conversing is 'itinerative' rather than 'iterative' insofar as conversing traces paths that can be followed but not predicted. Conversing is rhizomatic insofar as it conforms to the six characteristic principles Deleuze and Guattari stipulate for a rhizome: connections, heterogeneity, multiplicity, asignifying rupture, cartography and decalcomania.[14] All conversational turns are connectable (connection); conversations mingle signs and bodies (heterogeneity); a conversation is flat and immanent (multiplicity); a conversation's line of flight is primary and enables heterogeneity-preserving emergence (asignifying rupture); maps of emergence are necessary to follow conversations (cartography); and conversing is a mimetic process of lifting and transferring codes, images and texts, that is, a practice of tracing and representing (decalcomania).

Reciprocity's rhizomatic patterns of and processes for turn-taking consist in 'turning', that is, performing, distributing, integrating and transforming desiring-production and social-production. Conversing's turns are resources, instruments of access to and resources for intervening discursively in social-production. Sequences and series of turns become itinerative processes that articulate substance and form of content to substance and form of expression, which, in turn, perform, distribute, integrate and transform active and reactive forces and flows of desire. Turns, *in* whatever forms of expression, and *of* whatever substances of expression, as is the case with other valuable resources, are taken, given, invested, interrupted, erased, shortened, lengthened, ignored and denied itineratively. In this respect, conversing machines can be thought as media *of* and resources *for* enhancing and diminishing intensities of active and reactive forces at thresholds that articulate and disarticulate bodies of machinic assemblages of desire to subject positions of discourse formations of collective assemblages of enunciation. Said another way, conversing is a turn-taking machine for articulating form and substance of content (i.e. bodies, actions and passions) to form and substance of expression (i.e. regimes of signs and social institutions) in the itinerative process underwriting presuppositions and interdependencies of rhizomatic social-production. When a body intervenes by articulating to discourse, thereby taking a turn, it connects, conjoins and disjoins social-production and desiring-production. At the juncture of intervention, a becoming-turn terminates the preceding turn, thereby becoming a 'next' itinerative turn in the virtually endless process of conversing.

A becoming-turn is always already a potential monologue, a potentially endless becoming-narrative. At each juncture of conversational intervention and transition, reciprocity is actualized and embodied as a next turn. Conversational turns interrupt potential narrative monologues and constitute dialogue, that is, two or more desiring bodies discursively negotiating immanent conjunctural reality-effects. The concept of dialogue has at least two senses here: (1) dialogue refers to the uttering of a taken turn that intervenes in a becoming-narrative in the process of its telling, that is, its itinerative evolving, and (2) dialogue refers to a series of utterances articulated to more than one desiring body as turns become traces and maps of embodied memories. Turn-taking machines actually put into material-semiotic practice as social-production forms and substances of cultural, social, political, economic, psychological, emotional, aesthetic, erotic and spiritual (in short, 'libidinal') contents and expressions. Insofar as a turn crosses a threshold from the virtual to the actual, taking a turn is a choice, an act of immanent ethics; listening (or not) to a turn's utterance is also a choice with immanent ethical implications.[15] By 'choice' I mean that, to varying degrees, turn-taking machines reciprocally articulate collective assemblages of enunciation to machinic assemblages of bodies, and choice is both discourse-determined (semiotic) and content-determined (material). Remember that discourse formations of collective assemblages of enunciation have subject positions but no agency until machinic assemblages of bodies articulate to them. Once articulated, desiring bodies identify with and occupy subject positions with variable degrees of identification; discourse becomes 'live' as desiring-utterances, which are taken up in Chapter 5.

Subject positions of discourse formations do not exist prior to bodies of desire identifying with and occupying them; rather, they co-occur. It is in this sense that subjectivity and objectivity emerge simultaneously, and in this sense choice is discourse-determined. Bodies of machinic assemblages occupy and establish subject positions as a function of will to power and its primary manifestation, affect, that is, willingness to be affected. Identifying with subject positions of collective assemblages of enunciation, machinic assemblages of bodies become subjects *of* discourse, subjects *to* discourse and subjects *for* desire. Once identified *with* and *as* discursive subject positions, bodies of desire are not programmed to speak; taking a turn to speak (or not) is an immanently ethical choice. It is in this sense that taking a turn at conversing is subject-determined as much as it is discourse-determined; things can always be otherwise. The point to bear in mind here is that in taking a turn at conversing, a conversing subject misidentifies, dis-attends to, forgets or otherwise feigns ignorance about knowing the ways subject positionality is discourse-determined conjunctively. For conversing subjects, discourse formations are both invisible and inaudible insofar as conversing unfolds in keeping with patterns and thresholds of complex systems of discourse formations, that is, collective assemblages of enunciation thought of as abstract machines.[16] Uttering bodies are unaware of the ways in which discourse produces and positions them as by-products of conjunctive syntheses, that is, as subjects that experience identity possessively. An identity conjunctively produced as a by-product of a body occupying a discursive subject position retrospectively recognizes *that* identity as *their* identity.

Furthermore, a body experiences the forces and conditions responsible for conjunctively producing an identity that they retrospectively identify with to be forces and conditions they produced insofar as identity is experienced as inherently and always already having been in place. It amounts to an invisible reversal. Discourse constrains by positioning and managing available subject positions, but within those constraints, bodies of machinic assemblages choose whether to speak or to remain silent, when and how to speak and when and how to listen. So it could be claimed that conversing is locally administered and immanently monitored according to discursive conventions of engagement and principles of local governance. Even if parameters of some turn-taking machines are rigidly constraining, a subject chooses when to intervene by taking a turn (if at all), how to intervene (or not), and what to do by means of intervening.[17] In these ways, conversing can be thought of as a process of making immanent ethical choices by taking turns that select forms and substances of agonistic and antagonistic conflict. Yet much of the time formats of turn-taking and the ethical implications of their practices operate so routinely and so inadvertently as to go unnoticed. The focus of attention is almost exclusively on the substance and form of content while the form and substance of expression passes by largely un(re)marked; issues of the substance and form of content capture the most attention, substantiating and formalizing conflict. All the while, conversing substantiates and formulates its content in the very process of expressing it. When a conversing machine breaks down, it can be repaired either by attending to substantive and formal matters of content or by attending to formal and substantive matters of expression, or to both in different proportions. Much of the work of conflict resolution and trauma reconciliation, and of peacebuilding generally, is to attend simultaneously to the substances and forms of content *and* to the forms and substances of expression.

Subjects of and for conflict and trauma are so immersed in content that durational features and nomadic properties of expression go unnoticed as squandered immanent resources. Gaçaça transitional justice courts are minor communication machines deployed to recuperate those resources by thematizing and foregrounding nomadic properties of expressions of social-production. Thinking of conflict escalation/de-escalation and trauma incitement/reconciliation as reciprocal articulations of desiring-production and social-production opens spaces and durations for imagining conflict and trauma in ways that disarticulate fixed and sedentary identities, resulting in multiple nomadic identifications. Theorizing conversation, negotiation, mediation and dialogue as conversing machines brings into sharper relief immanent discursive expressions of content. Thinking of territorial assemblages, collective assemblages of enunciation, conversing machines, discourse formations, machinic assemblages of bodies and collective assemblages of enunciation generate schizoanalytic concepts of and for conflict, escalation, resistance, resolution, reconciliation and peacebuilding.

Conversational flows and traces

As sequences of reciprocal turns, conversing leaves traces of intensities of forces that articulate and disarticulate conflict and trauma as forms and substances of narratives and dialogues. Insofar as these intensities of forces are political, dominance accrues to a transcendent regime of signs; traces of narrative and dialogue constitute pragmatic maps of the politics of conflict and trauma. However, as nothing more than embodied memory of conversing's intensities, its sounds are reabsorbed by silence, and as nothing more than transcribed recordings of dialectical tracings of intensities of forces, transcriptions of conversing remain inert on the page. 'Take a dialogue [read conversation] and remove the voices . . . remove the intonations . . . carve out abstract concepts and judgments from living words and responses, cram everything into one abstract consciousness – and that's how you get dialectics' (Bakhtin 1986, p. 147). Generative tracings become transformational maps once narrative and dialogue are enunciated, that is, once desire either is spoken or written, or both.[18] As nothing but chronicles of narratives, conversations are series of unconnected monologues, and as nothing but sequences of utterances, conversations abstract into code, that is, into digitalized recordings of analogue desire, codes lacking affect.

It would be a mistake to theorize minor communication and conversing machines as totalities, as coherent, bounded and unitary phenomena. The conversational installation of machinic assemblages of bodies into subject positions of collective assemblages of enunciation records and maps multiple identifications. On a digital plane, that is, a plane of discourse, a body becomes a subject *and* an object (i.e. a subject *of* and *for* language as well as an object *of* and *for* language). Subject/object divisions are formatted conversationally and performed, distributed, integrated and transformed machinically in the processes of turn-production. Boundaries of subject/object divisions, and reciprocity sequences that constitute these boundaries durationally, are learnt socioculturally. Turn-taking practices that divide and multiply subjects and objects constitute the arithmetic of common sense and conventional wisdom. Forms and substances of turn-taking expressions quickly dissolve, acoustically and visibly but not mnemonically, into the background as a conversation's contents and expressions become increasingly foregrounded. The reciprocity of turn-taking is the primordial articulatory medium of expression for the contents of desire by means of the substances and forms of collective assemblages of enunciation. It is through the relative invisibility and inaudibility of turn-taking forms and substances that social-production and desiring-production come to be articulated in such subtle microphysical ways. Who would suspect something as seemingly innocuous as the forms and substances of the contents and expressions of turn-taking to be such highly generative circuits of power?

Dominant ways of thinking (major) communication posit rules and conventions, that is, rules of engagement and production, conventions of competence and performance. On this line of thinking, conversing is produced by following sociolinguistic rules governing sociocultural appropriateness and competence. But theories of discursive competence that account for how conversational turns 'actualize' virtual potentiality are underdeveloped. Instead of accounting for the unfolding emergent evolutionary processes of conversing, most extant theory emphasizes rules and codes as always already accomplished devices that explain sociolinguistic outcomes as products of particular rule-governed practices.[19] In this respect, rules do the work of keying the engines of sociocultural praxis of social-production. The dilemma is that those rules and conventions are themselves discursive products; rules and conventions are conceptual entities whose utility resides in their conjunctively synthetic retrospective accounts. Insofar as understandings of practices and processes are inherently incomplete, rules amount to rationalist devices that account for practical outcomes. Language, for example, can specify its grammar, but grammar is neither necessary nor sufficient for specifying language's minor communicative performances.

The most serious liability of rule-governed explanations of conversational production is that a rule operates as a presupposed solution to the difficulties posed by an inadequate theory of conversing, negotiating, mediating and dialoguing. To make rules operative, agency must be attributed to them. This presumably solves the problem of how bodies put communicative competence into performative practice, that is, bodies are presumed to have sufficient agency to follow rules. The relations of competence to performance are assumed to be more or less direct and unproblematic. The practices of conversing supposedly execute language by following rules. For Noam Chomsky, as for Ferdinand de Saussure, a theory of speech practices reduces almost legalistically to the function of obedient execution.[20] Practices of performance are simplified and reduced. It is this more or less directly executive relation between rule and practice that is the stubbornly irresolvable paradox for most communication theory and, by implication, for most conflict resolution and trauma reconciliation theory. Knowing the strategic rules and codes in a theoretical sense is an imperfect predictor of a subject's tactical, linguistic and communicative ingenuity. Locating communicative competence and performance as independent phenomena, either as discursive properties of an autonomous language external to and independent of bodies [as exclusive properties of collective assemblages of enunciation] or as cognitive properties of corporeal bodies [as exclusive properties of machinic assemblages of bodies] only postpones the realization that competence is inherently performative. Furthermore, performativity is a function of love, art, science and politics. Phrased alternatively, performing competence produces the conditions of possibility for intimacy and vulnerability, intuition and aesthetics, prediction and control, and strategy and tactics.

To have codes and rules as models of and for performative practice is to fall far short of being able to say much at all about everyday practical circumstances of minor communication's production and performance of conversing, negotiating, mediating and dialoguing. To account for everyday conversing in terms of rules is to maintain a position that practice is a product of rules, which is a position that privileges competence over performance. Systems of rules and codes of relations are placed in a master position; it is for communication to be conversationally obedient. The challenge is to account for conversing in terms of immanent minor processes rather than in terms of major codes and rules. It is crucial that conversing comes to be understood in terms of immanent flows of desiring-production and social-production performed, distributed, integrated and transformed through turn-taking machines, constituting striated space – in the case of Rwanda, that striated space consists in gaçaça transitional justice courts and their conjoined tasks of producing transitional justice, resolving conflict and reconciling trauma – effectuated by the stratification of the Rwandan state apparatus.

Sociocultural reality-effects, the ones that conversing performs, distributes, integrates and transforms are the articulatory manifestations of common sense and conventional wisdom. And those minor communicative articulations operate for the most part outside of conscious awareness in holey space; they are routine and operate underground, unnoticed. Recall that holey space is a third space of machinic assemblages, an underground space that can connect to smooth space and become conjugated by striated space.[21] In this respect, thinking minor communication as micropractices productive of holey space accounts for much of the social-productivity and desiring-productivity of gaçaça transitional justice courts. Conversing conjugates smooth space and striated space by articulating collective assemblages of enunciation and machinic assemblages of bodies. Minor communicative practices operating throughout holey space produce reality-effects invisibly and inaudibly, selecting substance and form of content and form and substance of expression outside of conscious awareness, in the third space of the machinic phylum of matter-flow. Forms and substances of conversing are simply overlooked, listened *through* rather than *to*, unless there is conversing/ontological trouble. That which ordinarily is listened *to* is the substantive and formal content expressed *through* forms and substances of turns expressed conversationally in routine ways that pass through unheard and unseen. Conversational/ontological trouble usually is assumed to be a function of substantive and formal contents rather than formal and substantive expressions. In the absence of trouble, conversing is assumed to be mundane, ordinary and routine – the small change of daily life, not worthy of thematic record keeping.

At sites and times of crisis and conflict, striated spaces and orders of reciprocity produced and reproduced by turn-taking machines deterritorialize, disarticulating relatively sedentary alliances of a relatively stable status quo, producing smoothing forces of intensive disorder, chaos and cacophony. Much comes to be performed, distributed, integrated and transformed during such moments; conditions can and do become otherwise. Disjunctures, ruptures, breaks and disarticulations warrant pragmatic attention; crises are moments of potential retracing, remapping, rediagramming and reprogramming. In actuality, conversations are reciprocity machines that overcode turn-taking formats responsible for distributing discursive subject positions. Conversing also overcodes in the sense of overriding heterogeneous codes, thereby producing unified substances and forms of and for stratification processes. Overcoding refers to multiple lines of force, influence and pressure that constrain and limit positionality and activity; but to claim overcoding is to claim neither determinism nor causality. Deleuze and Guattari insist that overcoding is a double articulation: the first articulation is the substance and form of content; the second is the form and substance of expression. Conversing further overdetermines the double articulation of a stratification process; it orders the articulation of content and expression reciprocally in accord with conversing formats. It is the overcoding of the articulation of content and expression that produces stratified phenomena such as centring, unification, totalization, integration, hierarchization and finalization (Deleuze and Guattari 1987, pp. 40–1).

Conversing is non-linear in its processual unfolding, much more rhizomatic than hierarchic or arborescent in its evolution.[22] Conversations, like rhizomes, grow from the middle; there are no beginnings and endings; there are only pauses and interruptions, and frames imposed externally. And although conversing's minor communicative practices are ideologically formatted and hegemonically circumscribed, conversing nevertheless wanders down blind alleys, slams into dead-ends, topples off cliffs, gets flipped over and turned around, becomes asphyxiated, repeats aimlessly and suddenly breaks off. It circles around and folds back on itself in ways that defy conventional assumptions of rationality, and when it ceases, conversed and conversing subjects dissolve into silence. Because conversational micropractices constitute, situate, trace and map positions of and for multiple subject identifications, keeping track of identifications and identities have material-semiotic implications in the seemingly mundane affairs of daily life. For many bodies, keeping track of identities and identifications has spiritual and metaphysical consequences. Losing track of identifications and identities risks losing (one's) place and opens the virtual potential and actual possibility of becoming lost spatiotemporally, dissolving into chaos, becoming indexically randomized, losing one's way, losing the thread, being left behind, forgetting (one's) location, and ultimately the nihilism of being erased (e.g. genocide). Consequently, when not conversing, it is pragmatically important to listen or otherwise attend sufficiently to follow along enough of the time to track lines of flight. Realizing (one's) conversing places as subject identifications and identities is usually a matter of propriety, but in Rwanda it became a matter of life and death.[23] Clearly the significance of this sort of reflexive, indexical and implicative discursive work in post-genocide Rwanda, both prior to and during gaçaça transitional justice courts, cannot be overstated.

Conversing bodies

In the course of rethinking space/time relations of social conflict, an overriding concern is the question of how conversing daily life might be engaged more nomadically, with greater improvisational ingenuity, without compromising immanent ethical standards. Strategic conversing (as opposed to tactical conversing) is thought of in terms of relations of spatial forces that are put into play when a body (i.e. a subject of will and power) is cut out and set apart from its interior relations. Strategy functions as a basis for generating exterior relations with space. Tactical conversing, on the other hand, is thought of in terms of durational relations, relations put into temporal play. Tactical ingenuity negotiates immanent relations with recollection-memory and contraction-memory, manifesting a practical agility for negotiating durational relations. Strategic ingenuity functions as a basis for negotiating extensive relations of differences in degree; tactical ingenuity negotiates durational relations of differences in kind. As discussed earlier, the social and behavioural sciences collapse durational/tactical relations into spatial/strategic relations, privileging the latter over the former. But the micropractices, that is, the verbal representations of daily conversing, are durational *and* spatial phenomena. Face-to-face conversations always take place in time; they are ways of bringing durational life to spatial existence, ways of actualizing material-semiotic conditions. Strata are what previously stratified practices produced; they are the prior conditions for ongoing stratifying micro- and macropractices. Micropractices are not transparently intentional; conversing – as is true of negotiating, mediating and dialoguing as well – produces results, but on the basis of inherited spaces and anterior conditions that inform the configuration of current conditions and circumstances.

Michel de Certeau's embodied subject is an artful dodger, a poacher of spatializing forms, a poststructural, posthumanist nomad.[24] It is a conversed and conversing embodied subject of partial and variable identifications capable of temporarily capitalizing on, even if not escaping from, the spatial constraints of durational recollection-memory and contraction-memory. Durational micropractices take place in the intervals between percept and affect whose embodied subjects negotiate immanence. Conversing bodies are producer-consumers in an axiomatic of capitalism – a commodified world of signs. In fact, distinctions between production and consumption for the most part are blurred, that is, consumers produce by consuming. Conversationalists become nomadic subjects in a world of signs, improvising with what is available to be appropriated, consummated and consumed. Sociocultural formations are stratified in accord with dominant macropractices that normatively configure groups, organizations and institutions as their substantive expressions. Macropractices that stratify Rwanda's institutional expressions directly and indirectly shape the practices not only for how those institutions administer services, but also for how Rwandan victims and survivors negotiate the emergent normative and structural contradictions of daily life. Our concern here is with micropractices that never become macropractically dominant. Resolving social conflict has everything to do with durational micropractices that interpolate, infiltrate and transform both bodies and spirits of conversing bodies in space and time.

Micropractices of conversing are durational incursions into spatial territorializations; duration and space intersect and articulate as desiring-utterances. Space is thought of extensionally either as stratified, bureaucratized and globalized worlds of cellular grids and information networks, or as transcendental sense. Ian Buchanan reminds us that 'the event is the sense we *make* of what happens' (Buchanan 2000, p. 79). Desiring-bodies become embodiments of social-production, taking up spatially distributed subject positions of spatially configured sedentary grids. Embodied bearers become positioned as discursive subjects in space and time, and they are obligated implicitly and explicitly to know and to keep to their places and to attend to time (i.e. Chronos of the proposition). Durational ingenuity temporalizes space, appropriating it even if never occupying it in any sedentary sense. Durational ingenuity is, in effect, living a life in time; nomadic bodies cannot 'afford' to live life in space as sedentary subjects. And yet, spatial subject positions are necessary, at least temporarily. Conflict becomes evident when body turns on body; for example, body A stands accused, blamed or suspected of something by body B, say, of having inappropriately appropriated body B's subject position(s). Diasporas are accused of illegally appropriating subject positions and material resources to which they are not entitled, depriving 'rightful' national bodies of both. Nomads are accused of poaching from positions that have been poached themselves, of taking advantages rather than being given them and of consuming resources (i.e. jobs, tax revenues, social services, housing, etc.) that 'rightfully belong' to national bodies. Strategic ingenuity accrues to dominant sedentaries (i.e. the nationals); it is *their* homeland, after all, 'by force' if not 'by right'. 'Entitlement must be earned,' so say sedentary strategists, much as priests claim that 'salvation' must be earned before entitlement can be claimed and owned. But entitlement is not earned, it is assumed, taken as/for granted. Entitlement is a transcendent position that can never be realized, any more than abundance can ever be produced from scarcity.

Tactical ingenuity, on the other hand, accrues to minoritarian subject groups, for example, nomads and immigrants. After all, it is *their* time being stolen, or with any luck bought and sold. Nomadic presence in space is tolerated insofar as mobile immigrant bodies are necessary for registering and recording time – and time is money. Incommensurable differences between tactical ingenuity and strategic ingenuity are pivots on which so many conflicts over immigration policies and practices turn. Whose time is it and whose space? What is the value of each? How are those values determined and by whom? These questions of desire, experience, will(ingness), resistance and resolve are taken up in greater detail in Chapter 5. Sociocultural forces and flows of desiring-production are encoded in and camouflaged by micropractices of conversing. Seemingly obvious, mundane, routine, normalizing quotidian practices and knowledges of a life constitute ontological and epistemological infrastructures of good sense and common sense, that is, hegemony's material manifestation on a micropractical plane. An engaged and sustained study of conversing machines and an engaged and sustained study of social conflict become one and the same enterprise. In one sense, hegemony consists in much more than conversing. In another important sense, however, conversing – taken to be machinic operations of sociocultural formats for turn-taking – is both a method and a process by means of which hegemony is perpetually reconversed and endlessly renegotiated. The silence of traumatic form and substance of content beyond the reach of collective enunciation may yet become incorporeally transformed substantively. Conversing's micropractices, in other words, endlessly perform hegemonic axiomatic codes that normalize irregularities, camouflage contradictions and resolve problems and conflicts, often without having to call specific micropractices into question. Conversing's subject positions are occupied by bodies of partial-identifications, that is, as themselves assemblages of identifications, not completely fixed and sedentary identities. They are subjects-in-process and on trial, negotiating the tensions of schizoid multiple identifications and paranoid essentialized identities.[25]

Stuart Hall paraphrases Louis Althusser's formulation of ideology as, 'systems of representation – composed of concepts, ideas, myths, or images – in which men and women . . . live their imaginary relations to the real conditions of existence' (Hall 1985, p. 103). Systems of representation function as codes of intelligibility, and conversations, as turn-taking machines, make sense (i.e. format and distribute, in the sense of Jacques Rancière's 'distribution of sense') of material conditions. Conversing punctuates immanence, producing intervals filled in by lines of subjectivity (i.e. affect, recollection-memory and contraction-memory) as the eternal turning and returning of difference. A turn's utterance is a multifaceted act of social-production discursively *in*formed by and *per*formed for (i.e. designed to address) other bodies in space and time. In those durational moments, utterances variably identify bodies. At one extreme of variability, a turn's utterance loses its good sense and common sense as it approaches the libidinality of transcendental sense, effectively disarticulating collective enunciation from desiring-bodies. At the other extreme of variability, an utterance manifests a high degree of discursive differentiation, marking changes in, and expansions of, circumstances and implications of intervals. The more highly differentiated a turn's utterance, the more complex and multifaceted the becoming-identifications of its embodied subjects. Language learning, then, is a body's immersion (i.e. its leap into) into transcendental forces and flows of the verbal representing of conversing. Experience becomes durationally and conversingly embodied in that manner; experience does not exist independent of its durational embodiment. In other words, it is not a matter of experience organizing embodied utterances from the outside; the converse is actually the case. Utterances organize and reorganize embodied sensation, symbolizing sublimated corporeal/material sensation as transcendental sense, good sense and common sense. Extensive social circumstances and their intensive cultural implications *in*form and *per*form utterances, conversing desiring-bodies and regimes of signs.

*In*forming and *per*forming as social-production, collective assemblages of enunciation conversingly articulate to machinic assemblages of bodies, at times intensively identifying with subject positions, at other times minimally identifying with subject positions. Ideology, in this fashion, becomes the discursive production of an assemblage's continuity of ideas, that is, the subject and object positions of a more or less sensible world of empirical consciousness and logical propositions. By cordoning off chaos, connecting events and distributing sense, ideology produces essentialized identities and coherent systems of ideas and affects in an otherwise incoherent cosmos. But an embodied subject always already is caught up in becoming, so ideology functions to narrate those processes, collectively expressing machinic desire by means of turn-taking that discursively fixes, identifies and positions embodied subjects. However, discourse is not reified language conceptualized synchronically as linguistics, that is, as a sedentary system; it is, rather, streams and flows of conversing.[26] Mikhail Bakhtin's study of Dostoevsky's poetics is instructive at this juncture. Bakhtin's concept of *hero* is neither a character nor a personality; rather, for Bakhtin, Dostoevsky's *hero* is discourse about itself and its world; a *hero* is not an objectified identity but rather something much more akin to autonomous discourse. We do not *see* so much as we *hear* a *hero*. That which we see and know as independent of such discourse is, as Bakhtin puts it, 'nonessential and is swallowed up (Deleuze and Guattari would say consummated-consumed) by discourse as its own material, or else remains outside it as something that stimulates and provokes' (Bakhtin 1984, p. 53). Dostoevsky's *heroes* utter themselves into the partiality of discursive reality in the process of living a life. Rather than creating finalized and complete monologists as *a priori* identities, Dostoevsky writes *heroes* who speak themselves into at least partial identifications with other worlds inhabited by other partials (objects and subjects) in processes of becoming-otherwise.

Desiring-bodies and collective assemblages of enunciation articulate, thereby actualizing material circumstances that structure and flesh out (i.e. embody) experience. Bodies speaking conversationally rather than monologically are speaking *with* a multiplicity of subject identifications rather than speaking *as* an identity *for* other identities and their group-subject identity. Conversing that is dialogical rather than monological is always already on a threshold of crisis and possibility. Embodied subjects are not finalized and determinate identities but subjects-in-process articulating to (i.e. identifying with) multiple worlds of other unfinalizable and partial-subjects of multiple identifications. The truths conversing subjects utter are truths of reflexive, indexical and implicative experience. It is into and against such ideological worlds that bodies become rational and libidinal forms as they articulate to discourse formations of collective assemblages of enunciation in the process of conversing. In those ways, utterances construe experience and distribute sense by tying a life together, at least temporarily, and sharpening some of its differentiations. To acknowledge that conversing is inherently ideological in this Bakhtinian sense is to acknowledge that conversing sustains relations of power and structures and stratifications in dominance. But to argue that all micropractices of conversing are ideological is not to claim that conversing and its social-production is nothing but ideology at work. Insofar as conversational micropractices are formats for codes that denote, manifest and signify the sense of the virtual conditions of existence, they mediate experience, and *that* mediated experience stands in virtually real relations to actually immanent conditions. Such micropractices put systems of codes and their representational capacities to work on social-production, and in that respect they function ideologically.

It is a given, then, that con-versing is always already oppositional and immanent to conflict and its micropractices are always already at odds. An utterance stands as a summons, or a challenge to what *is*. Ideology, as a system of variably coherent beliefs and ideas, spreads, informs and configures experience by means of discourse formations and conversational formats actualized in the service of differentiation, opposition and counter-claim as well as to unification, reconciliation and affirmation. Conversation thought of as conversing machines, as ideological actualization, is a medium through which history becomes inscribed and sociocultural formations reproduced. 'The theory of ideology invites us to see that language is not simply a structure which can be employed for communication or entertainment, but [is also] a sociohistorical phenomenon which is embroiled in human conflict' (Thompson 1984, p. 14).

Bodies of desire articulate to material conditions and social circumstances in which they are caught up. Insofar as conversing consists in the ways and means of sustaining exterior and interior relations of power and stratifications in dominance, conversing produces embodied subjects at the same time as it produces history and reproduces sociocultural formations.[27] It is in this sense that conversing is a double articulation, mediating desire and discourse. As epistemological and ontological maps of living worlds, their topography and *dispositions* are discourse formations that pass as the good sense and common sense of a material, semiotic and psychic world. As reformatted good sense and common sense, conversational micropractices are discursive machines for articulating content and expression, that is, desiring-production and social-production of everyday living.

Taking and returning to turns

A turn expresses content in the substance and form of a desiring-utterance; in the performance of its expression, a desiring-utterance denotes, signifies and manifests the very contents of conditions it is in the process of performing, distributing and integrating. Changing material-semiotic conditions and circumstances of conversing virtually and actually decodes and recodes, and at times deterritorializes and reterritorializes those conditions and circumstances, producing at one pole more or less steady-state stratified equilibria, and at the other pole more or less smooth intensified planes of nomadic consistency. Changes actualize from virtuality (i.e. changes actually become) in and through desiring-utterances, interpellating more turns to address and redress ever emerging intervals, differences, difficulties, mistakes and possibilities. Desiring-utterance, here, is a name for ways articulation cuts out and turns over substance and form of content, and expresses it performatively in forms and substances capable of deterritorializing and reterritorializing machinic assemblages of bodies and assemblages of collective enunciation in the process.

Taking turns of conversing entails turning back desiring-production *after* a desiring-body articulates to subject positions of discourse formations. Subject-reflexivity presupposes *phronesis*, a pragmatic wisdom about communicative capacities for actualizing social-production from desiring-production. Desiring-utterances produce identifications as by-products of becoming-enunciated; at one and the same time they draw on and add to collective assemblages of enunciation. As a by-product of the social-production of utterances, identities for bodies speaking from subject positions become inverted. Desiring-bodies, as positioned subjects of discourse formations, recognize and register their immanent identifications as identities. The self-reflexivity produced by machinic desire turning back on a desiring-body positioned as a subject *of* discourse functions as a conjunctive synthesis productive of identity, and identity is neither more nor less than synthesized, condensed and variable identifications. The work of subject-reflexivity is to forestall the morphing of multiple identifications into one-dimensional, closed sedentary identities imagined as unitary causal agents. Once conjunctively synthesized from multiple identifications, identities are always already at immanent risk, perpetually threatened with disarticulation by the flows of desiring-production, a condition of threat experienced as a perpetual identity crisis.[28]

Turns of desiring-utterances actually index subject positions with which bodies identify, effectively positioning bodies as subjects of desiring-utterances in time (i.e. tense) and space (i.e. locations). Bodies of desiring Rwandans consummate/consume signs of gaçaça events, and those signs (as discussed earlier) trigger material processes in properly attuned bodies; indexes are territorialized signs; symbols are deterritorialized signs; and icons are reterritorialized signs. Desiring bodies, as articulated subjects (i.e. as both subjects *for* utterances and subjects *of* utterances) consummate/consume indexical signs, symbolic signs and iconic signs, respectively, territorializing, deterritorializing and reterritorializing spatiotemporal significance of sites of exclusive disjunctive syntheses (i.e. of failed syntheses of connective and conjunctive syntheses productive of conflict and trauma). Deterritorializing in an absolute sense is a line of flight (i.e. a threshold between assemblages) to the plane of consistency, that is, of transcendental thought. Decoding territorial indexes is a method of resolving conflicts and reconciling traumas, not in the humanist sense of 'healing' and 'forgiving', but rather in the sense of escape, a line of flight between assemblages. Desiring-utterances of minor communication machines (re)form flows of desire, (re)sign signifiance, (re) distribute indexes of territorial signs, (re)integrate symbolic signs of deterritorialization, and (trans)form iconic signs of reterritorialization as experiments, as the trajectories of sense that articulations of desire and discourse produce.

Turns can be characterized in terms of their discursive properties, that is, the generative pragmatics of relations across utterances, the transformational pragmatics of relations of utterances to actions that mix and create new regimes of spatiotemporal indexes (i.e. their variable tenses), voices (active and passive), moods (indicative, interrogative and subjunctive), cases (possessive, objective and nominative), modalities (ontic and deontic) and agencies (direct and indirect), which condition possibilities for both diagrammatic pragmatics and machinic pragmatics. These communicative properties of desiring-utterances actualize tracings, mappings, diagrammings and programmings of singular articulations of machinic desire and collective enunciation onto immanent surfaces of empirical consciousness and logical propositions, utterance by utterance, turn by turn. Properties of minor communication actualize the discursive labour practices of transitional justice and reconcile collective trauma. There are no guarantees in the ways that tracing, mapping, diagramming and programming actualize virtual potential as actual empirical consciousness, which may or may not resolve conflict and reconcile trauma.

Collective enunciation and desiring-utterances

Language (rethought in terms of pragmatic experimentation) is the medium through which speech (rethought in terms of verbal representation) is machinically formatted for conversing, negotiating and mediating. Collective assemblages of enunciation are multi-planar media that its subjects (i.e. its bearers) assume they carry in common, but to which they have differential access. It operates as practical awareness, as implicitly held good sense (signifier) and common sense (signified and manifested). Desiring-utterances presuppose transcendental thought and verbal representation. In this sense, desiring-utterances articulate collective enunciation to desiring-bodies by means of reciprocal turn-taking. Michel de Certeau distinguishes between collective enunciation and desiring-utterances in terms of language and speech, and among four properties that separate them (de Certeau 1984, pp. 1–42). First, language takes place by means of speaking; speaking *realizes* language by *actualizing* portions of it as actuality; speaking and writing never exhaust language. Second, speech appropriates language in the act of speaking it, just as collective enunciation appropriates desiring-production without exhausting it. Third, speech presupposes a particular relational contract with an 'other', real or fictive, and desiring-utterances presuppose particular relations between subject positions, object positions and material conditions and their exterior relations. Finally, speech actualizes the present as time for an 'I' to speak (de Certeau 1984, pp. 1–42, *passim*). A speaking body instantiates present Chronos of the proposition to a life in that moment, no matter the form. Speaking takes place in an empty time of the present. In those ways, micropractices of conversing socially produce and reproduce conventions and cultural formations by means of articulating desire to discourse and thereby time to space. Conversing then can be thought of machinically as communicative practices for taking turns. How is all of this accomplished?

Discourse formations converge on, intersect with and articulate to bodies of desiring-production at sites of agonistic and antagonistic conflicts born of contested differences of value. The desiring-production of differences attract discourse, expressing those differences. As direct, indirect and quasi-direct discourse formations articulate to machinic assemblages of bodies of desiring-bodies, *space* ('here' and 'there') and *time* ('now' Aion and 'then' Chronos) manifest as *subject positions* (first-, second- and third-person singular and plural) and *voices* (active and passive). Bodies occupying subject positions and speaking multiple voices manifest as desiring-utterances of individual corporeal bodies as well as collective incorporeal bodies (e.g. legal bodies, governing bodies of nation-states). Desiring-utterances are enunciated collectively manifesting the communicative properties of *moods* (indicative, subjunctive and interrogative), *cases* (objective and nominative) and *modalities* (ontological and deontological). In these ways, desiring-utterances articulate the *agency* (transitive and intransitive) of *desiring-production* (subtraction, addition, division and multiplication) to the *subjectivity* (subject and object) of social-production.

In brief, discourse articulates to and reconfigures desire at sites of agonism and antagonism in the forms and substances of collectively enunciated utterances. The communicative properties of utterances eternally turn from empirical consciousness to transcendental thought and the primary order, and then return from the primary order to secondary organization and then to the tertiary order of empirical consciousness. Of pivotal significance to the work of reimagining conflict resolution and trauma reconciliation discourse is that any turn is capable of performing, distributing, integrating and transforming the spatiotemporal parameters of desire. Each of these kinds of utterances are taken up later in Chapter 5. If a past persists and remains immanent to present, as is the case with traumatic experience, a subject lives past as present, as frozen immanence. The ontological past (which *is*) and the psychological present (which *was*) conflate, collapsing into one another. It is not until past becomes distributed in, integrated with and transformative of the present that past can and does interpolate and inform the present by means of (i.e. in and through) conversing, negotiating, mediating and dialoguing. In effect, past experience becomes present memory; it does not continue as present immanence. The past can be argued about and fought over, celebrated and re-enacted, but it is only that which *was* present that can be changed. To attempt to resolve contemporary conflict by conversing, negotiating, mediating and dialoguing mythic pasts is Quixotic. Until and unless what *is* (the ontological) can be recognized and acknowledged in all its multiple present (psychological) reality-effects, and thereby granted propositional legitimacy in empirical immanence, and until desiring-utterances turn the past (what *is*) into 'here' and 'now' of a present (which *was*) – effectively conversing, negotiating, mediating and dialoguing what *is* (the ontological past) – what *might be* (virtual sense) remains illusion. History threatens to evaporate as the eternal return of the Same.

Chapter 5 concerns itself with how the articulation of desire and discourse is actually accomplished and how desiring-utterances perform, distribute, integrate and transform the spatial differences in degree and the durational differences in kind. As utterances unfold in forms and substances of communicative strings and series, they take shape as conversations, negotiations and mediations, that is, dialogue that interrupts conflicting narratives. Some configurations of communicative properties are more stable, fixed and sedentary; others are more unstable, mobile and nomadic. Nonetheless, when bundled together at sites of conflict, the communicative properties of desiring-utterances actually perform, distribute, integrate and transform actuality and virtuality. As discourse formations migrate to sites of social conflict and collective trauma, the communicative properties of desiring-utterances manifest as expressions of speaking subjects. Conflicts take on the embodied sounds of turning and returning desiring-utterances. Listening for and witnessing turns, that is, desiring-utterances of immanent conflict, provides clues to, openings onto and possibilities for interruptions of and interventions into conflict discourse. Of course, conflicts vary in form and content depending upon their immanent conditions. Communicative practices, then, are the media by means of which conflict manifests, and the form and content of desiring-utterances turn their conflicting subjects in the space and time of social-production.

Planes and properties of utterances

Recall from Chapter 3 that Bergson's conception and analysis of language is identical to the ways he thinks of recollection-memory and contraction-memory. Language as verbal representation corresponds to the secondary organization of virtual and transcendental thought, that is, the time of no present – Aion. We do not stand outside of language and use it instrumentally; rather, we leap into it, as Deleuze's Bergson phrases it. It is an immersion in pure becoming. Immersed in the transcendental sense of the virtual, a body actualizes as a subject of and for language in the process of psychologically perceiving sounds and images. For Deleuze, another phrase he uses to refer to *the virtual and the transcendental thought of pure becoming is verbal representation, which is the ontological foundation of language*. In effect, the secondary organization of the genesis of representation, that is, the organization of verbal representation of pure becoming, is the foundation of empirical consciousness and the logical proposition. That is why for Deleuze's Bergson only pure becoming (i.e. the time of no present, the time of Aion, of becoming-*was*) is psychological; the past of recollection-memory and contraction-memory is pure ontology (the always already *is*). An utterance, in its psychological pure becoming-enunciated, is taking place contemporaneously in the past, which it is in the process of dividing from the future; an utterance in this sense is thought of as an aleatory point or as a nomadic subject of unfolding conversing.

An utterance in the process of becoming-enunciation actualizes virtuality insofar as becoming-utterances actualize the convergence of affect, recollection-memory and contraction-memory on one line, and perception on a second line. Paradoxically, each becoming-utterance returns to itself as past. The present is active pure becoming of psychology; the past is impassive pure being of ontology. A becoming-utterance actualizes, that is, it articulates the past and present, the ontological and the psychological. Recall from Chapter 3, Bergson's formulation of the process of actualization, the adaptation of the present to the past, which he referred to as 'attention to life', a process consisting in five moments: (1) contraction-memory, a first moment of contact between the ontological past and the psychological present; (2) recollection-memory, a second moment of the past expanding in the present; (3) a dynamic affective attitude of the body that synthesizes contraction-memory and recollection-memory; (4) the fourth moment is the actual physical movement of the body; and (5) displacement, a moment during which the past is embodied in a present different from that which it has been, that is, the interval we discussed earlier (Deleuze 1991, pp. 52–3).

A becoming-utterance locates itself on the seam between the psychological and the ontological, between the pure becoming of the psychological immanence of transcendental thought, verbal representation and the virtual, and the pure being of the ontological immanence of language and empirical consciousness. Becoming-utterances manifest as 'attention to life' in the interval of actualization, perpetually articulating and adjusting the ontological which *is* pure being, to the psychological which is pure *becoming*, in the space of 'here' and the time of 'now'. A becoming-utterance manifests (i.e. takes place) in the interval between event (a preceding turn) and response (a next, imminent turn) becoming a response that fills in the interval by taking place, and in taking place it terminates the interval, becoming the immanent event of turn-taking-place-in-time and calling for a response in the interval its completion or interruption will actualize. However, an utterance manifesting (i.e. becoming-enunciated) 'here' and 'now' cannot denote nor signify the *space* of here or the *time* of now; it must by its very nature denote and signify some other *place* and *time*, that is, the signified of the signifier. Space is located in time and time indexes space. When a material plane of desiring-production intersects with an expressive plane of semiosis, spatiality and temporality converge and open intervals for potential articulations to take place in time. Desiring-utterances separate and divide 'now' from 'then' and 'here' from 'there' and there are countless virtual 'now is' and 'then is', and 'here is' and 'there is'. Discourses of different languages, for example, identify and locate subject positions, object positions and durations of actions in different places for different times. Time and space certainly are not universally uniform across different sociocultural formations, nor are places and durations universally uniform across agonistic and antagonistic conflicts.

For discourse formations of collective assemblages of enunciation of 'the' dominant English, *subject positions* can be first-person, second-person and third-person singular or plural. The *tenses* can be past, present and future, and those temporalities are expressed as stationary or as ongoing (i.e. past perfect, present perfect or future perfect) activity. And the *mood* of those tenses may be indicative (i.e. stating, indicating), declarative (i.e. exclaiming, pronouncing), subjunctive (i.e. supposing, hypothesizing) or interrogative (i.e. questioning, inquiring). For example:

> #1: 'I am willing to speak about what I did during the killings . . . about doing my job.'
> This is an utterance enunciated 'here' and 'now' (in the present progressive tense) with a first-person singular subject *position* and an active *voice*. The utterance is enunciated in the indicative rather than the subjunctive *mood*, and in the nominative rather than the objective *case*. Its *modality* is ontological (i.e. it states a condition of existence) rather than deontological (i.e. makes a judgement of moral obligation). Its *agency* is transitive (i.e. it is action that passes over to an object, a verb that takes a direct object to complete its sense) rather than intransitive, and its *process* of desiring-production is additive (i.e. it adds to possibility rather than subtracts from it, at times multiplying it).
> By contrast, consider utterance #2.
>
> #2: 'They hadn't been willing to meet with us and confess. . . . To ask us for forgiveness.'
> This is an utterance located 'here' at the time of its enunciation, but it refers to a 'then' of past-perfect time. The utterance is enunciated in a passive voice ('their' unwillingness to confess and to ask in relation to 'us'), and the utterance's case is objective (i.e. 'us' is the object of unwillingness); 'they' had not been willing to meet with, to confess and to ask 'us' . . . . The actively nominative subject position of this utterance is a disembodied 'they', somebody who is not materially present at the Aionic time of the utterance's enunciation. 'They' is spoken about in 'their' absence by a materially present manifested speaker signifying an unnamed denoted 'us'. Yet 'they' is the active subject and 'us' is the passive object with respect to 'their' unwillingness. The desiring-utterance is enunciated in an indicative mood. Had it been uttered in a subjunctive mood, it would have sounded like, 'If they hadn't been willing to meet with us. . . .'

The addressee of utterance #2 is an implied but unnamed second-person singular or plural body to whom it is being declared that an unnamed third-person plural 'they' is guilty of past-perfect unwillingness to meet with 'us'. The utterance's modality is deontological insofar as it judges negatively an ongoing prior violation (i.e. the past perfect) of an implied moral obligation to be willing to meet. It does not simply describe the facticity of a past-perfect ontological condition. The implication is that 'they' *should* have been willing to meet with 'us', confess and ask 'us' for forgiveness, hence the process of that utterance's desiring-production is subtractive, taking away from that which *ought* to be the modality.

Conversing a politics of turn-taking

Conversational turn-taking reproduces the very performative, distributive, integrative and transformative formats they order and organize. I am referring here to a circular organization, that is, a substance of expression that theoretical biologists and cognitive scientists call *autopoiesis*, a term coined to refer to the dynamics of autonomy proper to living systems that reproduce themselves recursively. Francisco Varela (1979) defines autopoiesis as

> . . . a network of processes of production (transformation and destruction) of components that produce the components that (1) through their interactions and transformations continuously regenerate and realize the network of processes (relations) that produced them; and (2) constitute it (the machine) as a concrete unity in the space in which they exist by specifying the topological domain of its realization as such a network. (p. 13)[29]

As minor communication machines, conversations perform, distribute, integrate and transform exterior relations of territorial assemblages. Those relations and forces are structured in and through (i.e. by autopoietic means of) turn-taking; daily life is punctuated by turns whose patterns and formats are micropractical arrangements for determining which subject positions have entitlements to which rights and which obligations in which territorial assemblages. What is done with a turn is integrally related to how and when a turn manifests semiotically and how it becomes embodied. Bodies are installed in available subject positions of collective assemblages of enunciation as conversed and conversing subjects. Coming to minor communication, then, is a coming to pragmatic (i.e. schizoanalytic), ethical, aesthetic, political, erotic and psychic immanence in ways that allow for engagement with and participation in rational, political and libidinal economies of everyday life. Resolving conflict and reconciling trauma are matters of love (i.e. both erotic and agapic), art (i.e. both creative production and aesthetic consumption), science (i.e. both prediction and control) and politics (i.e. both power and control) – in other words, the experimental articulation of social-production and desiring-production.

As a material-semiotic territorial assemblage, post-genocide Rwanda preserves the heterogeneity of its component parts while enabling affective transformation. Said another way, post-genocide Rwanda is a far-from-equilibrium system in near-crisis, that is, an assemblage near a self-ordering threshold situated somewhere between the stratifications of steady-state equilibrium and a smooth plane of virtuality outlining potential linkages among assemblages. The minor communication machines conversing the form and substance of gaçaça transitional justice courts actualizes some of those outlines of potential linkages, producing emergent affects by performing, distributing, integrating and transforming Rwanda's material-semiotic territorial assemblage. Gaçaça transitional justice courts articulate bodies and signs forming patterns of habit and socioculturally formatted conventions. Patterns of habit and sociocultural conventions, in turn, are composed of content-expression along one axis and deterritorialization-reterritorialization along the other. In short, schizoanalytic (i.e. pragmatic) effects of minor communication machines instantiate gaçaça transitional justice courts by means of conversing, negotiating, mediating and dialoguing exterior relations between regimes of signs and desiring-bodies producing emergent affects that, in turn, perform, distribute, integrate and transform multiplicities of relations reconstituting territorial assemblages.

There is in the very consummation-consumption of conversing, negotiating, mediating and dialoguing an ethics that instantiates space and time, actualizing good sense, common sense in common places for common durations. The qualitative temporality and quantitative spatiality of relatively stable near-equilibrium conditions of daily life are produced and reproduced as stratifications, that is, they are structured and ordered sequentially and linearly rather than genealogically and asynchronously. The practices of conversing machines in the process of creating strata (i.e. actualizing systems of homogenous components working in near-equilibrium conditions) are its methods of cutting out and turning over, of reversing the relations of discourse and desire, that is, reversing discursive productivity and embodied subjectivity. By reversing the relations of articulations, bodies as positioned subjects appear to *in*form and to *per*form reality-effects of daily life. In his critique of Michele Foucault's microphysics of power and of Pierre Bourdieu's concept of *habitus*, Michele de Certeau argues that discourse 'cuts out' a particular phenomenon (i.e. an event, a text) from its context and inverts it, 'turning it over'.[30] In Foucault's thinking, the 'it' that is cut out and turned over is the microphysics of surveillance and discipline. In Bourdieu's case, the 'it' is domestic practices of *habitus* and *disposition*. For Deleuze and Guattari, the 'it' is *event*.

For our purposes, conversing involves turn-taking that cuts out the substance and form of material matter (i.e. content) and articulates it to forms and substances of expression via utterances that turn (i.e. reverse by performing, distributing, integrating and transforming) content and expression into explanatory propositions that retrospectively make sense and appear to have been explained all along. Conversing, as minor communication, given this line of thinking, operates as a multi-versalizing (as opposed to a uni-versalizing) machine. Conversational forms and substances perform, distribute, integrate and transform patterns of dominance and subordination by means of enforcing rights and obligations of bodies occupying subject positions. In effect, turns take what they find – and what they find are countless striations and stratifications across territorial assemblages of exterior relations of active and reactive forces and their conditions of existence, machinic assemblages of bodies and collective assemblages of enunciation – from which they articulate desiring-utterances that turn, that is, rearrange relations to particular objects, bodies and conditions of material-semiotic worlds.

A turn materializes semiotically either as a radical experiment or as a repressive conformation; it may assert change by violating conventional forms and substances or it may insist on reinscribing them. By modifying the intensive affects of a body (i.e. its lattitude) as well as by modifying a body's differential rates (i.e. its longitude), conversational turn-taking machines always already condition fascistic and anarchistic potentialities and tendencies. They are potentially fascistic (paranoiac or 'paranoid') insofar as articulated bodies are obligated to perform conventional formats of turn-taking to demonstrate membership in a territorial assemblage. They are potentially anarchistic (schizophrenic or 'schizoid') insofar as turns may be taken in ways that violate conventions and that transform both practical and discursive good sense and common sense of empirical consciousness. Roland Barthes puts it this way: 'Language, as performance of the language system (*langage*), is neither reactionary nor progressive. It is quite simply fascist; for fascism is not the prohibition to say things, it is the *obligation* to say them. . .' (Barthes 1977, p. 14). Located at the border of actual and virtual reality, verbal representation actualizes virtuality discursively. A conversing turn draws from outlines of virtual relations and from striations of actual relations and articulates them materially and semiotically to bodies whose latitudes (i.e. sets of intensive affects of a body, what a body can do and undergo) and longitudes (i.e. differential rates of bodies' material elements, their speed and slowness) are affected in the process of enjoining assemblages. Every turn incorporealizes and conditions potential immanent, nomadic minor communication of rogue semiotics, and sedentary majoritarian state semiotics. In this sense, conversing articulates both schizoid potential of anarchy and paranoid potential of fascism. Pragmatically, a turn actualizes experimentation in the sense of evaluating what a body can do. Conversational turns are *ways* of modifying subject positionality in relation to active and reactive forces, *means* of shifting alliances and coalitions, and *methods* for accommodating rights and privileges. The question remains open for Rwandans: Can a body taking a turn make a rhizome?

5

Order-Words, Truth-Procedures and Desiring-Utterances

Chapter overview

Verbal representation (i.e. the nomadic subject of transcendental sense) is theorized as the articulation of desire and discourse capable of operating as truth-procedures and producing truth-effects. Bodies of machinic assemblages of desire and the utterances of collective assemblages of enunciation articulate in the forms and substances of questions that ask into order-words and their relations to desire, experience, will, resistance and resolve in ways that perform, distribute and integrate transcendental sense and empirical consciousness. Taking turns, that is, turning to and returning from the psychological time (i.e. Aion) of verbal representation and the ontological time (i.e. Chronos of the proposition) of affect and memory, produce intervals as durations for affect, recollection-memory and contraction-memory to fill in and to (re)punctuate. The selections of discourse formations, speech registers, communicative formats, vernacular conventions and their obligatory relations to the material-semiotic conditions of post-genocide Rwanda bring the concepts of truth-procedures and truth-effects to the struggle over order-words for transitional justice and sociocultural reconciliation of truth, peace, justice, healing and forgiveness with respect to gaçaça's extra-legal discursive processes.

Order-words and genocide

The elementary unit of discourse, whether indirect, direct or quasi-direct discourse, is an order-word, order both in the sense of giving a command and in the sense of creating order. '[T]he fundamental forms of speech are not the statement of a judgment or the expression of a feeling, but "the command, the expression of obedience, the assertion, the question, the affirmation or negation," very short phrases that command life and are inseparable from enterprises and large-scale projects. "Ready?" "Yes." "Go ahead"' (Deleuze and Guattari 1987, p. 76).[1] An order-word does not so much *refer* to a prior organization of thought and desire as it *creates* order and organization. 'Language is not life; it gives life orders. Life does not speak; it listens and waits . . . language does not operate between something seen (or felt) and something said, but always goes from saying to saying.' (Deleuze and Guattari 1987, p. 76). In this sense, order-words are discourse functions that are redundant with discourse formations, and desiring-utterances drawn from discourse formations are overdetermined by indirect, direct and quasi-direct discourse. Listen to an utterance of Pancrace, one of the Rwandan killers Jean Hatzfeld interviewed for his book, *Machete Season: The Killers in Rwanda Speak*:

> During that killing season we rose earlier than usual, to eat lots of meat, and we went up to the soccer field at around nine or ten o'clock. The leaders would grumble about latecomers, and we would go off on the attack. Rule number one was to kill. There was no rule number two. It was an organization without complications. (Hatzfeld 2005, p. 10)

Another killer, Pio, refers to the power of order-words as well:

> We met up in town, near the shops, and chatted with pals along the way to the soccer field. There they would give us orders about the killings and our itineraries for the day, and off we went, beating the bush, working our way down to the marshes. (Hatzfeld 2005, p. 10)

Order-words are capable of creating order and organization insofar as they are implicitly articulated to patterns of social obligation (and thereby to social-production), 'implicit or nondiscursive presuppositions' (Deleuze and Guattari 1987, p. 77), long-standing norms and conventions. When order-words are operating, they are modifying discourse patterns and presuppositions of social rights and obligations, which are often referenced in terms of ethical standards. Listen to Adalbert, another of the killers Hatzfeld interviewed:

> . . . the bravest young guys became leaders, the ones who gave orders without hesitation and strode eagerly along. Me, I made myself the leader for all the residents of Kibungo from the very first day. Previously I was leader of the church choir, so now I became a real leader, so to speak. The residents approved me without a hitch. (Hatzfeld 2005, p. 12)

The concept of order-word is not that far afield from the concepts of speech-act and illocutionary force. J. L. Austin (1962/1975) and later John Searle (1969) developed speech-act theory to account for, among other discursive functions, speech that accomplishes transformational modifications of immanent patterns and conditions. Given the appropriate context, uttering the words 'I do' illocutionarily transforms the status of a relationship of two persons from single individuals into a married couple. In the context of the 100-day Rwandan genocide, listen to the chanting and singing of order-words by the *interahamwe* gangs of young men in the throes of killing Tutsi men, women and children: 'Find them, find them, kill them all'; 'Kill them big, kill them small, kill them, kill them, kill them all' (Ilibagiza 2006, p. 78). Immaculée Ilibagiza, a young Tutsi girl who successfully hid during the genocide and had to listen to the *interahamwe* chanting nightly, offers her own theory of order-words:

> Young Hutus were taught from an early age that Tutsis were inferior and not to be trusted, and they didn't belong in Rwanda. Hutus witnessed the segregation of

> Tutsis every day, first in the schoolyards and then in the workplace, and they were taught to dehumanize us by calling us 'snakes' and 'cockroaches.' No wonder it was so easy for them to kill us – snakes were to be killed and cockroaches exterminated (Ilibagiza 2006, p. 78)

The irony is that these young Hutu *interahamwe* had become snake-like and cockroach-like during the genocide process; listen to Ms. Ilibagiza describe her experience of hiding and watching and listening to the *interahamwe*:

> We were lucky today. They searched all over the house and searched in every room. They looked through the yard and dug through the dung heap behind the cow pen. They crawled into the ceiling and under the furniture – they even stuck their machetes into my suitcase to make sure I wasn't hiding Tutsi babies. They were crazed, like rabid animals. Their eyes were crazed and red. . . . I think they'd been smoking drugs. (Ilibagiza 2006, p. 80)

Order-words are capable of accomplishing corporeal/material as well as incorporeal transformations insofar as they are resolutely articulated to implicit sociocultural obligations and presuppositions (Deleuze and Guattari 1987, p. 77).

Utterances of minor communication are required to modify, and at times, undermine problematic, obstructionist and heinous order-words, and to destabilize, decode and deterritorialize ossified and counterproductive sociocultural obligations and presuppositions, often immanent to narratives. The objective of the gaçaça process and its truth procedures of desiring-utterances was to subvert, subtract and erase the presuppositional constants that conditioned the possibility, and in many respects, the inevitability of those order-words and narratives in Rwanda. Desiring-utterances drawn from minor communication machines of vernacular discourse formations were the cutting edges of the nomadic verbal representation of transcendental sense capable of decoding and deterritorializing genocidal order-words and dehumanizing narratives. Deleuze and Guattari's (1987) concept for these unsettling utterances is *tensor* (pp. 99–100). Tensors are desiring-utterances articulated to an unconventional *connective logic*, that is, a syntax of connective synthesis – 'and . . . and . . . and' – as opposed to being articulated to a more *deontic logic*, that is, a syntax of 'ought to . . .', 'need to . . .', 'should . . .', 'have to . . .', and 'must. . . .' A tensor, then, is a desiring-utterance that causes discourse to tend towards its limits, towards the limits of its communicative features for expressing forms and substances of content at the edges of propositional thought and libidinal imagination.

Tensors, like order-words, are discursive functions, not magical words and phrases or super-discursive grammatical categories. Tensors are words and phrases that function to uproot and decode conventional forms and typical expressions. 'The tensor effects a kind of transitivization of [typical, sedentary] words and phrases, causing the last term to react upon the preceding term, back through the entire chain' (Deleuze and Guattari 1987, p. 99). This transitivization can be imagined as utterances acting upon preceding utterances and their presupposed sociocultural rights and obligations; dialogue of conversing interrupts monologue of narrative. Engaging an unfolding (or perhaps a repeating) narrative by entering into it with dialogue in effect takes a turn, and in so doing, transforms monologue into dialogue, enabling monological discourse to pass over into another form of discursive expression, that is, conversing. When an utterance becomes imbricated in a sequence of utterances constituting the dialogue of conversing, it has the capacity to function as a tensor, to react against prior utterances in the series of utterances constituting conversing, turning those utterances back on themselves, creating a break; the dialogue of conversing now unfolds along a different substantive and formative trajectory. With respect to the dialogue of conversing (as opposed to the monologue of narrative), there are more possibilities for tensors and order-words to react against order-words and formal syntactic and pragmatic conventions of preceding utterances than simply reversing and turning on its immediate predecessor. Tensors are capable of modifying the grammaticality and stylistics of enunciated indirect, direct and quasi-direct discourse formations in any number of ways. An order-word as simple as the conjunction 'and . . .' instead of 'but . . .' may play the role of a tensor very differently insofar as 'and . . .' functions less as a conjunctive synthesis than it does as a connective synthesis, enunciating all possible connections that it places into continuous variation. '[T]he tensor, therefore, is not reducible either to a constant or a variable, but assures the variation of the variable by subtracting in each instance the value of the constant' (Deleuze and Guattari 1987, p. 99). As such, tensors are not reducible to or coextensive with any properly linguistic category, even though the pragmatic value of tensors is clearly operative in most if not all discursive formations of collective enunciation.

Communicating, then, is not merely a matter of referencing and representing, like bees tracing a path to a source of nectar, nor is it a matter of representing what is known, like intelligence officers decoding encrypted messages. It is much more a matter of transmitting what has been heard, more on the order of incorporating, mapping and reframing hearsay, that is, saying what others have said in other ways. When Deleuze and Guattari (1987) conceptualize transmission as indirect discourse, 'the saying to the saying' (p. 78), they are referring to what constitutes the dialogue of conversing, whether or not it engages, intervenes or interrupts narrative monologue. Conversing, negotiating and mediating, as modes of minor communication, constitute 'the saying to the saying', transmitting hearsay, saying what is heard, what others have said, spreading rumours, gossip, slogans and ideological hatred. In short, dialogue is much more a matter of pronouncing and responding to order-words and asserting and advancing tensors than it is a matter of transmitting and exchanging the content of information. This is even more the case in agonistic, antagonistic and dehumanizing discourse. Articulations of discourse and desire are effected in and through order-words and tensors that are inbuilt syntactic structures and pragmatic properties of empirical consciousness and the infrastructure of discourse. Discourse commands by means of ordering and organizing narrative and dialogue, which, in turn, articulate to implicit sociocultural rights and obligations. In addition to orders and commands, order-words also question, promise, compromise, bluff, threaten, lie, demand, complain, accuse, deny, defer and propose (an admittedly incomplete catalogue of discourse's pragmatic functions).

The sociocultural plane of reality-effects is what takes on primary importance for us. Individual utterances and psychological characterizations of manifested speakers as individual persons supposedly authoring their original utterances are of much less interest. Assemblages of collective enunciation account for the sociocultural character of the redundant forms and substances of content and the redundant structures of enunciation. Order-words become apparent in the redundancy of the pragmatic acts and the discursive utterances of the conversing of unfolding dialogue. Redundancy, as I intend it here, assumes two forms – frequency and resonance. Frequency concerns the significance of information and substance, whereas resonance concerns the subjectivity of style and form.[2] Information (substance) and style (form) are, in these respects, subordinate to dialogical redundancy. Said another way, implicit sociocultural rights and obligations are immanent in and performed through discursive redundancies; they become actionable through discourse's conversing. 'There is no significance independent of dominant significations, no subjectivation independent of an established order of subjection and subjugation' (Deleuze and Guattari 1987, p. 79). Both signification and subjectivation are conditioned by the transmission of order-words on a plane of sociocultural experience with presupposed rights and obligations. There is no individual enunciating; it is not an individual action. Rather, enunciating is a collective phenomenon (Deleuze and Guattari 1987, pp. 79–80). Order-words inhering immanently in collective assemblages of enunciation take on primary importance in accounting for the immanent sociocultural character of discursive formations and their schizoanalytic pragmatics.

Redundancies are important considerations insofar as order-words are always already inbuilt in the infrastructure of discourse, which is to say in the habits of daily living, what Bordieu refers to as *habitus*.[3] In effect, order-words consist in the set of all possible incorporeal transformations that are capable of being articulated to bodies of desire of a given sociocultural formation. As a singular instance of this kind of collective inquiry, imagine dialogue as variations and modifications of order-words and the attributes those variations and modifications articulate to desiring bodies, now functioning as manifested sociocultural subjects. The transformations thereby produced are incorporeal, and materially real nonetheless in their effects. Without order-words, discourse (like language) would remain a pure virtuality, remaining unarticulated to social-production. The inherent indirectness and quasi-directness of discourse (without which content and expression would be devoid of signifiance, and substance and form would be devoid of subjectivation) is the condition that enables the virtual to become the actual and possible. The practical question for conversing, negotiating and mediating narrative concerns ways in which informational content and stylistic expression articulate such that the redundancies of the order-words and presupposed sociocultural rights and obligations can be decoded and eventually recoded. A preliminary move might be to negotiate explicit conditions that foreground and support discursive practices capable of decoding incommensurable narratives and recoding them along at least partially commensurable lines of practical workability. That is precisely what the gaçaça process accomplished. What follows is an examination of indirect, direct and quasi-direct discourse, the forms of dialogue for engaging narratives of injustice and trauma, dialogue that conditioned the possibility for Rwanda's experiment in the social-production of transitional justice and trauma reconciliation.

Indirect and direct discourse

The manifestation of the dynamic tensions between enunciated discourse (i.e. the spoken) and enunciating utterances (i.e. the speaking) are to be found in the modifications of the patterns of the collectively enunciated, which become manifest as turns of enunciating dialogue modify them. These modifications manifest on the fluid borders separating grammatical structure from stylistic form. Two primary patterns of enunciating operate on collective assemblages of enunciation at the border between grammar and stylistics – direct and indirect discourse.[4] The pattern of direct discourse makes explicit the intonations and other paralinguistic, affective and libidinal features of dialogue, and is limited to a reciprocal exchange of intonational features and substantive expressions of turns of an unfolding conversation. It is a kind of reciprocal affective infectiousness of enunciated actions and passions and the substantive expression of desiring-utterances. As it fades from sound, a desiring-utterance is absorbed by the recollection-memory of enunciated discourse, now available for contraction-memory, incorporation and modification by subsequent utterances. In these ways, direct discourse maintains a relatively clear-cut separation from indirect discourse and between enunciated discourse and enunciating utterances, even as each utterance registers its libidinal and affective understanding of its predecessors.

Direct discourse *embodies* value judgements and attitudes, whereas indirect discourse is analytical in the sense that it is discourse *about* the direct enunciation of value judgements and attitudes, and about other indirect discourse. The content and expression of overt conflict is expressed directly; the content of covert agonism and antagonism is expressed indirectly, even if those expressions may be direct. But the expression as well as the content of covert tension may be indirect as well. Most discourse is indirect; it is discourse *about* discourse, speech *about* speech (Deleuze and Guattari 1987, pp. 75–7). Discourse becomes increasingly intense as its direct enunciation of values and attitudes becomes more performatively apparent. On the other hand, discourse becomes increasingly dense as its indirect enunciation of references and representations become more analytically pronounced. Direct discourse is more libidinally and affectively intense, whereas indirect discourse is more analytically and propositionally dense. Indirect discourse amounts to an analytical registration of the enunciated discourse of others. The libidinal, emotive and affective features of desire become expressed in the substance rather than in the form of an indirect desiring-utterance, that is, in facial expressions, intonational patterns and paralinguistic cues. Indirect discourse, as it incorporates the enunciated discourse of others, does not directly transmit forms of content and substances of expression. Rather, the affective form of material content is incorporated into desiring-utterances and substantively expressed as embodied sociality. In brief, a material body's emotive and affective forms of content are manifested through a desiring-utterance's forms and substances of expression. In the process, the materiality of the forms and substances of machinic assemblages of bodies become articulated to the forms and substances of collective assemblages of enunciation of indirect discourse.

An example of direct discourse is an iteration of a chant collectively enunciated by dozens of *interahamwe* on the 'hunt' for Tutsi in hiding: 'Let us hunt them in the forests, lakes and hills; let us find them in the church; let us wipe them from the face of the earth' (Ilibagiza 2006, p. 77). Direct discourse would also be Ms. Ilibagiza's utterance in response to hearing that chant as she remained silent and in hiding in a Hutu pastor's bathroom behind a vestibule: 'Dear God, save us . . .' (p. 78). If such an intensely enunciated direct utterance were to be incorporated into a slightly less direct desiring-utterance, it might sound something like: 'And I cannot forget their chant – "Find them, find them, kill them all."' Subsequently, at a hypothetical gaçaça trial, she might have recounted experiencing terror and rage during that traumatizing event, articulating it with a more indirect utterance: 'I remember praying to God, trying to remember every prayer I had ever learned.' An even more indirect reference to and analysis of a directly enunciated utterance might sound something like: 'They were yelling and screaming that they wanted to kill us.' The compositional and often the inflectional particularities of questions, exclamations, declarations and other forms of direct discourse are omitted in indirect discourse. Those interrogative, exclamatory and imperative features of an enunciated utterance are translated instead into the discursive features of the content of indirectly enunciating utterances.

Indirect discourse moves in several different diagonal directions as it concerns itself with three rather different operations that modify enunciated discourse, whether that enunciated discourse was relatively direct or relatively indirect. One of these operational directions is the *referent-analysing modification of discourse* (Vološinov 1973, pp. 130–1). This pattern of modifying enunciated discourse opens a wide range of possibilities for a desiring-utterance to interrupt, to interpolate (not necessarily to mislead, however), to reframe, to retort and to comment on enunciated discourse without sacrificing a distinction between the turning of an enunciating utterance and its interpolation of enunciated discourse. Utterances that perform referent-analysing modifications of enunciated discourse rely on a relatively linear style of enunciation that requires a depersonalization of the discourse being modified. Modification of enunciated discourse is accomplished primarily in communicative contexts in which a (manifested) speaker is making sense, that is, explaining, comparing and putting into a particular perspective or frame of reference (the signified) the sense of others (the denoted).

A second direction along which indirect utterances move as they modify the patterns of enunciated discourse is referred to as *texture-analysing modification* (Vološinov 1973, pp. 131–2). This operational direction concerns itself with the libidinal and affective nuances, the emotional tones and textures of the enunciated discourse of others. Desiring-utterances that modify the texture of the enunciated discourse of others actually incorporate into those enunciating utterances some of the words, phrases and locutions that characterize its expressive, affective and libidinal features (i.e. the subjectivated and stylistic features) of the direct and indirect discourse of others. Referring to Immaculée Ilibagiza's prayerful direct utterance, her texture-analysing modification reads: 'It wasn't the soldiers who were chanting, nor was it the trained militiamen who had been tormenting us for days. No, these were my neighbors, people I'd grown up and gone to school with – some had even been to our house for dinner. Now they were crazy with killing' (Ilibagiza 2006, p. 77). In the process of modifying the enunciated utterances of others, a desiring-utterance is disclosing its understanding of that enunciated discourse. Texture-analysing utterances, of necessity, modify enunciated discourse in very performative ways by creating imagistic, libidinal affects; they are of course referring to the substantive content of the enunciated discourse being modified, and at the same time they are foregrounding the libidinal, emotional and affective texture of the enunciated discourse. Such is the primary work of desiring-utterances that modify the expressive texture more than the content of the text (i.e. the referential formative content) of the enunciated discourse of others. These desiring-utterances operate by countersignifying the authoritarian and rationalistic operations of referent-analysing discourse.

A third direction for the modification of the enunciated discourse of others is referred to as *impressionistic modification* (Vološinov 1973, pp. 132–3). This modifying operation concerns itself with the imagined thoughts and experiences of the supposed sources of enunciated discourse. A desiring-utterance that is impressionistically modifying the enunciated discourse of others is being rather free with both the propositionality and the libidinality of enunciated discourse. Such utterances, in the process of their enunciating, may abbreviate (sometimes radically so) both the referential-analytic and the texture-analytic properties of enunciated discourse. Impressionistic modification may only highlight a few of the themes of the enunciated discourse that are becoming modified. Here is part of a conversation between Immaculée Ilibagiza and the Hutu pastor who had been hiding her in his home: 'Oh, God, no! On the radio they told everyone to go to the churches and stadiums for protection' (Ilibagiza 2006, p. 87), to which the pastor replies, impressionistically modifying Ms. Ilibagiza's comment: 'They might have said that, but it wasn't to protect anyone. The killers were sent there with machine guns and grenades. The bodies were piled up as high as my house . . . the stench is unbearable.' (p. 87).

If a continuum were to be constructed for these three discourse modifying operations (instead of mapping the directions of their diagonal trajectories), referent-analytic modification would anchor one end and texture-analytic modification would anchor the other; impressionistic modification of discourse would fall variably between the two. Its precise location would depend on how much the impressionistic modifications relied on the referential or the textural properties of the desiring-utterances performing the impressionistic modification. Referring once again to the above utterance example, a hypothetical impressionistic desiring-utterance manifesting Ms. Ilibagiza reflecting on her conversation with the pastor might sound something like: 'Then again, the pastor may have been trying to frighten us just for the sheer pleasure of striking fear in our souls.'

Quasi-direct discourse

Quasi-direct discourse can be conceptualized most lucidly as part narrative/part dialogue discourse; it is the discourse of conflict resolving but not necessarily of trauma reconciling. The latter involves witnessing, that is, listening to life, which listens and waits rather than speaks. Resolving agonistic and antagonistic conflict requires dialogue to interrupt monologue, that is, the reciprocity of turn-taking conversing machines must be initiated if enunciated discourse is to be modified. Monologue and dialogue are operating more or less simultaneously, that is, each is partially interfering with the other, which creates the immanent tensions characteristic of quasi-direct discourse. Vološinov, who is framing much of his philosophy of language in terms of literary fiction and theoretical criticism, characterizes quasi-direct discourse as those instances in which both an author and a character are speaking simultaneously (pp. 141–59, *passim*). In effect, quasi-direct discourse is a discursive construction that holds and maintains the accents of two differently positioned and oriented subjects. In this sense, the discursive manifestation of mediating conflict (i.e. a mediator, an author) holds and maintains the accents of the incumbents (i.e. characters) of two or more radically different (antagonistic) subject positions. In this sense, quasi-direct discourse is both overt and doubly faced, and it expresses the form and substance of the content and expression of conflict and trauma. Desiring-utterances expressing trauma speak two voices – sometimes more than two – from two or more subject positions simultaneously; such utterances at times defy the denoted of good sense and the manifested and signified of common sense, making comprehension difficult if not impossible in terms of logical propositions of empirical consciousness.

Vološinov insists, as do I, that quasi-direct discourse not be thought of in terms of an individual consciousness, that is, as consciousness contained in and bounded by a psychologized individual corporeal body. Discourse, as I have been arguing throughout, has no *a priori* bodies, just as desire has no *a priori* subjects. Desiring-utterances are articulations of desire and discourse that locate and turn bodies of desire to subject positions of discourse. Discourse does not originate from within corporeal bodies. Consciousness, to the extent that as a psychologized concept it has any utility by itself, is most productively thought of as both transcendental and psychological, in accord with Bergson's configuring of memory and duration. Another way of characterizing quasi-direct discourse is to imagine the boundary between enunciated discourse and an enunciating utterance to be completely blurred. Think of *direct discourse* as a desiring-utterance that expresses affect as a nomadic subject, an aleatory point of verbal representation in Aionic time, that is, time with past and future but no present, the time of a psychological subject – not a transcendental subject. *Indirect discourse* is a desiring-utterance that modifies, conveys, transmits and communicates the substantive and formative themes of the enunciated discourse of others. *Quasi-direct discourse* is thought of as desiring-utterances dialogically mediating the monologically and narratively expressed agonistic and antagonistic experience of others, registering differences not necessarily expressed agonistically and antagonistically. An example would be a desiring-utterance mediating the direct and indirect expressions of agonism and antagonism and of witnessing without modification the (narrating of) experience of genocide.

In terms of conversing, negotiating and mediating, a desiring-utterance enunciates (i.e. it calls, hails or interpellates) a body to a first subject position, and another body either to a second or a third subject position, depending upon whether the utterance addresses a particular body as a second subject or pronounces to plural bodies as unspecified third subjects, that is, witnesses. Nonetheless, witnessing subjects, whether situated in second or third subject positions, may experience the intensity and density of a desiring-utterance as a composite of percept and affect that aligns with a plane of enunciation, that is, with a plane of quasi-direct discourse of a collective assemblage of enunciation. When a subject expresses, conveys, transmits or otherwise communicates an experience of witnessing the enunciated discourse of another embodied or disembodied subject, that expressing of experience may quote the enunciated discourse with a referential-analytic modification or describe it by means of a texture-analytic modification.

If an embodied subject were to attempt to express, convey, transmit or otherwise communicate via quasi-direct discourse its unmediated experience of another's enunciated utterance, it would sound as if that subject was thinking aloud, talking to his/her/itself, delivering a soliloquy, verbally hallucinating, responding to voices no one else can hear, that is, losing touch with reality (p. 148). Quasi-direct discourse is of practical value insofar as it mediates discursive experience to itself and to 'others' simultaneously. It is singularly suited to mediating direct experience of witnessing as – rather than after – it recedes into the context of enunciated discourse. Quasi-direct discourse is better suited to summon living impressions than it is to analyse references or textures of desiring-utterances. The pragmatic schizoanalytic significance of quasi-direct discourse consists in its stylistic substantive properties much more than in its formal grammatical properties. Vološinov (1973) insists that the living impression (i.e. the experience) of 'hearing the voices speak' (p. 148), as if in a dream, can be directly expressed only in the form of quasi-direct discourse. Imagination and fantasy – witnessing – gives rise to quasi-direct discourse, that is, to becoming-nomad, becoming-imperceptible, making transcendental sense.

Another distinguishing feature of quasi-direct discourse is that, unlike direct and indirect discourse, it neither requires nor accepts an enunciating verb, for example, 'said', 'felt', 'thought' (as in, 'she "said" that she was unwilling to meet . . .', or 'they "felt" disoriented and ignored . . .', or 'I "thought" they would storm out of the room.'). Quasi-direct discourse has no need for enunciating verbs because its function is not to report or convey, but to register and mediate experience directly. Said more explicitly, quasi-direct discourse is grammatically and pragmatically, that is, schizoanalytically, capable of allowing its manifested speaker to separate the point of view of his or her subject position from that of a speaker of enunciated discourse. This is one of the most sophisticated tasks for conversing, negotiating and mediating to accomplish. The ability of a witnessing subject to discern its discursive position and its point of view from the subject position and point of view of each of the conflicting subjects is subtle work requiring psychological involvement without ontological investment. To the extent that an embodied subject of desiring-utterances cannot distinguish various points of view from his or her own, impartiality and capacity to witness are compromised.

In all of these respects, quasi-direct discourse can be characterized as an adept accommodation of the dualism separating abstract referent-analysing and texture-analysing modifications of enunciated good sense and common sense of empirical consciousness from unmediated direct experience of transcendental sense. An embodied subject, with its stylistic and grammatical proclivities, does not exist outside of its material objectifications and identifications in discourse. It is the articulation of bodies of desire and subject positions of discourse that brings each to a life. Vološinov (1973) concludes his discussion of quasi-direct discourse by claiming that it is via quasi-direct discourse that, 'we recognize another person's utterance not so much in terms of its message, abstractly considered, but above all in terms of the character's accentuation and intonation, in terms of the evaluative orientation of his speech' (p. 155).

An ethic of witnessing and willingness

Truth-procedures consist in questions that condition reflexivity, that is, they condition the production of the consumption and consummation (a conjunctive synthesis) of the disjunctively produced and recorded experience of trauma (a disjunctive synthesis), a synthesizing process produced by the production of production itself. As discursive practices, truth-procedures condition re-examination of recollection-memory and contraction-memory; they are practices capable of locating seams in otherwise connectively seamless recorded experience of meaningless conflict and the trauma of collective schizophrenic experience, and of expanding those seams, thereby producing intervals between event and response. Those intervals convoke reflexivity, that is, the conjunctively synthetic production of the consumption-consummation of traumatic experience, giving rise to a nomadic subject of the virtual of transcendental sense that conditions the distributive, integrative and transformative potential of symbolizing and recoding trauma. Questioning disjunctively recorded experience of trauma constitutes a truth-procedure that produces legal, therapeutic and restorative truth-effects for a nomadic subject of transcendental sense 'being born of the states that it consumes and being reborn with each new state' (Deleuze and Guattari 1977, p. 16). Asking conjunctively synthetic questions productive of consumption-consummation of traumatic experience presupposes witnessing and willingness; that is why the production of willingness is of primary importance to the efficacy of truth-procedures, particularly when there is so little willingness and so much trauma to work with. Negotiating willingness and asking for it from those who have so little of it to give, requires witnessing their embodied, vulnerable expressions of trauma. Intervals are durations in which sense may be distributed differently, and that which has disintegrated may reintegrate differently, which may, in turn, condition incorporeal transformations, all of which may be more productive of therapeutic truths and restorative truths than of pure legal truths. For these potential truth-effects to be actualized, it is necessary for a witnessing subject to risk becoming-affected materially and psychically by the contents and expressions of the forms and substances of trauma. Dialogical interventions into monologically performative and narrative expressions take the form of transcendental–empirical questions for which there are no answers, only intervals for reflexivity and response.

Imagined along these lines, witnessing is a medium of and a resource for conditioning desiring-utterances productive of willingness, not of opinions.[5] Dialogical interventions based on choices to witness, to listen and to risk being psychically wounded independent of opinions regarding agreement and disagreement, to inquire into transcendental–empirical sense, the implications and entailments of events – these are communicative practices that condition an ethic of willingness. So, too, are inquiries that continue asking for willingness. Choosing to witness the truth-effects of trauma and to work into intervals of willingness – these are psychically arduous truth-procedures that divide body/core (i.e. mind/spirit), opening both to the interval, the inhuman, to that which is beyond the decisive turn of experience. Witnessing frames and conditions truth-procedures; their efficacy is a function of ethical discipline. But choosing the transcendental–empirical experience of witnessing, especially when doing so opens mind and body to the intensity and the density of trauma, rage, grief, aggression, shame, revulsion, resistance and accusation, is as empirically intuitive as it is psychically exhausting. As ethically embodied listening, witnessing performative and narrative expression of trauma is a choice to receive substantively and formally the contents of what an expressing body is manifesting (i.e. actions and passions), which may be experienced more as aggression, rage and grief of the schizoid depths than as verbal representation of transcendental sense. The reactive move is to defend against aggressive, threatening expression and to attend to the content rather than to the expression of trauma's truths, to rationalize, psychologize and otherwise modify expressive truth-effects as content and thereby to avoid libidinality. But the intensity of the psychic investments in trauma's expression gives its manifesting subject away to a willing witness.

Witnessing trauma's intense expression and its dense material content *is* its truth; witnessing it testifies to its ontological validity. Desiring-utterances may be presignifying libidinal expressions of psychic contents in the forms and substances of moaning, wailing, howling, sobbing or silence; the abundance of desiring-production exceeds the limits of language and presents symptomatically as the social-production of traumas.[6] A subject has choices about whether and how to attend to life, whether to attend at all and whether to witness or merely to listen, and what sense to make of desiring-utterances. *Power* flows through embodied subjects attending to and witnessing an event of truth, through a speaker witnessing and affirming resistance. On the other hand, *control* manifests through a speaker interrupting, ignoring or otherwise resisting resistance. No matter how psychically demanding, there is always a choice regarding how to respond to an event, what to do with/in an interval and whether to reciprocate and affirm an expression of trauma's truth by witnessing it.

Badiou (2001) contends that we have paid too high a price trying to found an ethics of communication, which is little more than an ethic of opinions and cultural relativism. Instead, he argues, 'the only genuine ethics is of truths in the plural – or, more precisely the only ethics is of processes of truth, of the labor that brings some truths into the world. There are as many subjects as there are truths and as many subjective types as there are procedures of truths' (p. 28). Truth-procedures, like philosophy, trauma reconciliation and conflict resolution, construct intervals for reflexivity and conjunctive synthesis to coexist. 'But this coexistence is not a unification – that is why it is impossible to speak of *one* Ethics' (p. 28). Witnessing desiring-utterances of subjects passionately attached to closed identities regarding Truth, reconciliation, amnesty and justice in Rwanda is capable of producing therapeutic truths, restorative truths, but often at the expense of *pure* legal truth(s), hence the international criminal justice's critical response to Rwanda's truth-procedures for producing truth-effects by means of gaçaça courts. Experience for Rwandans – Hutu and Tutsi – one assumes, is intensely personal and intimately local, and at the same time such experience is regionally territorial, even global in its reach. Witnessing trauma produces intervals from which different kinds of articulations manifest and different orders of questions emerge. Resolving and reconciling may be more a matter of witnessing *through* different truth-effects rather than listening *for* the legal Truth, but certainly not at the expense of restorative and therapeutic truths. (Recall Deleuze's description of a kind of witnessing with universal survey at infinite speed).

I am suggesting that most, if not all, asymmetrical violent social conflicts are produced when truth-procedures are ignored, oppressed or otherwise violated and an ethic of witnessing truths is abandoned; a third discursive subject position is erased, leaving no witnessing position for subjects to occupy. A territorial assemblage of impunity is the consequence, as has been apparent historically in instances of massacre and genocide. At that point, the agonism of truths of universal singularity morphs into the antagonism born of a commitment to a universal Truth of universal application, that is, as *the* Truth. The ethical project at those junctures is to inaugurate minor communication machines for witnessing and for resolving conflict and reconciling trauma, for intervening in performative monological narratives claiming *the* Truth. They are communicative interventions intended to transmute those narrative monologues into conversational, negotiational and mediational dialogue. It is by means of the reciprocity of conversational turn-taking that truth-procedures can be (re)introduced into the (violent) antagonism of competing Truth narratives. It is the introduction of truth-procedures as operators for witnessing and resolving conflict and reconciling post-conflict trauma that generate conditions of willingness sufficient for embodied traumatized subjects to engage. Confidence in a truth-procedure and willingness to engage with such procedures are conditioning resources for conflict resolving and trauma reconciling to take hold. If the interval for a truth-procedure is not produced, there can be little or no confidence in its potentiality and little or no willingness to bring its virtual reality to empirical consciousness. So, the questions become: How are truth-procedures (re)introduced into the incommensurable discourses of antagonistic narratives of *the* Truth? What are these truth-procedures? How do they sound? How are they actually performed? The task is not so much a matter of intervening in the form and substance of the content of narratives of *the* Truth; it is more a matter of intervening in the form and substance of their expression. It is by engaging a narrative's monological expression with dialogue rather than by advancing a counter-narrative that the incommensurability of truth-effects can be transformed.

Interventions into performative monologues with the dialogue of intervening turns (re)introduce and (re)model the fidelity, discernment and restraint of an ethic of truth-procedures.[7] This amounts to working in the immanence of truths of universal singularity on the one hand and simultaneously with the convergence of the diverging lines of interval and subjectivity on the other. Truth-procedures traverse differences without erasing them or transcending/dissociating them; rather, desiring-utterances of truth-procedures flow through differences, saturating them, transforming them without violating them. Communicative engagements/interventions of desiring-utterances, rather than trafficking in opinion and cliché, are interpolated into agonistic and antagonistic monologues, inviting degrees of confidence in the truth-procedures and convoking willingness to participate in their agonism and antagonism. I am arguing for the productivity of resolving conflict and reconciling trauma with communicative engagements/interventions held to an ethic of witnessing and of truth-procedures. To take a turn in a truth-procedure (e.g. to engage in conversing, negotiating and mediating) is to engage conflicting narrative monologues of *the* Truth. Witnessing is a necessary precondition for knowing if, when and how to engage as a witness by taking a turn and thereby articulating desire to/and discourse. Truth-procedures embody potential for conditioning confidence and willingness to the extent that their turns demonstrate evidence of witnessing and hold to the fidelity of a truth, discern a truth from its resemblances and restrain the imposition of a truth on contesting narratives (Badiou 2001, pp. 67–71).

As a turn-taking machine, a truth-procedure inserts subject positions into agonistic and antagonistic monological discourse, transforming it by means of conversing it, that is, creating at minimum a second subject position in a despotic and oppressive monologue, producing a contestatory, polemical and countersignifying discourse, in effect turning monologue to negotiation by means of inserting dialogue. In like manner, conversing an antagonistic negotiation creates a third subject position, that is, a witnessing position that manifests by taking a turn from a third subject position, in effect mediating an antagonistic negotiation. Similarly, conversing an antagonistic mediation manifests additional discursive subject positions in the discourse, in effect transforming it into multi-subject and polyvocal dialogue. Each subject position, once introduced, in effect mediates the others; the more subject positions manifested, the greater the mediating potential of the discursive truth-procedure. Conflict escalates when truth-procedures are violated and witnessing subject positions are vacated; immanent intervals collapse and responses to events go unmediated, becoming unreflexive, unthinking and reactive rather than active. Truth-effects take place in intervals and those intervals are the intersections of material and psychic immanence. Antagonistic factions are threatened by and angry about the imposition of *the* universal Truth, which is so egregiously oppressing and repressing them. The universal address of a truth to a subject to truth, along with its singular reception and its conversational application become confused, assuming that universal address implies universal reception and universal adherence, hence the need to bring (i.e. to impose) that truth, as *the* Truth, to (i.e. on) others. In effect, differences come to be heard not as the banality of infinite difference but rather as threats to their *psychological* identity, to *the(ir)* Truth and to *sacred* Morality.

A truth-procedure puts in place and sets in motion a turn-taking reciprocity machine that negotiates interruptions of agonistic and antagonistic monologues in ways that (re)introduce fidelity, discernment and restraint to antagonistic discourse. It is not unusual in protracted and violent social conflicts (asymmetrical or not) to find that fidelity to a truth has been abandoned in whole or in part, that simulacra of truths have been adopted and that all subjects are hard at work imposing on others their version of *the* Truth, usually militaristically rather than militantly (Badiou 2001, pp. 58–71). The task is to interrupt and engage monologue in ways that allow the expression (it is not a function of content) of a truth-procedure to take hold, to inform and perform resolving and reconciling practices, sustaining an ethic of witnessing truths as universal singularities, that is, as universal in their address, singular in their reception and conversational in their application. Working to resolve conflict and to reconcile trauma is work that dwarfs special interests of individual mortality. Conflict resolving and trauma reconciling work requires a commitment beyond the decisive turn of experience, a commitment that stems from experience of an Event and truth-procedures born of it, truth-procedures with the capacity to withstand failed projects, humiliation, vertical learning curves and material/spiritual exhaustion. The disciplined adherence to a truth born of an Event forms, informs and performs a truth-procedure and an ethic of witnessing. Committed adherence to a truth-procedure in the face of overwhelming difficulties and discouraging setbacks is oftentimes all that can be expected. What are the schizoanalytic implications of this shift from an objective-rationalist epistemological orientation to a transcendental-empiricist pragmatic orientation for conflict resolving and trauma reconciling? What would an ethic of truths and the turn-taking interventions of a truth-procedure look and sound like? What would emphasizing nomadic communicative practices of fidelity, discernment and restraint entail in terms of the theory and practice of conflict resolving and peacebuilding?

Questions articulating desire to discourse

The aims and objectives of the Rwandan post-genocide transitional justice experiment with the gaçaça process – to produce truth, peace, justice, healing, forgiveness and reconciliation – were as ennobling in their conception as they were fraught in their actualization. Phil Clark provides a nuanced account of the controversy attending the creation of the concept of gaçaça courts as a method for accomplishing those aims and objectives, and of the mixed reviews of their results (Clark 2010, pp. 98–131). Rather than entering into those debates, however, I have been mapping salient features of the Event of the Rwanda genocide and post-genocide transitional justice efforts onto Deleuze's transcendental–empirical account of the genesis of representation in order to address the above questions. The degree to which gaçaça courts were productive of truth, peace, justice, healing, forgiveness and reconciliation is the degree to which minor communication machines (i.e. conversation, negotiation and mediation) were instrumental in the social-production of transitional justice and collective reconciliation, their limitations and failures notwithstanding. Gaçaça courts provided an alternative to traditional courts of Law as an immanently ethical material-semiotic response to a corporeal/material Event of massive proportions, an opportunity for ontological questions to be asked, implicitly if not always explicitly, and for desiring-utterances to be stammered on the way to approximating responses that may never be adequate. Conversing, negotiating and mediating the dilemmas of truth, peace, justice, healing, forgiveness and reconciliation are interminable processes that can never be completed as accomplishments, but the alternative of not 'attending to life', of not making a good faith effort to make sense of collective psychosis, is unthinkable. Asking questions that invite ontological reflexivity, questions that ask victims, survivors, perpetrators and bystanders transcendental–empirical questions, asking for their willingness to witness desiring-utterances when they are forthcoming may be the best we can do.

Speaking and thinking reflexively depend less on propositional logic and rational judgements than they do on the schizoanalytic force of questions. In poetry and open form literature – that is, minoritarian discourses – we see and hear discourse's power to transform across a variety of senses (Colebrook 2002a, pp. 11–27). Asking questions of inquiry rather than questions of interrogation, asking for willingness and for good faith rather than settling for suspicion and accusation, asking for reflexively active responses rather than searching for reactive hidden truths, these are the productive conversing practices for negotiating and mediating antagonistic monologues of conflict and collective trauma. Witnessing opens opportunities to ask such questions. From a witnessing mediator's subject position, reality-effects are abundant, contingent, immanent, multivocal and variable. From a disputing advocate's subject position, reality is univocal, universal, foundational and endlessly reproductive of *the* Truth, which is isomorphic with identity, both of which must be defended and protected, often with life and limb. Antagonistic conflict is both a function of and an outcome of those tensions. For each material-semiotic system – each region of reality-effects – any other system of reality-effects that confronts and traverses it is suspect, if not wrong, simplistic, if not primitive, and dangerous, if not evil. And each of these 'other' material-semiotic 'realities', from within their one True reality, is *known* to be flawed, foreign, unstable, naive, short-sighted, dangerous and threatening (Docherty 2001, pp. 49–102).

Truth-procedures consist in utterances that inquire into desire, experience, will, resolve and resistance. Each body is afforded access to subject positions from which to manifest, to testify, to speak, to take an opportunity to tell what happened. Depending upon scale, complexity and history, the processes of experiencing (connecting), recording (disjoining) and consuming-consummating (conjoining) truth-effects are of variable duration, but all of these processes are psychically and communicatively labour-intensive. The question that remains perpetually open: To what extent are truth-procedures, such as conversing, negotiating and mediating accounts of genocidal atrocity and trauma, capable of registering reflexive, indexical and implicative truth-effects? Mediating is founded on the assumption that understanding/misunderstanding on the one hand and agreement/disagreement on the other are independent, qualitatively different operations, and *that* assumption is what conditions mediation's claim to neutrality, impartiality and fairness. Witnessing, intuiting and inquiring comprise the durational process work of recording and consuming-consummating the experience of machinic assemblages of bodies manifesting (i.e. speaking) the truth (i.e. signifying) of experience (i.e. denoting). Those processes, necessary to intuiting beyond the decisive turn of experience, condition the reconciliation (i.e. convergence) of percept and affect (i.e. body and spirit). Without consumption-consummation recognizing and acknowledging the ontological validity of the expression of content, mediating seldom takes hold as a truth-procedure. The pragmatic schizoanalytic question with which gaçaça courts in Rwanda grappled was how to separate the substance and form of expression from the substance and form of content in ways that sustained the founding assumption of mediation, that is, that understanding/misunderstanding and agreement/disagreement are qualitatively (not quantitatively) different operations, an accomplishment necessary for the production of legal truth-effects, therapeutic truth-effects and restorative truth-effects.

Mediation's method is to ask witnessing questions whose answers lead beyond the decisive turn of experience and conventionally majoritarian ways of making transcendental sense, good sense and common sense of conflict and trauma, questions asked from a third subject position of witnessing, that is, inquiring from a position of engaged but not invested witnessing, along the lines of Bakhtin's *superaddressee*. Think in terms of an engaged impersonal subject, a witnessing machine.[8] Deleuze and Guattari (1987) distinguish between mechanism and machine, relying on the latter to develop an active (rather than a reactive) intuitively immanent ethics of becoming and duration (Deleuze and Guattari 1987, pp. 333, 391, 457–8). Mechanisms are established on their own foundations of transcendence; they are, in effect, closed systems with determinate functions and fixed equilibria. A machine, on the other hand, is neither more nor less than its connections and exterior relations to other machines. It is not necessarily made up of any particular body or made for any particular purpose. Its *machinicity* is precisely its *indifference*, its *neutrality* and its *impartiality*. Mediating-machines capable of engaging without investing, capable of neutrality and impartiality inquire into desire, imagination, will, resistance and resolve without assuming closed and unitary identities and without attaching passionately to fixed subject positions. They identify *as* witnesses who have stepped outside of their own durations to 'attend to life' by becoming acutely aware of the durations of other forms and substances of life. They identify *as* nomadic processes rather than *with* sedentary identities, fixed positions and interior relations. Mediating-machines articulate identifications without condensing or collapsing them into closed unitary identities. Mediating-machines only work machinically, (i.e. *as* machines) when they articulate to other machines rather than to mechanistic identities.

In gaçaça processes, elected elders work as mediating-machines insofar as they occupy third subject positions as witnesses, but from those positions they also render judgements; they condition relatively uninterrupted narratives, counter-narratives and mixtures of semiotic systems (i.e. presignifying, signifying, countersignifying and postsignifying systems) for collective enunciation. Schizoanalytic mediating is engaged neither from a position of pure witnessing nor from one of pure judging, as is true of courts of Law. Gaçaça truth-procedures are machinic in different ways in their struggles to produce processual as well as procedural fairness, social justice, therapeutic truth-effects and restorative truth-effects, all the while conversing, negotiating and mediating local sociopolitical contingencies. The networks of machinic connections and identifications produce actual possibilities and virtual potentialities to which conversing, negotiating and mediating attend. Although mediating has proclaimed itself a neutral process (unlike conversing and negotiating), it continues to negotiate ways to make good sense and common sense of that claim in practice, that is, it struggles with how neutrality and impartiality of witnessing actually sound and work durationally. Inquiring into conflict to resolve it and witnessing trauma to reconcile it machinically expands intervals between event and response, traversing Aionic and Chronotopic time, varying tempo and multiplying response potential, and thereby enhancing ethical immanence, resiliency and creativity. Mediating produces distinctions across order-words, which, in turn, reframes virtual potential and reconfigures desiring-production and social-production. In this sense, mediating-machines are immanent processes of producing rather than formal mechanisms of production.

Machine, as that concept is invoked here, is not a metaphor; life *is* machinic, as is conflict, and, by extension, trauma. Machine is not simply one more metaphor by means of which liberal-humanists with noble intentions either insert themselves into the centre of conflicts or rely on it to justify inattention and inaction. There is no mediating that is not machinic; 'all life only works and *is* insofar as it connects with some other machine' (Colebrook 2002a, p. 56). What is too often lost in recoiling from the suggestion that mediating is a machinic process is that human life becomes and transforms through what is inhuman and traumatic (Braidotti 2006, pp. 153–58). Majoritarian mediating has been conceptualized in terms of how conflicting bodies rationalize their histories and their contemporary circumstances to make rational sense of experience. Mediating machinically, by contrast, deterritorializes the resolve of conflict by multiplying connections that transform it incorporeally, a process of becoming-imperceptible, a process without foundation and without an escape hatch to transcendence.[9] Resolving conflict and reconciling trauma are not matters of imposing order; rather each desiring-utterance is an offshoot of difference that expands actual possibility and virtual potentiality. An end to conflict, and of conversation, is difficult to imagine. Even though there is no inherently rational telos towards which mediating is striving, there is an internal and effective striving to inquire, to affirm life and power, and to multiply potentiality. Desiring-utterances take turns filling in intervals with affect, recollection-memory and contraction-memory. Inquiring into the truth-effects of conflicts in order to register them, to recognize, acknowledge and validate them, and to believe them without believing *in* them, affirms an inquiry into the productivity of desire, an inquiry that allows for immanence, fluidity and the connective, disjunctive and conjunctive syntheses of desiring-production to be addressed as the social-production of legal truths, therapeutic truths and restorative truths.

Questions of desire and imagination

Inquiring into desire from a witnessing third subject position begins by asking conflicting subjects about their relations with/to desire. Such questions are asked from beyond reason and rationality, from beyond the decisive turn of experience, with no answers presupposed, no bottom line and no blue sky. The terms and relations of a desiring-question, (i.e. 'What do you mean, "desire"?', 'What kind of a question is that?', 'Desire in relation to what?'), are not for a mediator to answer. Answers to questions of terms and relations are left open, to be determined in and by a response. Inquiry into desire is an invitation to pay attention to life and to dreams/imagination in order to deterritorialize attention focused on and embedded in the intensity and density of antagonism, and to decode sense and redistribute it to subject positions of reflexivity. The question of desiring-production invites interlocutors to an interval, to expand it, that is, to pause momentarily in the production of antagonism and to attend reflexively to active rather than reactive forces. The conflict and/or trauma will have moved and changed ever so slightly in the process of an interval's duration of reflexive hesitation, which is accomplished by asking questions of desire-imagination from a third subject position. What often becomes obscured in centripetal identitarian vortices of violent conflict is any reflexive sense of incorporeal transformation. Inquiry into desire asks for reflexive, affirmative, active centrifugal responses that open onto virtual potential and transcendental sense, loosening an embodied subject's passionate attachments to a conflict's centripetal identitarian forces. Things can always be otherwise, Deleuze tells us.

Questions of desire-imagination may be destabilizing, disorienting and deterritorializing to the extent that they arrive from someplace else and without apparent limits. The productive principle operative in questions of desire-imagination is that they do not know the substance and form of the expressions they are asking for. Witnessing questions arrive from outside the durations of antagonistic subjects; they are questions antagonists seldom ask of themselves or of one another. Their constraints and limitations, as questions, are determinations made by their responses. Questions of desire-imagination are deterritorializing and decoding in their effects, in large measure because they are asked from third subject positions of witnessing. Questions of desire-imagination come with no assurances that answers will ever be forthcoming; such questions may not be registered as questions until there is nothing left to lose, and perhaps not even then. The timing of their asking is crucial; *kairos* (the Greek concept for something taking place at precisely the appropriate moment) is implicated sensitively in the affect, recollection-memory and contraction-memory that fills in intervals between events (i.e. questions) and responses (i.e. answers). Reflecting on desire's abundance rather than on need's scarcity opens onto transcendental sense (i.e. the time of Aion), during which the good sense and common sense of what *is* (i.e. the ontological past) antagonism and trauma decode and transform. And in the same moment, questions of desire-imagination call embodied subjects to a first subject position, in the present tense, with an active voice, in a subjunctive mood of agency. 'What would it be like if you surrendered to and embraced your desire?' 'How would attending to life become different?' 'And then what?' . . . 'and then' . . . 'and then . . .?' From the discursive durations of active responses to desire, inquiry into subjectivation opens and unfolds questions that convoke narratives that transform transcendental sense into an empirical consciousness.

Questions of subjectivation and experience

A body of desire occupying a subject position of discourse on a plane of immanence appears to itself and to others, as a consequence of a conjunctive synthesis of consummation-consumption, to be the author of 'its own' experience. Questions of subjectivation inquire into experience (of, say, abuse, oppression, violence, trauma and genocide); they make reflexive use of order-words (i.e. words that both organize and order the sense of percepts and affects) to condition potentiality and possibility for transforming territorial assemblages of historical injustices caught up in contemporary injustices. Machinic desire articulates collective enunciation now capable of imagining will-agency and of transforming resistance-resolve. And desire-imagination produces all of this without forgetting memory, erasing history or denying reality-effects. Questions of subjectivation-experience inquire into narratives foregrounding will-agency. Movement from accusatory and polemical countersignifying semiotic systems to signifying and/or postsignifying systems does not presume that the abuses, violations and oppressions that give rise to antagonism and trauma have now somehow disappeared into forgetting or escaped from the politics of memory. To the contrary, performative narratives express the experience of subjection and subjugation. Questions of subjectivation-experience invite and request narratives that provide details, which, in turn, open up virtual potentialities and actual possibilities for different understandings. Detailed narrative understandings give rise to more questions without answers. Without witnessing narratives of tragic inevitability and victimization, performative narratives repeat, adding ever more detail, intensity and amplification to their expression.

Witnessing does not guarantee that performative narratives of tragedy and victimization will cease, but it does open the potential for expressing will-agency. The discursive transformation of resistance-resolve, however, may never take place, or may take place only after an incalculably long duration. If and when such subjectivation-experience shifts, there are no guarantees that the transformation of antagonism will not result in movement towards even more intense antagonism and perhaps even more widespread violence. Because of the unpredictable distribution of deterritorialized and decoded practices and processes, mediating is an unstable, indeterminate and foundationless process with no guarantees. Rarely does mediating open onto an orderly and predictable experiential topography. More typically it jumps across registers, meanders and backtracks, and stammers at the edges of virtual potentiality. In its narrative mode of inquiry, mediating expands potentiality and possibility as it captivates and carries along its narrating bodies in the flows of desiring-production. Imagining desire as both virtual potentiality and actual possibility produces countersignifying systems that open intervals onto which the vulnerability of will-agency may surface. It makes possible a kind of minor communicating, a thinking aloud together, and when it works, it interpellates others to third subject positions, that is, to mediating positions of witnessing.

Questions of will and agency

What happens to will-agency in this account of passionate attachments of embodied subjects to the forces of power to which they are subjected? Judith Butler (1997b) suggests a distinction between the concept 'subject' (as a linguistic category, a structure in formation and a place holder) and the concept 'individual' (as the individual body that comes to occupy the site and position of the subject) (pp. 10–11). An individual body becomes an embodied subject by assuming a subject position and in the process becoming subjected and subjugated to discourse, a process Butler calls subjectivation (a translation of the French *assujetissement*) (p. 11). In telling a story an embodied subject loses itself (becoming-imperceptible, as Braidotti phrases it) and becoming nomadic, an aleatory point searching transcendental sense for connections that may have already been made apparent. Resisting this process of subjectivation ensures its repetition, although never in identical forms and substances of content and expression. In the process of informing and performing as an embodied subject, subjectivation is thought of as a becoming-subject of will-agency. Butler (1997) marks another crucial distinction, this time between the power that inaugurates a subject (*pouvoir*) and the power that a subject exercises (*puissance*) (p. 12). The two are not continuous forms of the same power, that is, they are qualitatively different. This distinction conditions the possibility for resistance (i.e. *pouvoir*) and resolve (i.e. *puissance*), given that the immanence of subjectivation is the source of power for both agency and will. There is no continuity between what makes power possible (i.e. subjugation, *pouvoir*) on the one hand and the kinds of possibilities that power assumes (i.e. subjectivation, *puissance*) on the other. It is possible that the power assumed and appropriated in subjectivation (*puissance*) can work against the power that made that assumption inevitable (*pouvoir*). The conclusion Butler draws from this line of thinking is not that resistance is a recuperation of power, nor that recuperation is necessarily resistance, but rather that power is both at once, and *that* ambivalence constitutes the pivotal bind of agency (p. 13).

In moments of vulnerability to the narrative captivity of actual possibility and virtual potentiality, questions asking into will-agency, its limits and constraints, its incentives and promises, comprise an inquiry into will(ingness) rather than (cap) ability. Not '(what) can you do?', but '(what) are you willing (to do)?'; '(what) would you be willing (to do)?'; '(what) have you been willing (to do) to this point?' In effect, 'what would you be willing to consider doing and saying (i.e. becoming-) to experience the actuality of possibility (and by implication, the virtuality of potentiality) that you imagine-desire?' These questions invite an embodied subject to a discursive space of subjunctive reflexivity, to a subject position into which a body to whom such questions are addressed is invited to explore limits of subjectivation and to transgress those limits, that is, to expand the ontological parameters of will-agency. To inquire into will-agency is to specify the conditions and consequences of the anxiety of risk when duration and agency intersect as a subject of will in a moment of actual possibility. Identifying such moments presupposes intuiting them, which evinces artistic performativity as much as it does political knowledge and philosophical thought. Questions of will-agency are ways of asking into limits and possibilities of boundaries regarding subjectivation. Such questions call listening and witnessing bodies to will-agency. One way of responding to resistance to such calls is to respond to assertions of resistance with questions of resolve. Doing so places in continuous variation the variables that make an utterance an enunciation, which is the creative work of will-agency. In short, it is the work of making explicit the implicit presuppositions to (and with) which desiring-utterances are articulated; it is, in effect, the transformative work of uttering the non-discursive, unutterable and unimaginable. The dilemma is that there are no guarantees in willingness and contingency and there is a sense of comfort in familiarity, even if there are no guarantees in the known, no certainty in remaining sedentary and territorialized, no rationality in repetition and redundancy, no security in identity and sameness, and no power in control.

Mediating works with the tensions and ambiguities of subjugation and subjectivation; it operates in the interval between the two, an interval in which the forces of representation, understanding, suspicion and vulnerability struggle for dominance. That interval opens momentarily when, in responding to questions of desire-imagination, resistance-resolve is identified by intuiting and listening for/to willingness-agency. Utterances of articulated discourse and desire accept chance and necessity, and at the same time they have ethical import insofar as they consist in a selective ontology, one that presupposes some latitude of choice. Mediating is an ethical enterprise, then, insofar as its utterances enact a will to power that works both with and against resistance to limitations and oppressions. For Deleuze (1983, pp. 49–52), Nietzsche's concept of will to power is vulnerability, a willingness to be affected by the contingent forces of a life. Embodied subjects occupy no inherently sovereign, uncontested and *a priori* position in discourse. The intellectual and ethical task of mediating is to operate nomadically and flexibly in worlds of part-objects and supra-individuals, and to communicate in terms of the multiples and fractions of nomads and bricoleurs rather than in the unities and polarities of property owners and of architects.

Questions of will-agency concern themselves with choices and affects, potentialities and possibilities, constraints and transgressions. Given any set of circumstances, what are the virtual and actual choices? What are their limits? What fears constrain virtual potentialities and actual possibilities? What desires invite transgressions of those constraints? What longings do potentialities and possibilities call into place? What subjectivities are implicated in those longings? Such questions ask their interlocutors to abandon the known tracings of the familiar and to intuit detours not yet mapped. At such junctures, affects and percepts are primary. At issue is a fear of feeling as much or more than it is a fear of thinking. It is a nihilistic fear of dissolution, of identity's disarticulation and deterritorialization. For Nietzsche, the will to power and the affirmation of life entail willingness to be affected ultimately by fears of nihilism, yet a resolve to transgress (rather than to conquer or transcend) those fears and constraints, nonetheless. Mediating from a witnessing third subject position entails asking questions of resistance and resolve that invite first and second embodied subjects into those fears in the interests of multiplying choices by transgressing the constraints of identities and opening up potentialities and possibilities for multiple identifications.

Questions of resistance and resolve

Mediating engages conflict with a resolve that amounts to optimism of will born of the contingent nature of conflict, that is, conditions are never immutably fixed but can always be otherwise. Such resolve takes the form of resisting the forces of pessimism, cynicism and futility that mark protracted conflicts and that keep them interminably preoccupied with past victimizations, traumas and injustices. The irony is that focusing on past injustices perpetuates them, but not attending to past injustices risks escalating them. The double bind of agency that mediating negotiates is, on the one hand, not to deny, ignore or minimize past injustices, and on the other not to become consumed by the reactive forces of vengeance and retaliation. Nomadic wisdom entails knowing how and when to recognize and acknowledge past injustices (requiring intuition and *kairos*) and then knowing how and when to transform their second-person, past tense, passive voice, indicative mood narratives of blame and victimization into first-person, present tense, active voice, subjunctive mood narratives of accountability and obligation. In this sense, mediating is a form of resisting the resistance to transformation, a form of countersignifying semiotic system that calls for will and resolve to change, that is, to make things otherwise. Mediating operates in an interval (which is qualitatively different from a liminal space) between transcendental sense of the virtual and empirical consciousness of the actual, between desire and imagination where potential change and transformation are always already immanent. The present of empirical consciousness, that is, Chronos of the proposition, is informed by recollection-memory and contraction-memory performed with/through imagination.

Truth-procedures, then, embody the ontological, epistemological and axiological validity of truth-effects to the extent that desire, experience, will, resistance and resolve collectively enunciate subjects, objects and their material-semiotic relations. To resist, to deny, to deflect or to trivialize the validity of a conflict not only multiplies the probability of its perpetuation in other forms and substances, but also intensifies antagonistic interior relations, sharpens points of contention and magnifies its effects as it dreams the futile dream of transcending the reality-effects of immanence. Conflicting bodies lay claim to long histories of resisting systemic invalidations and injustices. As a transcendental–empirical experiment with truth-procedures (i.e. recognizing, acknowledging, witnessing, validating and perhaps even understanding) relying on indirect, direct and quasi-direct discourse, mediating expresses truth-effects (legal truths, therapeutic truths and restorative truths) of conflicting factions of territorial assemblages. Such discursive work produces experience of embodied subjectivation, of countering dissociation of body and mind and thereby of counting for something, of counting as one of visibility and of mattering. The potential truth-effects of truth-procedures notwithstanding, the process holds out no guarantees; it promises only to open the virtual to the actual.

As discussed in Chapter 1, much of Western thought is constructed on a transcendent foundation of Enlightenment principles and liberal-humanist values. It is the task of transcendent*al* empiricism to interrogate those transcendent foundations in the interest of freeing empiricism to operate immanently. Deleuze insists that the task of transcendent*al* empiricism is to understand how the experience of external reality and of transcendence is possible. The term 'empiricism' for Deleuze means a commitment to 'experience' as the starting point of inquiry, rather than beginning from presupposed foundational ideas and concepts. It does not found inquiry universally, nor does it limit itself to human experience. Rather it investigates the conditions of experience for the idea of transcendence to make sense, which is what we have been exploring in terms of conflict, trauma, discourse and process. That line of inquiry begins by identifying the relations among three elements: collective assemblages of enunciation, machinic assemblages of desire, and the identities and identifications of their articulations.

The first consists in various discursive formations; the second consists in bodies of desire; the third consists in the inevitability of conflict.

Desiring-utterances presuppose social obligations and are accomplished collectively. The relations between desiring-utterances and actions and passions are immanent to conflict. They are relations of redundant identifications rather than of identity. An order-word is the redundancy of an act and an utterance, not an expression of their identity. A significant implication of this line of thinking for communication studies, conflict resolution studies, transitional justice studies and trauma studies is that conversing, negotiating and mediating are not primarily matters of communicating in the sense of exchanging information. They are, rather, media for the transmission of redundancy, that is, of communicating order-words. The distinction to be made is not between information and noise, nor is it between communication and nonsense, but rather, as Deleuze and Guattari put it, 'between all the indisciplines at work in language and the order-word as discipline or grammaticality' (Deleuze and Guattari 1987, p. 93).

Creating intervals (not spaces) for the social-production of discursive truth-procedures requires preconditions or ground rules; there are no transcendent foundations. Military science and international relations sometimes refer to these preconditions as 'rules of engagement'. Negotiating preconditions temporarily determines the following parameters: Which bodies and factions are to be recognized and acknowledged? Who will be invited to engage? Who issues invitations and how are they sequenced? What processes and procedures are invoked? In what tenses are the processes and procedures to take place? What intensities of affect and percept are such processes to accommodate? With what agonistic and antagonistic forms and substances of content and expression will truth-procedures engage? How, if at all, are the truth-effects produced to be memorialized? To what extent is engaging voluntary? What are the consequences, if any, for transgressing the parameters of truth-procedures? And crucially, *how* and *when* are responses to these questions performed? It is over and against these process parameters that the order-words of truth-procedures are able to counter the order-words of genocide to produce truth-effects and accomplish the material-semiotic reterritorialization of Rwanda, to the extent that is possible.

Desiring-utterances and the gaçaça process

The gaçaça process can be characterized in terms of the tetralinguistic model of language that Henri Gobard developed based on the research of Ferguson and Gumperz (Deleuze and Guattari 1986, p. 23). Gobard's four languages (vernacular, vehicular, referential and mythic) rest on the collective assumptions that utterances have a conative and an emotive function (i.e. there are senders and receivers), a vehicular function (i.e. there is an exchange of information), a referential function (i.e. a verbalizable context), a poetic function (i.e. utterances are a selection of the best elements and combinations) and a metalinguistic function (i.e. there is an agreed-upon code for sending and receiving). For Deleuze and Guattari, Gobard's originality consists in his examining collective assemblages of enunciation (by which they refer to discursive formations, plus subjectivity, minus agency) rather than pre-existing systems of language, and machinic assemblages of desiring bodies (by which they refer to desire, plus agency, minus subjectivity) rather than universal subjects, objects, messages and codes. When collective assemblages of enunciation articulate to machinic assemblages of desiring bodies, they produce heterogeneous forms of power. Gobard assumes that these forms of power and functions of language are inseparable and that their articulations are capable of material-semiotic movements, deterritorializing and reterritorializing material contents and semiotic expressions. Importantly for our purposes, it is the power and function of language to move experience spatially and to affect it durationally that is crucial in accounting for the productivity of the gaçaça process and its capacity for producing transitional justice and for mediating collective trauma. Deleuze and Guattari refer to this new sociolinguistic approach as *geolinguistics*.[10] Its concern is with 'collective assemblages of utterances' rather than with individual 'subjects', with 'coefficients of deterritorialization' rather than with 'codes', and with the question of how a language comes to power, whether locally, regionally, nationally or globally, rather than with meanings. One entailment of this geolinguistic orientation is a focus on pragmatics rather than on syntactics or semantics, and for Deleuze and Guattari, this pragmatic focus is the orientation of schizoanalysis.

As mentioned in Chapter 4, for Henri Gobard, *vernacular language* is maternal, familial and territorial; it is the language of rural communities and is rural in its origins. In Rwanda, vernacular language is native Kinyarwanda, the native language of the farmers. Its spatial compass is 'here'. *Vehicular language*, by contrast, is urban, governmental and business discourse; it is the language of commercial exchange and bureaucratic transmission, that is, the language of Rwanda's first country-wide deterritorialization. In Rwanda, vehicular language is Rwandan French; its spatial purview is 'everywhere'. *Referential language* is the language of sense and of cultural reterritorialization; its referents are 'over there'. Rwandan referential language is a heterogeneous mixture of Kinyarwanda, Rwandan French and standard French. *Mythic language* is at the edges and on the cultural horizon pertaining to spiritual and religious reterritorialization. Its spatiotemporal reach is 'beyond' and it is enunciated predominantly in Kinyarwanda and artful Rwandan French. Phil Clarke, in his assessment of the gaçaça process, argues that the transitional justice process was productive to the extent that it allowed for all four of these 'languages' of collective assemblages of enunciation to articulate in different ways and at different times to machinic assemblages of desire in the achingly slow process of reterritorializing material-semiotic Rwanda (Clark 2010, pp. 308–55). Desiring-utterances manifest speakers in three subject positions (first-person, second-person, third-person), two cases (nominative and objective), two genders (masculine and feminine) and two numbers (singular and plural); they signify in two voices (active and passive) and in two modes (ontic and deontic); and they denote in two moods (indicative and subjunctive) and in ten tenses (present, past and future indicative moods; present-perfect, past-perfect and future-perfect indicative moods; present and past subjunctive mood; and present-perfect and past-perfect subjunctive moods). This geolinguistic orientation is well suited to an examination of gaçaça truth-procedures and the production of truth-effects.

Desiring-utterances range across the chronological tenses of daily life, accounting for and recounting events in the vernacular language of rural communities. Clearly, subject positions, speeds, rates, tenses, directions and qualities of desire and discourse are crucial to the artful conversing, negotiating and mediating of these events. Subject positions are active and passive; they are the direct and indirect objects (i.e. the would-be subjects) of verb phrases (i.e. agency), and their voices perform, distribute and integrate narratives whose forms and substances trace arcs of blame, victimization, restoration and reconciliation. Scarcity and impotence produced by oppression and exploitation constitute the emplotment of those narratives. The ontic modes of desiring-utterances pertain to entities (i.e. subjects, objects and relations) and the facts about them in the phenomenal world; deontic modes pertain to conditions of duty and obligation (i.e. judgements of morality). The deontic mode of performative, distributive and integrative turns of desiring-utterances concern moral obligations and duties of bodies with respect to justice and law as they are collectively enunciated in the interests of producing legal, therapeutic and restorative truths. Quantifying qualities and digitizing analogues are contested processes whenever deontic claims of rights and obligations are enunciated.

The moods of desiring-utterances, when indicative, are concerned primarily with establishing facts and conditions of participation in the genocide, with producing legal, therapeutic and restorative truth-effects regarding degrees of culpability and degrees of traumatization, with determining kinds of inequitable and unjust treatment, as well as with validating rights and entitlements. Subjunctive desiring-utterances, by contrast, speculate on conditions and pronounce conditionalities, that is, what 'may', 'might' and 'could' take place 'if' and 'when' particular rights are (not) recognized and acknowledged, and valued resources are (not) distributed fairly and equitably as measured by specified standards of fairness. Such speculations convoke questions posed in a deontic mode, that is, what 'ought to be', 'needs to be', 'should be' done? Deontic desiring-utterances open onto potentialities of and for transitional justice to be performed, distributed and integrated, and for incorporeal transformations of therapeutic and restorative truth-effects to be produced. The tensions between rights/obligations, potentialities/possibilities and inevitabilities/contingencies are at work in most desiring-utterances, and they are tensions never to be resolved. Which bodies have which rights and which entitlements; which bodies have which obligations and which responsibilities? By what formulae are rights and obligations to be negotiated and distributed? How are fair and equitable distributions of the sense of justice and reconciliation to be determined? How are charges of inhumanity and immorality articulated to machinic desire? Desiring-utterances circulate ontic details that substantiate deontic claims, (e.g. claims about identifications and identities, duty and obligation, morality and ethics, justice and law) and struggle with rationality and libidinality.

The questions that repeat in ever new ways are: How to respond to claims of rights and obligations, ethics and morality, justice and equity? How are such claims to be addressed? What is to be done? Rights to justice and fair treatment are warranted on the basis of foundational principles of morality, entitlement, reason and law. As contents of machinic desire become articulated to and expressed as desiring-utterances, data regarding inequalities and injustices become more widely realized.

Oppressed bodies with few if any resources are bodies narrated as nominative object positions with compromised if not seriously depleted agency. Keep in mind that the purpose of the gaçaça process was not simply to produce legal truths, but to produce therapeutic truths and restorative truths as well. The reality-effects of the past (which *is* present ontologically) must be recognized, named and acknowledged before a possible future and past (which was and will be and is always present psychologically) can be addressed subjunctively. The tenses of desiring-utterances are present, past and future declarations indicative of psychologically past yet ontologically present conditions of immanence enunciated collectively as accounts of events competing for ontological recognition as truth. Desiring-utterances are offered as narrative truths to be witnessed, recognized and acknowledged. Resisting those desiring-utterances counts as ontological resistance; the stakes for both enunciating and witnessing turns of narratives in this instance are life and death. And yet they are resisted, often passionately, by other bodies in the gaçaça process, usually Hutu bodies accused of genocide, but at times Tutsi bodies resisting participation, bodies whose identities are threatened if narratives of a desiring-utterance are true; the accused Hutu become *génocidaires*; the Tutsi plaintiffs risk retraumatization and retribution.

An ethical response to a desiring-utterance is to witness its truth-effects. And yet – and here is one of the intuitive contributions of witnessing rather than merely listening politely and pretending tolerance – it is necessary that witnessing take place outside of Aionic time of verbal representation. Witnessing bodies must step outside of their own duration to become ontologically aware of the duration of others still immersed in their psychological worlds. Such witnessing abstracts the form of expression (i.e. the regime of signs) from the substance of expression (i.e. facial expression, tone of voice, paralinguistic features), and from the substance (i.e. bodies) and form (i.e. actions and passions) of content as well, becoming removed from the psychology of agreeing and disagreeing, the better to attend to (ontological) life. Although desiring-utterances are enunciated as declarations of truths told to dominance, in effect challenging hegemonic narratives, they nevertheless expect to be witnessed and believed *as* truth, even if not believed *in* and agreed *with*. Decoding and deterritorializing relatively fixed territorial assemblages of identities and interior hegemonic relations produce countersignifying regimes of signs constructed from vernacular, vehicular, referential and mythic discourse formations. They express hypocrisies, dilemmas, contradictions, paradoxes, double-binds and injustices that collectively forge agonistic, antagonistic and violent relations. Tensions between libidinal passions of oppression and injustice, and propositional discourses of domination and control thereby become contested.

During the interval of the unfolding gaçaça process, countless conversations, negotiations and mediations varying in degrees of formality and informality were taking place across Rwanda. These conversing machines of minor communication collectively engaged vernacular, vehicular, referential and mythic discourses, which accounts for gaçaça's relative success and productivity; transitional justice and collective reconciliation were not simply a function of the discursive processes of trials. The process was productive – criticism from the international criminal legal community notwithstanding – in large measure because the goals of Rwanda's experiment with the social-production of transitional justice included the production of three forms of truth and their attendant truth-effects. The gaçaça process, as a machine for the social-production of truth-effects, was designed to make sense of genocide events, and of the Event of genocide itself, by means of desiring-utterances decoding and recoding reality-effects as legal truths, therapeutic truths and restorative truths of experience. Truth-procedures are inquiries, questions and answers that make qualitatively different kinds of sense, which is to say that desiring-utterances make sense differently, punctuate transcendental thought differently, thereby producing different kinds of truth-effects. What follows is a discussion of the different ways by which responses turn those questions to (i.e. produce) truth-effects.

It is important to emphasize at the outset, however, that unlike psychoanalytic theory for which it is consciousness and intentionality that determine reality, for schizoanalytic theory it is the transcendental unconscious that determines the reality of empirical consciousness. Articulations of desire and discourse may not primarily or even secondarily be produced and expressed in the forms and substances of logical propositions. Their productive expressions of bodily actions and passions may as readily be savage, barbaric, uncivilized, unreasonable, dangerous, unconventional, libidinal and incoherent. The salient question becomes: What are the pragmatic, schizoanalytic features of collective assemblages of enunciation that, when they articulate to machinic assemblages of bodies, produce conversing turns whose forms and substances of expression are capable of circulating substances and forms of content throughout territorial assemblages of conflicting active and reactive forces? In doing so, how do they condition potentiality for decoding and recoding transcendental sense, ontological good sense and logical common sense, which, in turn, reterritorialize material-semiotic territorial assemblages?

Performative turns

When desire and discourse *perform* their articulations, turns effectively perform sense; they express and make sense analogically, as presignifying signs of that which cannot be said, at least not yet, and not in so many words of good sense and common sense. The expression of the substance and form of a turn's content is performative to the extent that enunciating a desiring-utterance is isomorphic with what it does. Performative turns of desiring-utterances are not 'about' something else; they do not represent, refer to, or 'mean' something other than what they do.[11] They are expressive turns, expressing the actions and passions of the bodies manifesting them. Performative turns call attention to themselves. They are libidinally and psychically expressive and they signify in manifesting, but cannot be said to transmit information or transfer meaning. Instead, they produce truth-effects. They may break through to empirical consciousness, shattering good sense and common sense of what is taking place spatially and what is unfolding durationally. They demand recognition and acknowledgement by asserting themselves forcefully as the product of production. Among other functions, performative turns register rage, demonstrate resolve, express hilarity, mock hypocrisy, resist oppression, scream in pain, insist on truth, stand up to dominance, press for change, refuse oppression and mark injustice.

Whatever form and substance performative turns productively express as desiring-utterances, they are staged as immanent becomings. I am not alluding here to 'staging' in the sense that theatrical performances are staged productions. 'Performativity' and 'performance' are not the same things. 'Whereas *performance* encompasses a broad range of social behaviors, forms and effects, *performativity* refers more specifically to the complexities and subtleties of discursive practices, to often unconscious investments and desires that circulate in all discourses, and to the decisive effects that various modes of discursive actions have on individual and group subjectivities and identity formations' (Strine 1998, p. 313). In the theatrical sense, performativity is the production of an often-promoted, rehearsed and/or repeatedly performed, usually scripted property brought to market for an audience's aesthetic consumption, and for a profitable return on investment for its producers. In the quasi-legal gaçaça sense, performative articulations are improvisationally immanent. Performative turns may engage vernacular narratives, interrupting and turning them (in)to conversations, negotiations and mediations, punctuating their local sense and redirecting their course. They may engage and interrupt vehicular and referential discourses of bureaucratic and cultural life. They may be planned, but are usually not rehearsed; more typically they demand attention and resist assumed conventions of daily life. Immanent local conditions may obstruct the flow and circulation of desiring-production in ways that subtract resources and value from some factions and add them to others in the process of social-production. The political economics of a hegemonic bloc direct the circulation and flow of the libidinal economics of desiring-production away from and around certain bodies, thereby depriving them, and towards and through other bodies, thereby privileging them (e.g. obligating Tutsi to occupy plaintiff subject positions during the gaçaça process while simultaneously obligating Hutu to occupy defendant subject positions).

Now consider the syntax of articulations turning performatively. Assume that agonistic and antagonistic relations have become unbearable and that oppression, discrimination, exploitation, abuse, betrayal, violence and trauma have become commonplace. An enormously important ontological problem that traumatized bodies struggle to solve is how to resist these conditions, how to speak truth to dominance and violence, and how to consume-consummate experience incorporeally, remaining off to the side of it as its by-product rather than to be consumed by it, consummating with it by dissociating and transcending it. Suspicion, fear, rage, depression and self-loathing are becoming pervasive. Violence and threat of violence are ever present. The challenge is to engage oppression and injustice from traumatized subject positions in ways that transform and produce libidinal and psychic potential, not merely rationally circumscribed possibility. Traumatized assemblages of desiring bodies, both micro-political (e.g. families) and macro-political (e.g. a nation-state), are deterritorializing and becoming unstable, psychically decoding, operating on logics of suspicion, mistrust, doubt and fear. Performative turns resist those threats and address oppression and injustice in direct and indirect ways that demonstrate, produce and express their truth-effects. Performative turns are not always enunciated from first-person subject positions, in an active voice of present tense and indicative mood. Affective expressions of experience, historical/mythical renditions, retraumatizing enactments, primary order eruptions, spiritual pronouncements, as well as narrative accounts are all examples of the ways in which performative utterances may turn. To the extent that they produce and express truth-effects of genocide, rape, torture and betrayal, performative utterances often turn beyond the reach of majoritarian discourse. The libidinality of desiring-production may be too intense, too primary to articulate to conventional regimes of signs of social-production; it may remain as presignifyingly semiotic, performatively paratactical rather than communicatively syntactical.

A shocked, silent, mad, numb or catatonic (collective) body may stammer, stutter, scream, demonstrate or otherwise express truth-effects.[12] Performative turns are nomadic; they circulate throughout traumatized territorial assemblages, often expressing narratively without recourse to dialogue, disseminating with little or no interest in witnessing, or engaging in anything other than the forceful production and assertive expression of intense libidinality, yet at times withdrawing into catatonia. In this transcendental–empirical sense, performative turns assert and affirm truths not yet and perhaps never to become collectively enunciated; they may have remained implicit, silenced by fear. When and if desperation overtakes nihilism, that is, when libidinality completely overwhelms rationality, truths become performatively enunciated. A subject of/to truth speaks truth (i.e. power) to domination and oppression (i.e. control), risking everything for anything (any chance for things to become otherwise). A subject of/to truth may be a collective body (e.g. a family, a community or an institution – legal, financial, political, intellectual, governmental or religious), or it may be an individual corporeal/material body. Confronted and challenged are hegemonic claims of legitimacy, good sense and common sense of the strata of governance, mechanisms of power, distributions of resources, conventions of inclusion and customs of recognition. Whatever forms and substances of content that performative turns express, however, they connect part-objects into indefinite series by means of a syntax of 'and . . . and . . . and . . .', that is, a connective synthesis of the production of production. A truth-effect articulated performatively may actually haemorrhage discourse, gushing out, pushing and crowding additively and at times multiplicatively; they also manifest as numbed silence.

Distributive turns

Turns of desiring-utterances also *distribute* sense by dispersing it centrifugally, decoding signifying signs, releasing desiring-production and setting it in motion, freeing it to circulate, decoding the sense of objects, subjects and their exterior relations. Performative turns synthesize desire and discourse connectively; their narratives are self-generative until their determinate connective syntheses of 'and . . . and . . . and' are disjoined into 'or . . . or . . . or . . .', that is, interrupted, ruptured, broken or otherwise arrested in anti-production. The disjunction of a performative turn makes a mark, a sign, as a record of sense for recollection-memory. Bear in mind that it was first German and then Belgian and Catholic colonization of Rwanda that interrupted and ruptured pre-colonial connectively synthetic relations between bodies subsequently identified and recorded by those colonial forces as Hutu, Tutsi and Twa, subsequently producing and recording countless illegitimate disjunctive syntheses generated by the fundamentally illegitimate disjunction of colonialism. These disjunctions established disjunctively exclusive relations between 'superior' Tutsi and 'inferior' Hutu, completely discounting Twa, and initiated the circulation and intensification of *ressentiment* and bad conscience, distributing the transcendental sense, the ontological good sense and the logical common sense of colonially reified identities and their illegitimate 'interior' relations. That illegitimate exclusive disjunction established the quotidian colonial relations that evolved into pre-genocidal and eventually genocidal interior relations, and in many important respects continues to stratify and affect the illegitimate forms and substances of the contents and expressions of post-genocide Rwandan daily life today.

In the process of decoding and recoding colonial, pre-genocidal and genocidal narratives, and reterritorializing deterritorialized Rwanda, the communication machine that was the gaçaça process began repunctuating transcendental sense and distributing different forms and substances of good sense and common sense by making available discursive subject positions for genocide victims, survivors and *génocidaire* suspects to occupy and from which to be manifested as speakers of legal, therapeutic and restorative truths of traumatic experience. Opportunities to articulate desiring bodies to collective enunciation effectively liberated good sense and common sense from virtual transcendental sense. The communication machine of the gaçaça process interrupted the production of connectivity, that is, it halted the productivity of the connective synthesis of the interior traumatic relations of genocide, producing a disjunctive synthesis (i.e. a synthesis of anti-production) that effectively repunctuated transcendental sense, creating potential for making different sense by modifying the quality and quantity of the desiring-production drawn to the social-production of truth-effects. The forms and substances of disjunctively synthesized sense articulate to the forms and substances of collective assemblages of enunciation, and those articulations distribute sense as turns, via direct, indirect and quasi-direct discourse, to different orders of reality-effects and different orders of truth-effects. Different orders of truth-effects, in turn, opened onto different transcendental and empirical forms of life, and continue opening.

For bodies occupying privileged subject positions within a dominant regime of signs, as was true for colonial Tutsi, then for post-colonial, pre-genocidal and genocidal Hutu, and now for post-genocidal Tutsi, decoding the good sense and common sense of a hegemonic regime of signs threatens stratified relations in dominance by interrupting their flows and decoding their striated identities. A paranoid fascistic dominant order such as Rwanda's, prior to and during the genocide, was produced by the neurotic and ultimately psychotic repetition of the same. Distributive turns productive of anti-production and of exclusive disjunctive syntheses interrupt that repetition and return of the same (i.e. the production of production with its syntax of 'and . . . and . . . and . . .'), producing difference instead (i.e. the production of recording with its syntax of 'either . . . or . . . or . . .'), a creative and productive process of the interruption of flow and the repetition and return of difference. The fear of, and resistance to, disjunctions is that the production of difference will dissolve order into chaos – and it will, however repressive that order may have been – and cause autonomous identities to co-mingle as identifications. For bodies oppressed by a hegemonic regime of signs – as was true initially for colonized Hutu and subsequently for post-colonial Tutsi and Hutu sympathizers in Rwanda prior to and during the genocide – taking a countersignifying turn that disjunctively synthesizes connectively synthesized sense and redistributes difference, engaging that fear was and is a fearful proposition. Turns productive of anti-production, that is, exclusive disjunctive syntheses, break flows of desiring-production and the interior relations of social-production they recode and redistribute, producing different reality-effects and truth-effects. Communicative properties of distributive turns invoke different order-words, thereby altering the intensity, density, orientation, speed, duration, form and substance of transcendental sense, good sense and common sense, effectively repunctuating and redistributing that which performativity had brought to the immanence of empirical consciousness.

Distributive turns circulate repunctuated segments of transcendental sense, good sense and common sense. Remember that performative turns assert and thereby actualize Aionic time, that is, becoming-imperceptible. They perform the psychological reality and validity of Aionic time, a transcendental time of past and future with no present. The nomadic subject of transcendental sense and verbal representation manifests truth-effects by performing them. The distributive circulation of disjunctively produced sense is capable of expressing series and sequences of the contents of machinic desire. Machinic assemblages of desire distribute heterogeneous forms of representational and phantasmagorical images, qualitative and quantitative formulae, vivid and fading memories, individual and collective body parts, aesthetic and hallucinatory visions, dreams and nightmares, sensual forms, erotic impulses, revulsions, aversions, anticipated fears, imaginary scenarios, flashes of rage, indices of accumulations and depletions, collections and chronicles, partial records of tragedies and triumphs, scattered archival materials, sacred and profane places, memorial sites, commemorative objects, and conjunctions of madness, absurdity and brilliance. These are only some of the forms and substances of machinic desire the disjunctively recorded signs of which now circulate distributively. Distributive turns effectively reterritorialize quantities and recode qualities as resources distributed to agonistic, antagonistic and violent sites, where inequity, injustice, discrimination and oppression are or have been operating, leaving their marks.

Integrative turns

In ethical response to the Event of genocide, in the interval opened up by its cessation, President Paul Kigame's RPF-backed government inaugurated the gaçaça process as a truth-procedure, in effect creating a communication machine capable of producing a sociocultural conjunctive synthesis of consumption-consummation productive of legal truths, therapeutic truths and restorative truths. The gaçaça communication machine produced legitimate discursive subject positions in collective assemblages of enunciation for accused, victimized and surviving bodies of desire to manifest and witness the trauma of genocide. The gaçaça process was a communication machine for articulating bodies, objects, discourses, relations and experience, producing opportunities for surviving bodies to consume and consummate the composite experience of genocide and of becoming a subject off to the side of trauma rather than being consumed and consummated by trauma, that is, integrating, naming and thereby making sense of having passed through the Event of genocide rather than remaining traumatized in its timeless time. The syntax of these integrative turns of conjunctive syntheses is, 'So it was . . .', 'So that's what happened . . .', 'So that's what it was . . .', 'So that was my experience . . .', 'So that was me . . . .' – in effect a coming together of fractured, dissociated sense.

Rather than doing nothing in response to the material-semiotic, the embodied-psychic deterritorialization and devastation of post-genocide Rwanda, the gaçaça communication machine began to make collective sense of collective psychosis, integrating disjoined, scattered fragments of distributed sense. The gaçaça process opened an interval of ethical immanence by creating a diagram for a machinic assemblage of desiring-bodies to articulate to/with a collective assemblage of enunciation, conditioning the production of performative turns of monological narratives of genocidal trauma and the possibility for dialogic engagements and interruptions to produce legal, therapeutic and restorative truths. In the process of its self-production and self-organization, a machinic assemblage of traumatized bodies articulated to a self-producing and self-organizing collective assemblage of enunciation, taking performative, distributive and integrative turns at making sense of the Event of genocide. Desiring bodies manifesting as speaking victims, survivors and suspects/defendants took turns articulating to a collective assemblage of enunciation, effectively integrating shattered and scattered sense, intuiting attunement beyond the decisive turns of traumatic experience, and conjunctively synthesizing (i.e. consuming-consummating) trauma, continuing the agonizing and antagonizing process of coming from transcendental sense to terms of good sense and common sense of empirical consciousness (i.e. of coming to terms with trauma) and thereby approximating legal truths of transitional justice while attempting collective reconciliation in the production of therapeutic truths and restorative truths.

In its most minoritarian sense, desiring-utterances of transitional justice and collective reconciliation may sound as off-handedly innocent and profound as the desiring-utterance of Cassius Niyonsaba, a 12-year-old schoolboy from N'tarama Hill: 'Papa was a primary school teacher, Mama a farmer. In my father's family, it's only me who's still alive. In my mother's family, it's just only me as well, who's still alive. I no longer remember how many big and little brothers and sisters I had, because my memory is too taken up by so many deaths, it's not handy with numbers anymore. That slows me down in school, too' (p. 9). This boy's desiring-utterance integrates the forms of an indefinitely large number of contents expressed and implied as a matter of fact. The moods of integrative turns are predominantly indicative. Listen again to Cassius Niyonsaba: 'Now I live among her [a neighbor's] children and other children on their own like me. When we children talk, someone may mention the genocide, so then each one starts to tell what he saw. That can take a long time. Now and then someone wants to change a detail, but usually we repeat the same memories to one another. Talking together clears away pain and sadness' (p. 15). His desiring-utterance, in its way, is compelling evidence of the transcendental–empirical productivity of the vernacular language of minor communication machines that have been unfolding as rhizomatic offshoots of Rwanda's gaçaça process.

Afterword – Schizoanalysis and Nomadic Discourse

A pragmatics of human communication

By way of concluding this Deleuzean thought experiment in the formulation of a social ontology of social conflict and collective trauma, I examine the axioms of the conventional understanding of the pragmatics of human communication before moving on to imagine a schizoanalytics of nomadic discourse. There are important differences between the two in terms of the ways in which we think of violent social conflict, whether and how we attempt to resolve it and how we engage the collective trauma that violent social conflict – particularly asymmetrically violent conflict such as genocide – inevitably produces. The axioms of the pragmatics of human communication and the principles of the schizoanalytics of nomadic discourse are similar, however, in that communication is at one and the same time a contributor to many forms of conflict, the medium through which such conflicts take shape, the resource for managing, resolving or otherwise engaging conflicts, and the methods for imagining and implementing resolutions. Conflicts and their resolutions in effect are integral, ever-present, indwelling and inherent forces of life. Resolving conflicts consists in putting into practice mobile and flexible discourse, and conversing is the minor communication machine that accomplishes this work. Several different forms of discourse and the knowledges that they presuppose are taken up here in the interest of rethinking and reimagining a pragmatics of human communication in terms of a schizoanalytics of nomadic discourse capable of more productively engaging and possibly resolving contemporary violent social conflicts.

Contemporary historical context

In the United States, from the 1930s through the 1950s, the academic discipline of rhetoric and speech, whose intellectual heritage reaches back to the pre-Socratic, classical Greek and classical Roman periods, framed itself as the study of all possible means of suasory discourse. It drew heavily from classical Aristotelian rhetoric and Platonic philosophy. Platonic philosophy was critical of Aristotelian rhetoric, claiming it was mere sophistry. Platonic philosophy, on the other hand, claimed for itself the noble calling of a search for truth. Rhetoric, unlike philosophy, supposedly pandered to the more superficial aspects of human thought and value. Aristotle argued that rhetoric was a pragmatic tool necessary for the cultivation of civilized, democratic forms of life and governance taking shape in the several emerging Greek city-states. Subsequently, rhetorical studies came to include the public discourses of classical Rome, British forms of public address and parliamentary deliberations and American public address and political debates.

From the 1950s to the present, the modern study of communication grew from its classical rhetorical roots by translating the instrumental concerns of Aristotelian rhetoric into the more contemporary metaphors of technical rationality, engineering, information theory and cybernetics. In effect, the study of rhetorical pragmatics shifted to the study of communicative efficiency and the effectiveness of message transmission. Throughout the 1960s, the social scientific framing of communication borrowed heavily from psychology, social psychology, sociology and cultural anthropology. Information theory (i.e. the science of redundancy) was developed at Bell Labs to solve the problems of inefficient message transmission over telephone lines. Cybernetics (i.e. the science of feedback) was developed to solve the problem of inefficient weapon systems for the military. This intellectual hybridization was in keeping with post-World War II enthusiasm for the promise of developing a human science of society and its communicational dynamics. Communication studies came to focus on how public opinion takes shape and how public and private attitudes change. Both concerns were important following the second World War, into the Korean War, throughout the Cold War, and remain important today with the war on terror and its violent consequences. Most contemporary rhetorical and communication theories assumed the *a priori* existence of speakers as the originators, that is, the sources of ('their') messages. Speakers are assumed to be capable of authoring and transmitting original messages and of listening to or otherwise receiving the messages of other speakers, messages encoded in utterances if spoken or in sentences if written. A spoken utterance may be as fleeting as a sigh or a glance, or as durational as a filibuster or a political campaign. A written utterance may be as short as a word or as long as a novel. Utterance size and duration are determined in large measure by the dimensions of the frame of analysis. The implication is that messages encoded in utterances originate with inventive speakers and authors.

Communication currently is understood as a turn-taking system (or 'machine') consisting in sequences of reciprocal messages, each of which originates with an individual speaker who utters them. These messages are presumed to represent other subjects, objects, places, times and things. Interpretation, then, is crucial to the communication process insofar as it is interpretation that produces the meanings of messages encoded in utterances that contain clues for understanding the intentions of their speakers. The psychosocial make-up of speaking and listening subjects is assumed to be responsible in large measure for the interpretation of meanings, what those meanings represent and what meanings 'their' speakers intend. One of the assumptions of this conventional way of understanding communication is that conflict is often a problem of 'misunderstanding' meanings and 'misperceiving' intentions. Misunderstandings and misperceptions spell practical trouble, one form of which may be conflict. Insofar as they are assumed into existence and represent problems, the argument is that misunderstandings and misperceptions can be remedied, even if not resolved, with better understandings and perceptions. Better understandings and perceptions, in turn, are to be arrived at by communicating more rationally and openly. But, of course, more problems of misunderstanding and misperceiving arise in the process of solving and resolving the problems arising from prior misunderstandings and misperceptions. Both are assumed to be inherent properties of human communication. The ongoing process of feedback and error correction, then, is itself fraught with problems. Communication creates problems in the very process of correcting itself; it creates the conditions of possibility for subsequent conflicts in the process of resolving immanent conflicts. The consequence is that meaningful messages not perfectly interpreted (which, of course, they never are) create misunderstandings and misperceptions that grow into different problems, causing even more conflicts that then must be resolved in their turn. But if meanings can be interpreted with higher fidelity, it is hoped that understanding is more likely to occur. And better understanding supposedly leads to more subtle solutions and wiser resolutions. Nuanced understandings, then, are presumably the products of ever more rational thinking, communicating and behaving.

During the 1940s and 1950s, Gregory Bateson (1972/2000) and several of his colleagues had begun rethinking communication by taking cybernetic science and information theory in several very different directions.[1] In research projects ranging from dolphin communication to schizophrenia and from alcoholism to dysfunctional family communication, Bateson and his colleagues were much more interested in studying what communication *does* (i.e. its pragmatic properties) than in what it *means* (i.e. its semantic relations), or in how it is *structured* (i.e. its syntactic relations, its grammatical relations and its rules of internal coherence). In 1967, Paul Watzlawick, Janet Helmick Beavin and Don D. Jackson published *Pragmatics of Human Communication*, signalling a turning point in the ways in which the study of human communication was imagined as a social and behavioural science. The intellectual conversation into which *Pragmatics* was published, however, was not much interested at that time in questions of pragmatics. Questions of syntactics and the prospect of discovering essential structural properties of language were of much greater interest. The assumption was that an adequate syntactic theory of linguistic competence would render a pragmatic theory of communicative performance superfluous. There would be no need to study superficial communicative performance if the deep structure of language and its generative rules could be discovered.

During the late 1950s and well into the 1970s, Noam Chomsky's (1957, 1965, 1972) work in structural linguistics and generative grammar was becoming the dominant way of thinking about language and, by extension, about communication. Chomsky had no interest in the pragmatics of communication, which he claimed was merely the performance of surface variations of language expressions (i.e. *parole*, speech). His concern was with syntax and the syntactic properties and relations of language (i.e. *langue*) understood as the deep structure of linguistic competence. Remember that the intellectual influence of structuralism was pervasive at the time, on the Continent as well as in the United States. Hopes were pinned on determining the deep structures of, and the grammars for all manner of phenomena – from cultures, to narratives, to language itself – as the most promising way of understanding the seemingly endless variety of observable behaviours, actions and their patterned expressions. The formal relations among synchronic elements at the deepest and most essential levels of competence promised to account for myriad surface features expressed diachronically.

In the 'Introduction' to their book, Watzlawick et al. (1967) acknowledge the seeming audacity of proposing at the time a systematic inquiry into the pragmatics of human communication (i.e. the relations between communication and behaviour) (pp. 13–16) prior to the completion of systematic inquiry into syntactics and semantics. Nonetheless, Watzlawick et al. proceeded to theorize and to demonstrate a pragmatic approach to human communication, focusing on problems of systemic interaction and therapeutic communication. Their frame of reference relied heavily on the concepts of information, feedback and redundancy. They postulated an unformulated code – what they called a 'calculus' – of human communication whose rules are adhered to in successful communication but that are violated in unsuccessful communication (pp. 39–43). Consider the axioms that Watzlawick et al. posit for this pragmatic calculus and some of the ways in which pathologies of communication (i.e. unsuccessful communication) may result from violations of those axioms.

Axiom 1: The impossibility of *not* communicating

The first of these axioms is the impossibility of *not* communicating (pp. 48–51). Anything one does or does not do, says or does not say, can be, and almost always is, interpreted as meaning-full (i.e. communicating something). Interpretations have behavioural (i.e. pragmatic) and other consequences, and those consequences, in turn, are interpreted by others as meaningful, and so on, indefinitely. Others are always looking for and listening for what a subject's body signifies and what its voice means and intends. One important implication of this axiom is that the significance and meaning of communication lies not in the intention of the speaking subject, but rather in the interpretation by a listening subject; significance and meaning are at least partially revealed in the subsequent turns of other speakers who were former listeners. Another important implication of this axiom is that once a body enters into language at birth, and particularly once that body becomes a subject *of* and a subject *to* language, it begins to speak its 'mother tongue'. A body subjected to language becomes a subject of language, both in the sense of becoming a subject *of* language, and subjected *to* language. An infant body, once it becomes a speaking subject, cannot *not* communicate. Everything an infant does is full of meaning for the caretakers and for others. And from then on, that subject's body cannot escape language, for better and for worse. A subject's body is assumed to be capable always of occupying subject positions of language (i.e. the slots reserved for proper nouns and pronouns), and in that sense a subject's body is subjected to language at the same time it becomes a subject for language.

Axiom 2: Content and relationship levels of communication

The second axiom is that communication has two dimensions: a dimension of content and a dimension of relationship. The latter qualifies the former, and at the same time the former shapes the latter. The unique qualities characterizing a relationship between two subjects influences, constrains, enables and thereby at least partially determines how the content of any turn of communication is interpreted and what its meanings are taken to be. Similarly, the content of any turn at communication cannot do other than influence the nature of the relationship between a speaking subject and a listening subject. This is another way of claiming that communication is inherently meta-communicative (i.e. that communication has the capacity to be about the content and about the relationship simultaneously). Communication is internally reflexive and externally representational (pp. 51–4). Communication transmits the content of information in the context of a relationship that articulates the conversing parties. Furthermore, all communication of content is a comment on the relationships among those involved, and those relationships, in turn, shape and influence content and the ways in which content is interpreted. The relationships between content and relationship is thereby simultaneously reciprocal and mutually causal.

Axiom 3: The punctuation of the sequence of events

The third axiom is that the nature of a relationship is contingent upon the punctuation of the sequences of communication (pp. 54–60). All communication is distributed by means of turn-taking exchanges, and turn-taking punctuates the communication it distributes as forms and sequences of conversing. Turn-taking distributes spoken discourse among bodies of desire that become subjects in the process of speaking from the subject positions (i.e. the places of pronouns) that discourse provides. Certainly a conflict can be imagined as a sequence of exchanging turns (as is detailed in Chapter 4) that punctuate discourse into different kinds of communication, a claim that holds true for sequences on any plane of analysis. For example, an action intended as a defence for one party is often interpreted as an offensive action by another. Party A's intended defensive move is interpreted by party B as party A's attack on party B. And party B's defensive move against what it takes to be party A's attack is interpreted by party A as party B's attack on party A. Such death spiral sequences, unless interrupted and re-punctuated, spiral out of control into war and mutual destruction. Punctuations determine where narrative sequences begin and end; they shape and influence the perpetuation or diminution of conflict and the narratives that account for them. Narratives, in turn, account for what happened, what it all means and how narratives of punctuated events shape and position their subjects in larger sociocultural and political-historical assemblages (pp. 54–9, 93–9).

Axiom 4: Digital and analogic communication

The fourth axiom posits that human beings communicate both digitally and analogically (pp. 60–7). Digital communication breaks the continuous analogue flows of communication into sequences. Consequently, digital communication (i.e. what we say) is characterized by a complex and powerful syntax, but lacks a sophisticated semantics of and for relationships. Analogue communication (i.e. how we say what we say), on the other hand, is characterized by a rich semantics of and for relationships, but its syntax of and for content is underdeveloped. For Watzlawick et al., digital communication has a powerful logic of syntax capable of structuring content in sophisticated ways. Analogue communication, on the other hand, has a sophisticated semantics of relationships consisting in not only body movements (i.e. kinesics), but also posture, gesture, facial expression, voice inflection and intonation, rhythm and cadence, and any other analogue qualities of which a body and its voice are capable of manifesting (p. 62). In terms of the third axiom, the relationship dimension is communicated analogically, whereas the content dimension is communicated digitally.

Perhaps the most significant difference between analogue and digital communication is that the former has no capacity for a simple negative (i.e. there is no expression for *not*), whereas the latter has the capacity for negation. Furthermore, analogic communication contains no qualifiers; there are no ways to indicate which of two different meanings is implied. Nor are there any tenses; there are no markers or indicators that distinguish between past, present and future. In many ways, analogue communication and signifying semiotics function similarly. Signifiers signify; they do not represent meanings. Signifiers connote chains of metonymic associations, whereas words denote referents; words represent things. Signifiers are incapable of signifying the negative. There is no *not* in semiotic systems of signifiers. Lacking in digital communication, however, is an adequate vocabulary for qualities and shadings of relationships. Any attempt at a literal translation of digital communication into analogue communication is destined to fail. Such attempts result in rough approximations at best. The same can be said for translating analogue communication into the domain of digital communication.

Axiom 5: Symmetrical and complementary interaction

The fifth of Watzlawick et al.'s (1967) axioms of communication pragmatics posits that all sequences of communication are either symmetrical or complementary (pp. 67–70). The former is a pattern based on maximizing equality by minimizing difference; the latter is a pattern based on maximizing difference by minimizing equality. For example, if one subject threatens a second subject, the latter responds with a counter-threat. The attempt is to minimize difference and maximize equality. Similarly, if one subject makes a concession, the second subject follows suit. Again, the attempt is to minimize difference and maximize equality. Think here of the 'tit for tat' strategy for bargaining. Complementary communication, on the other hand, maximizes difference and minimizes equality. So, for example, if one subject threatens, a second subject defers or relents. The more the second subject relents, the more the first subject threatens. Likewise, the more accommodating the first subject, the more greedy and acquisitive the second subject becomes. Think here of the vicious spirals of domestic violence, or of certain kinds of aid and assistance. All too frequently, aid and assistance produces dependency by enabling weakness and exaggerating strength.

Parenthetically, this is another way of framing the structure of the equality/liberty dialectic that founds democratic theory and practice (Mouffe 2000, pp. 17–35). Gregory Bateson (1935, 1936) first reported on these interactional phenomena in his fieldwork among the Iatmul in New Guinea. He referred to these interactional patterns as 'schismogenesis', defining them as processes of differentiation in the norms of individual behaviour resulting from cumulative interaction between individuals (p. 67). He emphasized that these 'schismogenetic' patterns of behavioural interaction became more fixed and defined the more frequently they were enacted, thus becoming an increasingly fixed cultural pattern. Lewis Richardson (1956) incorporated the concept of 'schismogenesis' to account for the logic of war and peace.[2] When aggression, for example, is met with aggression, which, in turn, is met with more aggression, and so on indefinitely, the pattern is symmetrical. When aggression is responded to with submission, which then triggers more aggression, triggering, in turn, even more submission, and so on indefinitely, the pattern is complementary. The extremes (i.e. the potential pathologies) of these interactional patterns take the form of symmetrical escalation and complementary rigidity, both of which are elemental properties of the logics of conflict and resolution on any analytical plane. Uninterrupted, both symmetrical and complementary patterns can destroy relationships on any plane of analysis.

Limitations

The strengths and limitations of these axioms and of this path-breaking move away from an abiding preoccupation with the semantics and syntactics of language and onto the plane of a pragmatics of human communication are that they are structuralist and thereby sedentary in orientation. Watzlawick et al. (1967) were concerned primarily with accounting for the patterning of recurring, ongoing communication, which they referred to as the *structure* of communication processes (p. 118). These structures of patterning and recurrence were then modelled as *systems* in accord with the properties of general systems theory.[3] Unlike most structuralist thought at the time, however, they insisted on the importance of time, whose companion, they assumed, was order. The organization of human communication was demonstrated in time, over time, as order, and they relied heavily on general systems theory for their conceptual and theoretical orientation. The component parts of a system were conceptualized as individual humans. Their attributes were not intrapsychic variables but rather communicative behaviours. And communicative relationships held the system together. So, their systemic thinking was cast at an interpersonal level of communication, and the proper objects of their systemic analysis were persons communicating with one another (p. 120). The position from which these systems were described was of necessity *outside* the system. The orientation was distanced and objective. Consequently, the lines drawn distinguishing a system from its environment, or a system from its sub-systems were wholly dependent on the interests and proclivities of an outsider, an objective observer of an interpersonal communication system over time.

More particularly, this version of communication pragmatics models itself as an open, living, organic system rather than as a closed, mechanistic (not to be confused with 'machinic') system. A 'mechanistic' system is one that can be 'wound up' somehow, fuelled externally; it then operates more or less automatically until it runs down. A 'machinic' system, as Deleuze and Guattari imagine that concept, is a mutually causal system operated by desire at the same time the system operates desire. It is a system with agency but without subjectivity. Once language as discourse articulates to machinic desire, bodies of desire become subjects of and to language, producing discourse. The properties of open systems that most interest Watzlawick et al. are wholeness, feedback and equifinality. The property of wholeness assumes that all the component parts of a system are to some degree interdependent such that a change in the attributes of any component part influences all the other component parts in unpredictable ways. An important part of their research programme was to discern patterns within unpredictability. The difference between a heap and an open system is that the parts of the former have no necessary interdependent relations. The parts of an open system, on the other hand, are not only interdependent, but also collectively open to influences from and changes in their environment.

The implications thereby are that an open system is greater than the straightforward sum of its parts and that the relations among component parts are multilateral, not unilateral. Open, living systems are assumed to be mutually causal, simultaneously reciprocal and multilateral hierarchies of objects, attributes and relationships that can be arbitrarily divided into and hierarchically organized as environments, systems and sub-systems. These features are made possible because of the property of feedback; outputs of a system are fed back into it as inputs. It is important to note that Watzlawick et al. are conceptualizing information systems rather than material systems; the causal connections are reciprocally multidirectional.

Equifinality is the third feature of open systems, which posits that unlike closed, mechanistic systems, open organic systems are not dependent upon their initial conditions for their successive operations. Simply put, the same results can come about from different initial conditions. And alternatively, the same initial conditions can result in very different end states (i.e. multifinality). In this sense, open systems are indeterminate; system parameters predominate over initial conditions. The system is its own best explanation of what is taking place and what is going on at any given moment. As an open system, patterns of communication over time change not because of some set of initial conditions, but because of the properties of the communication processes. Watzlawick et al. (1967) then devote much of the remainder of their book to explaining family dynamics in terms of open interactional systems characterized by these axioms and their theorems.

A schizoanalytics of nomadic discourse

For the purposes of reimagining communication as discourse, and conflict resolution as process, it is necessary to move away from semantic and syntactic concerns towards pragmatic and performative concerns, from individual personal selves to collective subjectivity. It is a move to more adequately acknowledge that communication is a mode of labour that has material effects in a material world. Communication gets things done, it generates processes, and it produces objects and subjects. A serious limitation of a communication paradigm devoted primarily to semantics is the presumption that understanding, consensus and collaboration are 'natural' conditions of the world and that agonism, antagonism, violence and war are aberrant, 'unnatural' conditions. The latter conditions are to be worked on until the former conditions can be restored. I am arguing that such thinking rests on a transcendent foundation of wholeness and that it is an idealization, a persistent and longstanding dream. If and when wholeness is temporarily approximated, it is the product of considerable communicative labour. Immanence and difference, not transcendence and wholeness, are the realities of life; parts, not wholes, constitute the dynamics of life.

A transcendent paradigm has little to say, for example, about how communication works when consensus, collaboration and common understanding are nowhere on the horizon. When antagonistic relations are manifest, when conflict is escalating precipitously, or frozen in resistant repetition, in defiant redundancy or dysfunctional patterns, what is to be said and done? When the libidinal forces (i.e. desire, will, imagination, resistance and resolve) of conflict are dominant and are determining the speeds, directions and intensities of conflict, what interventions, if any, are possible? Is it possible to alter these flows of desire and their circuits of distribution, integration and transformation? To begin to address those challenging questions, I draw from the pragmatic empirical-philosophical thinking of Gilles Deleuze and Felix Guattari (1977, 1987, and 1994). In their critique of formal linguistics, Deleuze and Guattari (1987, pp. 75–110) open up ways of imagining communication, conflict, settlement, information and pragmatics that are pivotal for this project of reimagining conflict and discourse.[4] Their focus on linguistics rather than on communication might seem off the mark initially, given their earlier critique of Chomsky's work (pp. 75–110, *passim*). But their work proves to be invaluable once we make some modifications and extensions, which is what this section aims to accomplish. The proper study of language does not so much concern itself with the exchange of information as it does with the transmission of *order-words*.[5] The concept of order-word refers to the articulation of every utterance to implicit presuppositions regarding social obligations.

We will return to these concepts shortly. Remember that singular utterances fashioned from discourse formations transmit not only order-words, but also the indirect discourse of hearsay, reported speech, partial quotations, clichés, slogans, aphorisms, conventional wisdoms, and bits and pieces of narratives.[6] Discourse formations, when coupled with machinic desire, result in mobile forms of discourse that are capable of producing substantive changes in a material world; this is what I mean when I refer to a pragmatics of nomadic discourse. The utility of the concept of discourse formation becomes apparent in the immanence of their articulations to the contents of desire. Deleuze and Guattari juxtapose communication and philosophy. They identify communication with concerns about consensus and opinions, and philosophy with concerns about dialectics and truth, much as Plato had done earlier. I contend that, at least with regard to conflict resolution and trauma reconciliation discourse, communication and philosophy are one and the same. Conflict discourse wrestles with both dialectics and truth, and at the same time with consensus and opinions. They are not necessarily autonomous domains. Certainly communication can be, and popularly has been imagined largely in terms of corporate and governmental marketing, mass media advertising and entertainment; in short, sophistry of all sorts that panders to mass tastes of the lowest common denominator, disregarding concerns for truth. Just as certainly, much of contemporary conflict resolution wisdom privileges consensus, collaboration and cooperation, often at the expense of debate, argumentation and settlements, as well as other dialectical forms of agonism.[7] The pragmatics of nomadic discourse and its articulations to desire entail some rather different implications. For Deleuze and Guattari, language operates in a fluid and fluctuating world of continuous variations, speeds, intensities and lines of flight.

First principle: Universal singularities

Jean-Jacques Lecercle (2002) extracts three pragmatic principles from Deleuze and Guattari's characterization of a world of continuous variations (pp. 159–65). Those principles constitute the elements of a mobile pragmatics of nomadic discourse. A first of these principles is that there are no universal generalities, only universal singularities. There are no constants, no invariants and no clear distinctions between competence and performance. Nomadic discourse is an articulation of forms of discourse to movements of desire.[8] Nomadic discourse has no transcendent foundation in the form of linguistic or communicative universals. Rather, it is transient, itinerant, ambulant, mobile, artisanal communication that moves towards and arrives at sites that are deterritorializing, decoding and in conflict, that is, sites that are becoming stripped of meaning and sense. These decoding, unsettling territories consist in fragments of all sorts that come to assume the value of territorial properties. This conception of nomadic communication is a better theoretical fit for the conditions and circumstances of conflict assemblages such as Rwanda's genocidal crisis. The pragmatic challenge is how to disarticulate parts of discourse formations that constitute conventional and sedentary forms of conversing, negotiating and mediating. The rationale for disarticulating sedentary discourse formations is to allow for the possibility of more nomadic and unconventional utterances to be put into play. A pragmatics of nomadic discourse is one way of imagining unconventional, non-linear, asynchronous utterances as interventions into conventional, linear, synchronous utterances.

The first rule of an assemblage is to discover and specify the topography it envelops.[9] A pragmatic function of assemblages is to extract territories from topographies and then to foreground the territorial places against a backdrop of the topographical spaces from which they are extracted. For another example, Copenhagen's conflict assemblage extracts the Arab Muslim centre-city community and places it back against the topography of Copenhagen. In this way, assemblages territorialize, settle and map enveloped topographies. They also deterritorialize, unsettle and unbundle them for strategic and tactical purposes. Assemblages have no permanent status, so they can be rendered invisible by disarticulating desire and discourse. Assemblages become invisible and silent once they are deterritorialized. The territorial places that assemblages extract from topographical spaces constitute planes of struggle, the bits and pieces of material reality that constitute the contents of machinic desire.[10] Individual policies and regulations become of paramount importance at times and fade from significance at other times. In other words, those territorial places are also planes of temporality that constitute the durations, rhythms, intensities and speeds of conflicting relations.

Assemblages are collections of these tensional planes. Imagine this thinking in terms of a dynamic and mobile geometry. The geometry consists in planes of reality-effects. These planes are parallel at times, they intersect at times and at other times they move off in directions that may never converge. Planes have a variety of surfaces and topographies, some mapped and some not. There are open spaces, places within spaces, and some spaces become closed and others collapse. There are planes on which sedentary, that is, settled, occupied, homesteaded spaces are already territorialized; those sedentary spaces are in perpetual tensions with nomadic, mobile, deterritorializing forces that operate in time rather than in space. There are planes on which discourse formations struggle with discourse formations and collective enunciation; planes on which libidinality struggles with rationality; and planes on which speeds and intensities struggle with one another. Assemblages, in effect, are sites at which planes converge, at times intersecting and at other times colliding. For assemblages in conflict, the relations between and among the various planes are unstable. They struggle with tensions in attempts to map topographical surfaces, determine discursive formations, harness machinic desires and gauge temporal intensities of all sorts of reality-effects. Planes of desire and planes of discourse intersect, co-mingle and articulate to one another at times, and disarticulate at other spaces and times. However, deterritorialization perpetually unsettles the territorialization of supposedly stable topographies, destabilizing them along flows of desire that are escaping the sedentary circuits of collective enunciation.[11] On the side of territorialization is the semiotic structure of collective enunciation and its discourse formations. On the side of deterritorialization are the cutting edges of desire's lines of flow. The consequences of their intersections and articulations are the stammerings and the paratactics of nomadic discourse, that is, the production of unconventional, new, unprecedented utterances and partial utterances in the process of becoming created in the immanence of conflict.

Second principle: Politics of language

The second pragmatic principle of nomadic discourse pertains to the micro- and macro-politics of language all along the continua of reality-effects. An utterance can be thought of as a micro-political action, and in the moment of its becoming uttered, it is coming to have macro-political consequences. The same principle holds for conversing, negotiating and mediating. Unlike the pragmatics of human communication, the pragmatics of nomadic discourse is immanently political and globally accessible; consider the internet and the instantaneously global effects that individual utterances can have. In fact, the topographical, spatial, libidinal and temporal articulate to the communicational, linguistic and discursive, producing myriad reality-effects. Micro- and macro-political utterances exert corporeal and incorporeal forces on the contents of machinic desire throughout the material and immaterial worlds. And those forces of machinic desire interpellate, that is, call for or hail various discursive formations of collective enunciation.[12]

Imagining desire in machinic rather than humanistic terms is to imagine desire as a process without a subject. Individual bodies of humans and collective bodies of social formations cannot be said to *have* (i.e. possess) desire. Desire does not originate from within bodies, somehow driving and motivating them. Nor is desire a function of lack or absence. I may crave what I lack, but craving is not the same as desiring; craving is a function of needing what I do not have. Desire is not produced by lack or insufficiency; it is, rather, becoming 'full of life', forces of life overflowing their merely material, mortal bodies. Desire is an abundance of life that overtakes and often overwhelms material bodies of desire. Occupying subject positions of discourse enables desire to be coded as utterances of discourse formations drawn from the collective enunciation of sociocultural formations. When discourse without bodies and desire without subjects articulate and couple, bodies of desire become subjects of and subjects for discourse.

In an interview with George Stambolian, Felix Guattari (1996) responds to Stambolian's request to define 'desire', and he does so by invoking the concept 'machine'.

> For Gilles Deleuze and me desire is everything that exists *before* representation and production. It's everything whereby the world and affects constitute us outside of ourselves, in spite of ourselves. It's everything that overflows from us. That's why we define it as flow. Within this context we were led to forge a new notion in order to specify in what way this kind of desire is not some sort of undifferentiated magma, and thereby dangerous, suspicious, or incestuous. So we speak of machines, of 'desiring machines,' in order to indicate that there is as yet no question of 'structure,' that is, of any subjective position, objective redundancy, or coordinates of reference. Machines arrange and connect flows. They do not recognize distinctions between persons, organs, material flows and semiotic flows. (p. 46)

Contents of desiring-machines (including bodies of all sorts) are hailed by and come to be identified with subject positions of discourse formations. Identities are produced as by-products of these articulations. A desiring-machine without a subject remains a non-subjective, or better an a-subjective process. A discursive formation without machinic desire remains a semiotic shell, an empty structure with no life.[13] It is only when a conflict assemblage is occupied by the bodies of machinic desire articulated to discourse formations that a series of identities and identifications are produced. Subjects and objects become embodied identities on uneven topographical surfaces of conflict assemblages. And these subjects and objects move at variable speeds with differential intensities.

Machinic desire circulates contents and bodies of desire in accord with libidinal forces. For example, scars, memorials, *genocidaires* relocated back into villages, utterances remembered from gaçaça trials, killing fields and rape locations are objects or bodies of desire that circulate throughout contemporary Rwandan daily life. As these part-objects articulate to discourse, they become subjects of signifiance, they can be said to be meaningful and that they produce reality-effects. Desire cannot say what it means because it has no discourse and no subject positions from which to speak. Desire is a-subjective, a-synchronous and non-linear. Subject positions are provided by discourse formations, and when the libidinality of desire articulates to the rationality of discourse, desire (libidinality) pushes the limits of discourse (rationality).

One of the ways by which desire is realized is when it couples with discourse. The plane of discourse consists in systems of expression organized around subject positions.[14] The plane of desire resembles a collective of objects moving as a unit with boundaries that are unstable and perpetually change, like a flock of birds taking flight, or a fog bank or cloud formation. Discourse formations are linear series and sequences organized around their subject positions.Machinic desire articulates to subject positions of discourse formations, which produce materially embodied utterances fitted more or less precisely to just *this* singular set of circumstances. This accounts for the fact that reality-effects are realized improvisationally; subjects must make-up reality-effects on the fly, as circumstances develop. Rationality accounts for moments of territorialization and structure. At times, bodies of desire identifying with subject positions of discourse produce relatively stable and unitary identities. At other times, when libidinality is dominant, desire's deterritorializing effects overwhelm the territorializing effects of collective enunciation and discourse formations. Instead of a desiring body remaining identified with a synchronous subject position of territorializing discourse and sedentary relations of power, what gets produced is a subject of machinic desire – a libidinal subject.[15]

There are, of necessity, political consequences for reimagining desire and discourse, communication and conflict in these decidedly immanent and nomadic terms. When desire overwhelms discourse, the possibilities for change, transformation and revolution open lines of flight that deterritorialize settlements. When rationality overtakes desire, relative order and regularity prevail. When it overtakes rationality, when unchecked and unconstrained by discourse formations, desiring-production takes the forms of disorder that threaten to deterritorialize settlements, erase history and liberate memory from trauma.

Third principle: Immanence of articulation

A third principle of a pragmatics of nomadic discourse is that there is no ghost in the machine, so to speak. Or as Deleuze and Guattari would say, there is no abstract machine that is internal to language. They are alluding here to Chomsky's argument that there is a deep structure yet to be discovered in the human brain and that generative grammars of this deep structure can be imagined as algorithms of competence that generate the performance of endless series of grammatically correct sentences. But human bodies, it must be remembered, do not often speak in grammatical sentences. We utter expressions of discourse formations, utterances that are drawn from collective enunciation in the immanence of the articulation of desire to discourse. Collective enunciation and discourse formations are not constrained by formal rules and relations of grammar and syntax. In fact, utterances may include paratactical stammering, howling, moaning, ranting, chanting, repetitions and silences. There is no necessary internal coherence to utterances of nomadic discourse. There are only assemblages that envelop topographies, extract territories and produce articulations of discourse to desire. The point is that language is driven from outside itself rather than somehow from deep within itself. Collective enunciation and discourse formations articulate to the machinic content of desire, imagination, will, resistance and resolve.[16] In brief, discourse formations of collective enunciation articulate to machinic contents of desire, and the embodiments of those articulations become utterances of desiring identifications and identities, that is, subjects of desire, imagination, will, resistance and resolve.

Nomadic discourse comes into being in the intervals between material excitation and semiotic response, between libidinality and propositionality. Material bodies become caught up in and subjugated to the articulation of flows of machinic desire and the structures of discourse formations. Sedentary discourse captures and binds the flows of machinic desire, whereas nomadic discourse overruns sedentary structures. The flow of machinic desire in accord with its libidinality cannot be captured and contained once and for all by structures of propositional discourse. Territorialization is only temporary; the deterritorializing forces of machinic desire are always already at work. A body of desire answers the call of discourse to occupy a subject position. Those articulations generate material forces that account for the inherent instability and open-endedness of identities and settlements. These inherently unstable identities and settlements are at times constituted and at other times torn apart by the tensions of the forces of libidinality, propositionality and rationality struggling with and against one another. Nomadic discourse, then, circulates between planes. These planes constitute assemblages of conflict, and nomadic discourse maps the articulations of those planes, marking both planes as potential settlements and possible lines of flight. It is in this sense that discourse can be imagined as collective and indirect (i.e. saying what others have said, speaking hearsay, slogans and clichés), and desire can be imagined as a-subjective and machinic (i.e. processes with agency but without subjectivity). Nomadic discourse as indirect communication answers calls of machinic desire, produces subject positions as locations for identifications with subjectivity and produces identity as relatively stable unity. Nomadic discourse travels along lines of flight, paths leading both towards as well as away from conflict. Sedentary discourse occupies established, unitary circuits of centralized agency, formal power and official authority. Nomadic discourse immigrates into and emigrates out of sites of ruptures and unsettled territorialization; sedentary discourse has lost its force, or is in the process of losing its hierarchical hold on bounded settlements. When a rupture violates ordinary knowledge and common sense, when it is identified as a radical breach, it often is referred to as an 'event'.

Not all ruptures are referred to as events, and not all named events are referred to as conflicts, but those events that are named as conflicts in effect rip open holes in ordinary knowledges of structure and order, exposing what Alain Badiou (2000) calls exceptional realms of singular truths. Truths that emerge from such events take over the bodies of their subjects and persist through the testimonials, declarations and proclamations of what have become embodied subjects to singular truths. In this sense, subjects bear a truth revealed to them in the rupture of an event. Subjects to truth and an ethic of truths can be considered subjects to a truth, subjects bearing a truth, subjects overwhelmed by a truth and subjects for whom ethics consists in remaining true to a truth as it plays out during a life. Subjects in conflict are subjects to truth, and those truths differ from one embodied subject to another. Mediating conflict in an effort to resolve and/or reconcile trauma requires working agreements and temporary settlements that do not violate truths born of events. Subjects to truth have the capacity of choice during an interval, and it is choice that makes agreements and settlements across truths possible. The constraints on those choices, of course, vary from situation to situation, from one contingent moment to another. An embodied subject to truth is accountable for its choices and the consequences of those choices insofar as choice cannot be avoided. Granted, choices are made under an extraordinarily wide range of conditions, and a subject has no determinate control over what happens prior to a moment of choice. In effect, an embodied subject cannot control what befalls it, but it can choose what to do in response to what befalls it, however horrendous the available choices may be.

Three syntheses of libidinality/desire

How do 'events' happen? How are we to think in terms of 'things happening' and 'choices being available?' How do conditions 'take place' such that 'things befall' a subject of discourse? And exactly when does choice become possible for a desiring-body to become a subject of discourse? In their early work, Deleuze and Guattari (1977) theorize three syntheses of desire – a connective synthesis that produces production, a disjunctive synthesis that produces recording and a conjunctive synthesis that produces consumption-consummation. Throughout the preceding chapters, I have relied on these syntheses to address the above questions. Conflict assemblages and their embodied subjects transform immanence without transcending it by means of these three synthetic processes of desire (remember that desire is defined as all that comes before subject and object, before representation and production). The first of these three syntheses of unconscious thought is the connective synthesis, or the production of production. Deleuze and Guattari (1977) proposed that the syntax of partial objects and flows of desire was an open series of the conjunction 'and' (and . . . and . . . and. . .) with no period. Connective syntheses of production connect flows of desire, producing desiring-production.

Disjunctive syntheses of recording punctuate flows of desiring-production at the junctions where the flows are blocked, broken, interrupted or otherwise disjoined. Blockages, breaks, stoppages and interruptions of desiring-production are recorded or otherwise delineated. This second synthesis of transcendental unconscious thought is the production of recording, which is an indefinite series of alternatives (either . . . or . . . or . . .), with each 'or' marking or recording a disjunction of the flow of 'and . . . and . . . and'. In effect, desire records disjunctures and marks them at those sites. Those recordings of disjunctive syntheses are both consumed and consummated in the process of conjunctive syntheses, and the consumption-consummation of the recordings of disjunctures produce identity as its by-product. This third synthesis of the transcendental unconscious is the production of conjunctions, a retrospective naming of subject identities. The syntax of conjunctive syntheses is (Oh, so that's what it is/was . . ., so that's who I am/was . . ., so that's what's going on . . .).[17]

The flows of desire comprising two truths connect, producing the production of desire resulting from the connective synthesis. Let's say the two truths are axiomatic capitalism and authoritarian democracy in contemporary Rwanda. Their connective synthesis is productive until there is a disjuncture, a division of the flow. Let's say this disjunctive synthesis consists in the events that take place in Rwanda between early April and early July of 1994. The connective synthesis, that is, the production of production is broken. A hole is ripped in the good-sense and common-sense knowledges of everyday life. Life and time come to a standstill. This disjunctive synthesis is marked and recorded in any number of libidinal and propositional ways, materially and psychically/spiritually. One way is on the surfaces of memory. Duration stretches out and that event comes to be made sense of, that is, it is both consumed and consummated producing a subject identity and memory as by-products. That identity makes sense, in retrospect, of the recorded marks of that particular disjunctive synthesis. 'Oh, so that's what it was.' 'So that's what happened.' 'Oh, that's who they were.' A conjunctively produced subject identity becomes a name of an event, and choices can now be made in the retrospective light of a memory of that identity.[18]

Subject identity, then, is a conjunctive synthesis (i.e. an articulation) of discourse and desire materializing as utterances of affects (i.e. unformed affections), percepts (i.e. unformed perceptions) and concepts (i.e. unformed conceptions) (Deleuze and Guattari 1994, pp. 163–99). Connective syntheses of desiring-production are interrupted, stopped or disjoined in some way by singular conditions and circumstances. Those disjunctions mark and record themselves, leaving signs that, when taken in (i.e. consumed) and put together (i.e. consummated) by bodies of desire, produce recognition (i.e. subject identifications) that conflate as immanent identity. As signs, marks and traces of recordings are consumed and consummated conjunctively, they leave behind identities as by-products, as marks of hot spots. Said another way, analogue flows become digitized, consumed and consummated resulting in 'retrospective identification' of what it was and what happened. Conjunctive syntheses simultaneously consume and consummate signs, marks, records and tracings that produce a recognizing and knowing identity. Once identified, the signs take on the appearance of having been there all along and are only now coming to be recognized by a pre-constituted and already existing subject 'with' identity. Conjunctively produced identities and the synthetic processes producing them become inverted. Instead of identity being recognized as a product of desiring-production, however identity misrecognizes itself as a causal agent; a subject with identity produced by itself. But a conjunctive synthesis of consummation-consumption is a virtual and actual reversal of experience as memory.

In this sense, memory is both immanent structure of feeling and immanent structure of experience enunciated in the process of becoming articulated to discourse. Identity and subject may be produced simultaneously when bodies of desire become articulated to discourse and its subject positions. And this holds true for unconventional discourse formations as well as for non-discursive articulations such as dancing, singing, tagging, demonstrating, street theatre, performance art, rioting and myriad forms of resistance and affirmation.[19] A conjunctive synthesis, then, is a retrospective identification of events recorded on the surface of immanence as memory, be it individuated or collective. These three syntheses of desire describe the pivotal dynamics of libidinality and propositionality in the co-constitution of memory, trauma, narrative and identity.

Immanence in effect is a recording surface, that is, a plane produced in the process of its marks and signs being recorded. A plane of immanence is not an *a priori* condition. It is instead produced by conjunctive articulations of marked and recorded disjunctions. An example of such a plane being produced might be the developing memory of a human, the development of a strip mall, the collective experience of a city under siege by an enemy, etc. Accounts of disjunctively synthetic recording articulate psychic intimacy (i.e. desiring-production) to material sociality (i.e. collective enunciation), in effect reconfiguring, conversing, negotiating and mediating their elements. Conflict and its narratives, then, are inevitable functions of desire as they are connectively formed, disjunctively recorded and conjunctively consumed-consummated. Disjunctions mark and record themselves, leaving signs that when taken in (i.e. consumed) and put together (i.e. consummated) by bodies of desire produce recognition (i.e. identification) as immanent identity. The question of psychic and material malleability remains open. The relations of force articulating memory to identity are perpetually disarticulated and rearticulated, deterritorialized and reterritorialized, decoded and recoded, producing changes in structures of feeling and senses of events. And these perpetual syntheses of connection, disjunction and conjunction involving memory and identity produce openings onto planes of potentiality and possibility for conversing, negotiating, mediating and dialoguing incorporeal transformations.

Individual, local, intra-state, inter-state, national, international and global conflicts connect, disjoin and conjoin synthetically at all levels of process, whether those processes are products of subjugated groups or the productions of group-subjects.[20] Planes of experience can be mapped across scales of analysis in the form of bits and pieces of discourse, vignettes and stories from narratives whose outcomes hold possibilities. A Rwandan conflict assemblage is imbricated across all scales of analysis in quite different ways, from a young Tutsi girl returning to school with Hutu children, to village gatherings during which any mention of the genocide or of Hutu and Tutsi is forbidden, to worldwide transmission of images and texts of economic development in selected regions around Kigali, the capital of Rwanda. To better understand how modifications of discourse formations actually modify desiring-production and social-production, it is necessary to account for the ways in which desire and discourse articulate and, in turn, how modifications of discourse and desire engage with and modify conflict assemblages. That is the project on which I am now at work.

Notes

Introduction

1 See (Deleuze 1990, pp. xiv, 20–2, 181, 244); for supplemental discussion, see (Baugh 2005, pp. 284–5).
2 For a psychoanalytic interpretation of asymmetrically violent social conflict, see (Volkan 1997). For his internationally renowned journalistic accounts of the Rwandan genocide, see (Gourevitch, 'The Life After', *The New Yorker* May 4, 2009, pp. 36–49); for his initial reporting on the Rwandan genocide, see (Gourevitch 1998); see also (Semelin 2007, pp. 10–27). For a current and comprehensive collection of classic philosophical essays on violence, see (Lawrence and Karim 2007).
3 (Deleuze 1990, pp. 96–9); for valuable supplemental elaborations, see (Rajchman 2001, pp. 7–23); (Colebrook 2006a, p. 6); and (Hughes 2008, pp. 34–5).
4 I am drawing on the independent discussions of the transcendental unconscious of Joe Hughes and Cliff Stagoll; see (Hughes 2008, pp. 155–8) and (Stagoll 2005, pp. 282–3).
5 I am referring here to Hughes' explication of Deleuze's transcendental empiricism; see (Hughes 2008, pp. 20–47, 163–4, 156–7).
6 See Bruce Baugh's discussion of the intersection of transcendental empiricism and politics in (Baugh 2005, p. 285).
7 For Deleuze's reading of the rules of Bergson's method of intuition for addressing either non-existent problems or badly analysed problems, see (Deleuze 1991, pp. 13–35).
8 For a detailed discussion of truth, peace, justice, forgiveness, healing and reconciliation as six pivotal transitional justice themes and the debates contesting the best ways to actualize each in post-genocide Rwanda, see (Clark 2010, pp. 29–46).
9 Historian Gérard Prunier estimates that the 'least bad possible' number of Tutsi deaths was 850,000; see (Prunier 1998, pp. 264–68). Allison Des Forges puts the number of Tutsi dead at 500,000; see (Des Forges 1999, pp. 209–12). The generally accepted number is around 1 million mostly Tutsi, but many moderate Hutu are included in that estimate as well.
10 For vivid descriptions of this brutality, see (Clark 2010, pp. 12, 15) and (Prunier 1998, pp. 16–23).
11 For Deleuze and Guattari's discussion of this point, see (Deleuze and Guattari 1987, p. 411); for their broader discussion of nomadology and the war machine as it contrasts with the forces of State military institutionalization, see (pp. 351–436). For a widely cited account of Rwandan sociopolitical and cultural history leading up to and including the most recent genocide, see (Prunier 1998, pp. 264–8). For a synopsis of this history, see (Clark 2010, pp. 12–19). For a critique of this dominant narrative account of the Event of genocide and for a decidedly more leftist interpretation of the Rwandan genocide, see (Herman and Peterson 2010).

12 Deleuze and Guattari differentiate 'nomadic war machine' from 'state-sponsored armies' by arguing that the former is a nomadic phenomenon without subjects, a phenomenon that is part and parcel of any assemblage in which desire is variously territorialized and deterritorialized at different times, whereas the latter is a consequence of the state appropriating the nomadic war machine and subjectifying it by organizing it into armies under state control and command. See (Deleuze and Guattari 1987, pp. 351–423).

13 Recall that Deleuze and Guattari insist that signs and signifiers cannot be equated; they distinguish three sorts of signs: territorial signs are 'indexes', deterritorialized signs are 'symbols', and reterritorialized signs are 'icons'. See (Deleuze and Guattari 1987, p. 65). See also (Eltringham 2004, pp. 18, 19) and (Clark 2010, p. 17).

14 For an account of France's role in the genocide, see (Wallis 2007, pp. 51–78). For Lt. General Dellaire's account of his command of the UN Peacekeeping forces, see (Dellaire 2003).

15 For Lt. General Dellaire's first-hand account of these events, see (Dellaire 2003, pp. 221–62).

16 Lt. General Dellaire's account is a compelling on-the-ground narrative; see (Dellaire 2003, pp. 293–327).

17 For Clark's thorough account, see (Clark 2010, pp. 19–28); for supplemental detail, see (Des Forges 1995, pp. 45–6).

18 For a more complete and detailed account, see (Peskin 2008, pp. 207–31).

19 For a discussion of the plans to ban Mouvement Démocratique Républican (MDR), see (HRW Briefing Paper, Kigali, May 2003).

20 The following is my synopsis of the narrative that opens Phil Clark's superb critical ethnographic study of the gaçaça courts in post-genocide Rwanda. This particular narrative is a record of his field observations of gaçaça at Kigali Ngali, Bugesera, 19 May 2003. I have truncated his extended example, and I want to acknowledge at the outset how indebted I am to his study for so much of the material I draw from throughout *A New Philosophy of Social Conflict*. See (Clark 2010, pp. 1–4).

21 For a journalistic account of the war crimes of Rwandan journalists, see (Temple-Raston 2005).

22 I am also relying on Cliff Stagoll's entry for the concept Event in Adrian Parr's *Deleuze Dictionary*. See (Stagoll 2005b, pp. 87–8).

23 Much is being made of the concept of transformation in the ongoing mediation and dialogue debates. See, for example, (Bush and Folger 1994), (Ellis 1999) and (Ellis 2006). A critical review of that transformational discursive experiment is spirited and informative, both in terms of what is addressed and what is not; see (Nader 2001).

24 I want to thank Brian Polkinghorn for bringing this growing disjunction to my attention.

25 'Machinic' is a Deleuzean concept (to be distinguished from mechanistic, organic, or systemic metaphors) for processes that can be characterized in terms of agency without subjectivity. This concept will be developed with greater specificity in subsequent chapters. For Guattari's recently translated collection of essays on the machinic unconscious, see (Guattari 2011 [1979]). For other informed explications of this concept, see (Grossberg 1997, pp. 83–90), (Colebrook 2002b, pp. 55–67), (Wise 2005, pp. 77–87) and (Bonta and Provtevi 2004, pp. 54–5).

26 For an elaboration on these three dimensions of the concept of contextuality, see (Grossberg 1996, pp. 102–5).

27 For an excellent example of the enormous productivity of this kind of mapping of articulated relations onto contextual spaces of incommensurable difference, see Jody Williams's essay in (Hopkins 2000, pp. 185–205). Jody Williams is the 1997 co-recipient of the Nobel Peace Prize, along with Bobby Muller, for her work as the chief strategist for the International Campaign to Ban Landmines, an alliance consisting of the Vietnam Veterans of America Fund (which Bobby Muller initiated), Handicap International, Human Rights Watch, medico international, Mines Advisory Group and Physicians for Human Rights. Williams' discussion of the discipline of her work to articulate relations onto contextual spaces of incommensurable differences is passionate, compelling and extremely informative.

28 For a superb example of fieldwork conducted in Northern Ireland during the height of The Troubles, see (Feldman 1991).

Chapter 1

1 In the following account of the genesis of representation and the transcendental unconscious, I am relying heavily on the work of Joe Hughes and his insightful reading of three pivotal Deleuze texts; *The Logic of Sense, Difference and Repetition*, and with Felix Guattari, *Anti-Oedipus*. The following synopsis of the primary order of the pre-predicative life of the transcendental unconscious is drawn from these texts. See (Hughes 2008).

2 For a vivid account of the body-without-organs as the nascent ego, see (Hughes 2008, p. 29), see also (Deleuze 1990, p. 187).

3 For explication of these crucial relations in Deleuze's thought, see (Deleuze 1990, p. 149ff), (Lecercle 2002, pp. 1167ff and 173ff) and (Buchanan 2000, pp. 73–89).

4 Several essays in a collection on international peace building speak directly to this point and provide unambiguous advice to privileged Northerners and Westerners at work with international conflict resolving, peace building and collective reconciliation initiatives. Hizkias Assefa, Harold H. Saunders, Elise Boulding and Adam Curle advise well-meaning First World Liberals not to engage in such work in order to save the less fortunate, to feed their own egos, to build their reputations, to pad their vitae, or to profit from lucrative consulting and training contracts. Instead, they recommend that those culture workers remain in their own Western and Northern countries and work to change policies and practices that contribute directly and indirectly to conflict, violence, poverty, terrorism, wars and genocide that people in the South and East live with on a daily basis. See (Lederach and Jenner 2002, pp. 283–319).

5 For one of his later and more succinct explications of this commitment, see (Deleuze 2001, pp. 25–33).

6 See Deleuze's 'Third Series of the Proposition' in (Deleuze 1990, pp. 20–2).

7 For his discussion of this movement, see (Deleuze 1990, p. 219); see Hughes's reading of this feature of sublimation (Hughes 2008, p. 37).

8 See (Deleuze 1990, pp. xiv, 12, 20–1, 78).

9 For a more nuanced explication of the relations among the primary order, the secondary organization and the tertiary order, see (Deleuze 1990, pp. 70, 72, 81, 86); see also (Hughes 2008, pp. 20–5).

10 For a discussion of the mortal dangers of the return of the same in terms of the holocausts of Nazi Germany, Rwanda and Yugoslavia, see (Semelin 2007, pp. 33–8). For the return of the same with particular reference to trauma and reconciliation, see (Humphrey 2002, pp. 105–24).
11 For a discussion of the four characteristics of Deleuze's concept of plane, see (Stagoll 2005, p. 205).
12 See Chapter 2, 'The Logic of Sense' in (Hughes 2008, pp. 20–47) for an extended explication of these genetic dynamics.
13 For a description of the Umuvumu Tree Project, see (Larson 2009, pp. 50–9). For a much more inclusive discussion of contemporary conflict resolution initiatives throughout Africa, see (Uwazie 2003) For an in-depth investigation of a restorative justice model in post-colonial Nigeria, see (Elechi 2006).
14 For a provocative discussion of the role of religion and its implication in 'cleansing' and 'purification' forces in the production of asymmetrical violence, see (Semelin 2007, pp. 81–92).
15 For a discussion of conflict emerging in smaller and smaller identity units and cellular grids embedded within larger and larger political assemblages, see (Lederach 1997, pp. 3–19). His prediction foreshadows the US war on terrorism and its belated remembering of the difficulties involved in fighting a conventional war (i.e. state-sponsored military action) against an enemy organized as fluid, transitory, nomadic networks that blend into familial and community/tribal populations (i.e. nomadic war machines).
16 For an analysis of these and related contemporary dilemmas, see (Naím 2013, pp. 218–53).

Chapter 2

1 This synoptic account of the chronology of events of the Rwandan genocide is drawn from (Semujanga 2003), (Hatzfeld 2005), (Hatzfeld 2006) and (Semelin 2007).
2 For an unapologetic account of Rwandan economic development, see (Crisafulli and Redmond 2012).
3 The phrase 'deliberative democracy' is perhaps most closely associated with (Guttman and Thompson 1996) as a strategy for addressing moral disagreements. They maintain that parties in moral disagreement can reach morally acceptable decisions if all sides engage in rational deliberations guided by six principles – reciprocity, publicity, accountability that regulates the processes of politics, basic liberty, basic opportunity and fair opportunity. These principles supposedly enable citizens to reach provisional moral agreement that all parties can recognize.
4 I am synopsizing here the first three chapters of section 1 of *Anti-Oedipus*; see (Deleuze and Guattari 1977, pp. 1–22). These three syntheses are used for several different purposes throughout *A New Philosophy of Social Conflict*.
5 For a more detailed treatment of these contrasts, see (Mouffe 2000, pp. 83–90).
6 *Interahamwe* translates as 'those who stand (and fight) together'; *inkotanyi* translates as 'invincible', the name given to the Tutsi rebels who organized in Uganda in 1988 and fought against Habyarimana's dictatorship. They formed the basis of the Rwandan Patriotic Front. See (Hatzfeld 2005, pp. 28–33).

7 Jacques Rancière's theorization of dissensus and the distribution of the sensible may be closer to Mouffe's conception of combative democracy among friendly enemies than they are to the concepts of dialogical, deliberative, or third-way democracy; see (Rancière 2004, pp. 52, 56, 62, 65, 85).

8 Mouffe is directing much of her critique at Anthony Giddens and is referring to his book on third-way politics; see (Giddens 1998). For a transcendent communication approach to mediation and conflict resolution, see (Pearce and Littlejohn 1997, pp. 151–216).

9 Deleuze and Guattari (1987, pp. 367–74) call this kind of thinking nomad science, a mode of thinking at odds with decidedly more sedentary, conventionally neoliberal and liberal-humanistic ways of thinking; see (Deleuze and Guattari 1987, pp. 367–74). The latter is thinking that – having arrived at some geographical, conceptual or affective space – makes a place of that space by laying claim to it, drawing its boundaries, declaring its identities and defending its borders, that is, reterritorializing it. Boundaries, identities and borders become justified given nomadic transgressions, incursions and flows that become all the more threatening once sedentary bodies have settled in. This settling in (i.e. reterritorializing) establishes bodies as identities (the strata of the organism), meanings as hierarchies (the strata of signifiance) and forms as accountabilities (the strata of subjectification). This results in sedentary, state-sponsored wars that deploy militarized armies of the state against nomadic war machines in the interests of defending sedentary ways of life against deterritorializing ways of the nomads, whose primary function is not the waging of war but rather of living nomadically. For a detailed discussion of the strata of the organism, of signifiance and of subjectivation as they pertain to an application of Deleuzism, see (Buchanan 2000, pp. 120–7).

10 Amartya Sen provides an extended discussion of non-violent strategies for negotiating multiple identities; see (Sen 2006). For a personal account of the rigours of living multiple identities in a globalized world, see (Maalouf 2000).

11 President Oscar Arias Sanchez of Costa Rica and Harn Yawnghwe, representing Aung San Suu Kyi of Burma (now Myanmar) at a Nobel Peace Laureates conference at the University of Virginia, comment on the role of the United States selling arms to developing, non-democratic regimes with egregious human rights violation records, in (Hopkins 2000). On different configurations of European democracies in terms of how they structured governmental institutions and addressed forms of conflict during the decade of the 1990s, see (Steiner 1998, pp. 115–61) and (Sklair 2002, pp. 84–117).

12 For a collection of essays that call into question the instrumental worth, the economic conceptions and the constitutionalism of democracy, see (Christiano 2003). Of course there are crucial distinctions to be made between political liberalism and classical theoretical liberalism. The latter considers individuals to be free, autonomous, rational actors pursuing their own self-interest. Modern theoretical liberalism is closely associated with John Rawls, whose concern it was to modify classic liberalism by including social issues such as poverty, health and education. That these logics and their discourses cannot be reconciled is abundantly clear when, say, Rawls and Habermas are read against one another. In the end, Rawls privileges liberalism and Habermas privileges democracy. Neither attempt at reconciliation of the two traditions is successful. For the details of this debate, see (Rawls 1993) and (Habermas 1996). For an extended discussion, see (Lakoff 2002).

13 Elias Canetti's classic study of crowds and power is an investigation of ethological more than sociological categories of social formations; see (Canetti 1962, pp. 15–90, 169–200, 281–99); and for a detailed discussion of the discursive features characterizing each of those forms of discourse, see (Vološinov 1973) whose work I take up in Chapter 5.

14 Felix Guattari's diagrams of schizoanalysis are particularly instructive at this point, particularly two of his essays, 'Assemblages of Enunciation, Pragmatic Fields and Transformations' and 'Reference Points for Schizoanalysis'. See (Guattari 2011 [1979]), pp. 45–73, 149–98).

15 I am rehearsing an argument Chantal Mouffe makes based on her reading of Derrida on this point; see (Mouffe 2000, p. 12). For provocative dialogues with Jürgen Habermas and Jacques Derrida (the former on fundamentalism and terror, and the latter on real and symbolic suicides) shortly after the events of 9/11, see (Borradori 2003).

16 For the more traditional and conventional social, behavioural, economic, diplomatic and military discourses of peacebuilding and conflict resolution and for social scientific methodological strategies for conducting such research, see (Druckman 2005). For a comprehensive historical account of conflict resolution methods, see (Barrett and Barrett 2004).

17 For a thorough review of the social and behavioural science research on conflict and conflict resolution done from the mid-1940s through the late 1990s, see (Deutsch and Coleman 2000). The social and behavioural sciences, of course, have engaged in several important post-World War II debates that have altered their respective curiosities over the intervening decades. One such debate with a direct bearing on this study of conflict, resolution, desire and communication is the textual turn in cultural anthropology; see (Clifford and Marcus 1986), (Marcus and Fischer 1986); and (Clifford 1988).

Much of the more contemporary ethnographic work in cultural anthropology is an exception to this critique. For a social science and ethnographically oriented cultural anthropology concerned with alternative dispute resolution and conflict analysis, see (Avruch 1998) and (Avruch 2013). For first-person accounts of Hindus and Muslims in a Bangladeshi village, see (Roy 1994). For an analysis of more than 12,000 pages of negotiation transcripts from the Waco conflict between US government forces and Branch Davidians, see (Docherty 2001). For an extensive collection of national and international cases of multi-party mediations, see (Crocker et al. 1999).

18 Avruch and Black point out that Burton's first eight needs do not have a common theoretical genealogy (they are drawn from sociobiology, psychology and stimulus-response behaviourism) and thus lack coherence and result in an epistemological jumble. But for Burton, the social benefits derived from his universal needs constitute a non-negotiable foundation (Avruch and Black 1987, p. 92). Burton defines universal human needs as 'those conditions or opportunities that are essential to the individual if [s/he] is to be a functioning and cooperative member of society, conditions that are essential to [his/her] development and which, through [him/her], are essential to the organization and survival of society' (Burton and Sandole 1986, p. 59).

19 'Abduction' is a term Gregory Bateson borrowed from C. S. Pierce; it refers to a diagonal and oblique method of constructing knowledge based on consistencies and pattern. It is neither inductive nor deductive. It is not linear, either vertically

or horizontally. Rather, 'abduction' is non-linear, circuitous, metonymic and associative. For a more detailed discussion of abduction, see (Harries-Jones 1995, pp. 177–80).

20 Gilles Deleuze 1988 [1970], p. 49; see also (Deleuze and Guattari 1987, pp. 256–7); and (Bonta and Protevi 2004, pp. 49–50).

21 See (Hall 1980, p. 325); for a complementary implementation of articulation, see also (Laclau and Mouffe 1985).

22 I am referring here to the will to purify and destroy that several historians and philosophers claim to be the energy that drives so many of the political uses of genocide. See (Semelin 2007). For Gilles Deleuze's reading of Nietzsche's conception of active and reactive forces and the tragic, where Deleuze responds to the problem of the will to power, to Nietzsche's conception of *ressentiment* and bad conscience, and to the Overman, see (Deleuze 1983, pp. 111–98). For her extension and refinement of J. L. Austin's (1970, 1975) speech-act theory, particularly with regard to illocutionary and perlocutionary forces, injurious speech and sovereign performatives, see (Butler 1997, pp. 43–102) and (Butler and Athanasiou 2013, pp. 97–130). Deleuze's Nietzschean world is made up of forces and relations between forces; Judith Butler's Austinian world is made up of performatively political enunciative forces. Contents of machinic assemblages of desiring bodies engage these active and reactive forces in the process of articulating to subject positions of discourse formations, thereby enjoining and engaging a collective assemblage of enunciation.

23 Francis Jacques proposes a relational and dialogical theory of desire that he locates between the Hegelian idea of desire as a natural necessity (in which consciousness moves through appropriation and negation to self-consciousness) and the Levinasian idea of desire as an ethical awareness (of both separation from the other and respect for the other), an awareness that opens outward with no return to self. Jacques formulates his concept of desire in relational terms and argues that it flows along the lines of relations with others; see (Jacques 1991, pp. 74, 56–114).

Chapter 3

1 For a critically sensitive discussion of the ethical and practical challenges of Rwandan women participating in gaçaça trials, see Meghan Brenna Morris, *The Courage to Come Forward: Factors Related to Rwandan Women Bringing Cases of Genocide Rape to Women's Courts* (PhD dissertation, UC Berkeley, Fall 2011).

2 Jacques Semelin draws relations between transforming humans into animals and then exterminating the 'animals' in the interests of purifying a sociocultural formation, see (Semelin 2007, pp. 87–92).

3 Throughout much of this and the following section, I trace rather closely and in linear fashion Deleuze's reading of Bergson's *Time and Free Will, Matter and Memory, Creative Evolution* and *Mind-Energy* with particular focus on the first two chapters of Deleuze's text, 'Intuition as Method' and 'Duration as Immediate Datum'; see (Deleuze, 1991, pp. 13–49. I am also relying on Valentine Moullard-Leonard's nuanced study of Deleuze and Bergson complementarities and contrasts in their formulations of transcendental thought and the virtual; see particularly Chapter 4 (Moulard-Leonard 2008, pp. 89–104).

4 Tamsin Lorraine relies extensively on Deleuze's reading of Bergson, particularly with reference to the concept of the interval in her explication of Deleuze and Guattari's immanent ethics and feminist cartographies; see (Lorraine 2011, pp. 1–29; 57–113).
5 For Deleuze's elegant discussion of Bergson's example of the duration of a sugar cube, see (Deleuze 1991, pp. 31–2).
6 I make much more use of Deleuze's figuring of intuition as the methodical movement of emerging from our own duration when I take up the concept of 'witnessing' and 'mediating' in Chapter 5. For now, see his discussion of that process in relation to Chronos and Aion (Deleuze 1991, pp. 32–3).
7 For his synoptic account of the two forms of time, see (Hughes 2008, pp. 25–7); Hughes elaborates these conceptions throughout his text.
8 I am referring here to her sustained discussion of ethics, trauma and counter-memory (Lorraine 2011, pp. 115–45).
9 I am faithfully following Hughes' explication of Deleuze's reading of Nietzsche's formulation of the eternal return; see (Hughes 2008, pp. 37–8).
10 For Deleuze's discussion of these two facets, see (Deleuze 1991, p. 34).
11 I am referring here to Bergson's first chapter of *Matter and Memory* and his decomposition of Representation. See Deleuze's discussion of that section of *Matter and Memory* and *Time and Free Will* (Deleuze 1991, pp. 53–4).
12 Although he does not address trauma directly, Deleuze's discussion of the eternal return of difference rather than of the same is of pivotal importance to my conception of trauma; see (Deleuze 1991, pp. 59–60).
13 At this point I am drawing on (Deleuze and Guattari 1987, pp. 399–400).
14 For a more technical explication of the relations of evens and singular truths, see (Badiou 2001, pp. 40–57; 2005a, pp. 127–45; 2005b, pp. 173–261; and Hallward 2003, pp. 107–51).
15 For a detailed explication of an example of a radical break and a subsequent incorporeal transformation with respect to St Paul, see (Badiou 2003, pp. 4–30).
16 I am referring specifically to Jean Hatzfeld's two volumes, one with accounts from the Rwandan killers and one with accounts of Rwandan survivors; see (Hatzfeld 2005, 2006).
17 For a collected account of these concepts, see (Bonta and Protevi 2004, pp. 107–8).
18 (Bonta and Protevi 2004, p. 120) explicate these relations in greater detail.
19 A more complete historical account of this moment is available in (Semelin 2007, pp. 187–8).
20 (Semelin 2007, pp. 184–6) provides more detail of this crucial moment.
21 Erinn Cunniff Gilson makes a compelling argument for an ethics between Deleuze and feminism; see (Gilson 2011, pp. 63–88).

Chapter 4

1 For their thinking of smooth and striated spaces and stratification, see Deleuze and Guattari, *ATP*, pp. 385, 441, 474–5, 479, 481, 492; For a more extended discussion of 'uneasy peace' in this context, see Bonta and Protevi, 2004), p. 144.

2 Josias Semujanga provides an in-depth historical contextualization of the Rwandan genocide; as a Rwandan born historian, he provides a somewhat different interpretation of the Event than do several of the more influential historical accounts written by Europeans; see (Semujanga 2013, pp. 78–90).

3 Phil Clark, contributing to the Cambridge Studies in Law and Society series, bases his book on extensive post-genocide fieldwork throughout Rwanda; see (Clark 2010, pp. 15–19).

4 For a more detailed account of the 1996–97 war in DRC, see (Human Rights Watch, 'What Kabila is Hiding: Civilian Killings and Impunity in Congo' October, 1997); see also (Clark 2010, p. 23). For detailed accounts of conditions in the refugee camps in Zaire, see (Halvorsen 1999, pp. 307–20).

5 For a detailed analysis of this second Congo war, see (International Crisis Group, 'Scramble for the Congo: Anatomy of an Ugly War', New York: International Crisis Group, 20 December 2000); see also ('The Worst War', *The New York Sunday Times*, Sunday, 16 December 2012, p. 7).

6 Deleuze and Guattari write: 'Could it be that it is at the moment the war machine ceases to exist, conquered by the State that it displays to the utmost its irreducibility that it scatters into thinking, loving, dying, or creating machines that have at their disposal vital or revolutionary powers capable of challenging the conquering State?' (Deleuze and Guattari 1987, p. 356). A nomadic war machine can be thought of as a counter-force to state-sponsored and sanctioned military apparati. The state seeks to appropriate the power (*puissance*) of a nomadic war machine, incorporating it into the state's sovereignty (*pouvoir*). A war machine as such, however, is external to the state, and its object is not war. Ironically, it could be argued that, its name notwithstanding, its object is creativity thought of as a smooth space maintained via pragmatic battles rather than wars, tactical movement without strategic possession, nomadic mobility through territory without sedentary occupation of it. Josias Semujanga writes of 'war machines' and 'propaganda machines' with no reference to Deleuze and Guattari, evidence of the power of those concepts; see (Semujanga 2003, pp. 31–47).

7 Six years after the genocide, the creative, self-organizing war machinic forces of the gaçaça process manifested in form and substance as the expression of the content of injustice and trauma in the attempt to produce transitional justice and to reconcile collective trauma.

8 I have in mind here the models of the five strongest truth commissions, that is, South Africa, Guatemala, Peru, Timor-Leste and Morocco. In each instance, the granting of amnesty was an enormously contentious issue that each of these truth commissions debated differently, given differences in actual material-semiotic conditions and local circumstances. Although gaçaça was not officially sanctioned to hear genocide cases until 2001, debates regarding its possible utility began shortly after the genocide, during 1995. Amnesty was rejected early on as an option on the grounds that it would inflame genocide survivor's desiring revenge/justice. For a thorough treatment of truth commissions – the five strongest mentioned above as well as twenty other less successful truth commissions – see (Haynes 2011, pp. 27–74). For a collection of essays addressing the morality of truth commissions, see (Rotberg and Thompson 2000). For a discussion of post-violence reconciliation on third-party intervention and forgiveness,

see (Rigby 2001). For essays addressing the localization of innovative transitional justice processes, see (Shaw and Waldorf 2010). For a detailed historical account of the debates surrounding the emergence of gaçaça in post-genocide Rwanda, see (Clark 2010, pp. 55–63). Marie Breen Smyth examines the conditions that predispose and prevent post-conflict recovery of truth and the production of justice, focusing on Northern Ireland; see (Smyth 2007). For an edited collection of provocative essays addressing the problems of theorizing post-conflict reconciliation, see (Hirsch 2012). For a study of reconciliation focusing on the politics of atrocity, see (Humphrey 2002).

9 For their elaborations of 'conceptual personae', see (Deleuze and Guattari 1994, pp. 63–5, 67–8, 71, 75, 77).

10 I am referring specifically to their usage of this relation between order-words and regime of signs in (Deleuze and Guattari 1986, p. 18).

11 The following description of the eight principles of a regime of signs is drawn from (Deleuze and Guattari 1987, pp. 117–20). For a synoptic discussion of 'regime of signs', see (Bonta and Protevi 2004, p. 134).

12 For a comparison of two of their formulations of schizoanalysis/Pragmatics, see (Deleuze and Guattari 1987, pp. 139, 145–6).

13 See (Deleuze and Guattari 1987, pp. 372–4). Eugene Holland points out that 'Evolution is thus a matter of what Deleuze and Guattari call "itineration" rather than "iteration" or reproduction according to universal law: it traces a path that can be followed rather than predicted' (Holland, 'Nomad Citizenship and Global Democracy', in Fuglsang and Sørensen (eds), 2006, p. 193). Holland's extension of Deleuze's and Guattari's distinction between 'itineration' and 'iteration' – the former characteristic of nomad science, the latter characteristic of Royal science – contextualizes and clarifies the differences, which is precisely my point here.

14 For their discussion of the six principles of connection and heterogeneity, see (Deleuze and Guattari 1987, pp. 7–14).

15 Tamsin Lorraine's treatment of theory, subjectivity and duration is founded on Deleuze and Guattari's immanent ethics; of particular relevance to my work is her discussion of feminist cartographies, bodies, time and intuition (Lorraine 2011, pp. 57–113).

16 For complementary discussions of discourse that bear on my formulation of conversing, see (DeLanda 2006, pp. 75–80) and (Deleuze and Guattari 1987, pp. 508–14).

17 For an ethnomethodological and conversation analytic explication of turn-taking, see (Sacks et al. 1974, pp. 696–735).

18 I am following the lead of Mladen Dolar here in his study of voice as he moves beyond Derrida's examination of phonocentrism and beyond the two conventional conceptions of voice as a vehicle of meaning and as a source of aesthetic appreciation to a third understanding – voice as a lever of thought. In doing so, Dolar focuses on linguistics, metaphysics and ethics of voice. Several of the implications of his conceptualization of voice as a lever of thought are extended in Chapter 5; see (Dolar 2006).

19 Perhaps the most notable exception to this critical claim is Pierre Bourdieu's work theorizing the logic of practice. In his earliest work on theory and logic of practice, he critiques objectivist theories as inadequate insofar as they are structuralist, atemporal representations. He writes: 'To restore to practice its practical truth, we

must . . . reintroduce time into the theoretical representation of practice which, being temporally structured is intrinsically defined by its *tempo*. The generative, organizing scheme which gives . . . improvised speech its argument, and attains conscious expression in order to work itself out, is an often imprecise but systematic principle of selection and realization, tending through steadily directed corrections, to eliminate accidents when they can be put to use, and to conserve even fortuitous successes'. . . . 'Because it produces its science of the social world against the implicit presuppositions of practical knowledge of the social world, objectivist knowledge is diverted from construction of the theory of practical knowledge of the social world, of which it at least produces the lack' (Bourdieu 1977, p. 4). For more extended discussion of temporality and structure, see (Bourdieu 1977, pp. 1–29).

20 I am referring here to Noam Chomsky's earlier work theorizing linguistic competence and performance; see (Chomsky 1957, 1968).

21 For discussions of holey space, see (Deleuze and Guattari 1987, pp. 413–5) and (Bonta and Protevi 2004, pp. 95–6).

22 Gilles Deleuze and Claire Parnet write: 'That's it, a rhizome. Embryos, trees, develop according to their genetic performation or their structural reorganizations. But the weed overflows by virtue of being restrained. It grows between. It is the path itself. The English and Americans, who are the least "author-like" of writers, have two particularly sharp directions which connect: that of the road and of the path, that of the grass and of the rhizome. . . . Henry Miller: "Grass only exists between the great non-cultivated spaces. It fills in the voids. *It grows between – among other things*." The flower is beautiful, the cabbage is useful, the poppy makes you crazy. But the grass is overflowing; it is a lesson in morality. The walk as act, as politics, as experimentation, as life: "I spread myself out like a fox BETWEEN the people that I know the best," says Virginia Woolf in her walk among the taxis' (Deleuze and Parnet, *Dialogues II*, 2002, p. 20). For a more extensive discussion, see (Deleuze and Guattari 1987, pp. 75–110).

23 Another example of the significance of this kind of conversing work is Allen Feldman's cultural, critical, ethnographic, theoretical work with the narratives of the body and political terror in Northern Ireland, see (Feldman 1991).

24 For his discussion of tactical and strategic ingenuity in relation to *la perruque*, or the art and skill of poaching and living in time, see (de Certeau 1984, pp. 29–42, 143–63, 165–76).

25 Julia Kristeva formulates this dialectical feature of conversations as the practice of producing symbolic language from semiotic desire. For Kristeva, *thetic subjects* leave an oceanic yet turbulent subjects-becoming domain of the *semiotic chora* (that which comes before language) and enter into the domain of the symbolic, the domain of language, logic, order, patriarchy and hierarchy. And the tensions between the semiotic and the symbolic never ultimately resolve. Instead, a thetic subject, as Kristeva insists, is a subject in process and on trial. Individuals are not fixed and unitary subjects; they are, rather, multiple, fluid non-linear processes – 'possible worlds'. Desire translates the semiotic into the symbolic, producing that which cannot go without saying. In that sense, conversational micropractices discursively digitize and thereby render symbolic the analogic *semiotic chora* (Kristeva 1984, pp. 21–106, *passim*). Stephan-Paul Martin takes up in literature, gender and politics what Kristeva addresses in psychoanalysis, namely, the semiotic chora and the thetic subject (Martin 1988, pp. 117–214, *passim*).

26 For an extended critique of linguistics along Deleuzean lines of thought and an assessment of the harm it has done, see (Jean-Jacques Lecercle 2002, pp. 8–40, 62–98).
27 For a discussion and critique of this perspective, see (Žižek 1994, pp. 1–33).
28 In addition to Kristeva's discussion of a thetic subject perpetually in process and on trial, see (Jacques 1991, pp. 56–114).
29 For their elaboration of autopoiesis and cognition, see (Maturana and Varela 1980 [1972]); for a more extended discussion intended for lay readers, see (Varela et al. 1991) and (Maturana and Varela 1992).
30 Michel de Certeau conceptualizes this phenomenon of cutting out and turning over in (de Certeau 1984, pp. 29–42, 165–76).

Chapter 5

1 Deleuze and Guattari are quoting Oswald Spengler here (Spengler 1932, p. 54).
2 'Redundancy' is one of many places where Gregory Bateson's work on cybernetics complements Deleuze and Guattari's thinking; the concept of plateau is another. For a consideration of these conceptual correspondences, see Bateson's cybernetic thinking regarding pattern and process, epistemology and ontology, and immanence and transcendence (Bateson 1972/2000, pp. 405–73).
3 For his detailed explication of *habitus* and its relations to structure and symbolic power, see (Bourdieu 1977, pp. 72–95, 143–58, 183–97); see also (Bourdieu 1980, pp. 52–65).
4 The following discussion of indirect and direct discourse follows the thinking of V. N. Vološinov's philosophy of language; see (Vološinov 1973, pp. 125–33, *passim*).
5 I am referring here to Alain Badiou's critique of contemporary ethics as a category of pious discourse, and communication ethics being preoccupied only with opinions. See (Badiou 2001, pp. 21–3, 48–52).
6 I am making reference here to expressions such as Alan Ginsburg's poem, 'Howl' and Gil Scott-Herrin's performative work with what would become 'beat', 'rap' and 'hip-hop'. But I am also referring to utterances and other forms of enunciating and expressing that exceed conventional linguistic conventions of syntax, semantics and grammaticality. Consider the annual days of remembrance in Rwanda during which ceremonies, expressions of collective grief and trauma exceed conventional linguistic expressions.
7 For Badiou, these are the requirements for an ethic of truths to be maintained and for a Subject to truth to sustain itself; see (Badiou 2001, pp. 40–57).
8 Mikhail Bakhtin contends that an utterance has three audiences – its addressor, its addressee and its superaddressee. The latter may be presumed to be either an actual or a virtual body, that is, a potential earth-bound corporeal interlocutor or a transcendent interlocutor, that is, a deity. For his explication of these relations, see (Bakhtin 1986, pp. 132–58).
9 Rosi Braidotti argues compellingly for an ethics of becoming-imperceptible that makes a similar case for an eco-systemic ontology; see (Braidotti 2006, pp. 133–59).
10 Deleuze and Guattari explicate this *geolinguistic* approach in their chapter on minor literature in (Deleuze and Guattari 1986, pp. 16–27).

11 Judith Butler extended speech-act theory, introduced by John Searle (1969), J. L. Austin (1970) and (1975), to feminist critical theory and discourse studies by recognizing the performativity of illocutionary force, enabling her to interrogate linguistic vulnerability, injurious speech, implicit censorship and discursive agency. See (Butler 1997).

12 Deleuze differentiates stammering from stuttering, that is, the stammering of language itself as opposed to a subject stuttering in enunciation; see (Deleuze and Guattari 1986, pp. 28–42) and (Deleuze and Parnet 1987/2002, pp. 1–35).

Afterword

1 See (Haley 1963), and (Sluzki and Ransom (1976) for examples of Bateson's influence on psychotherapy and family therapy, respectively.

2 This was an early attempt to formalize the analysis of war and foreign politics; see (Richardson 1956, pp. 1240–53). For another early but a more game theoretical and less mathematical approach to bargaining along these lines, see (Schelling 1963, 1978, pp. 7–43, 81–133).

3 Watzlawick et al. (1967) rely heavily on general systems theory as it was formulated in the 1950s and early 1960s by Bertalanffy 1950, 1956 and 1962; they also rely on the early work of Hall and Fagen 1956, who define a system as 'a set of objects together with relationships between the objects and their attributes' (p. 18). Objects are the component parts of the system, attributes are the properties of the objects and relationships tie the system together. See also Anthony Wilden, *Systems and Structures*.

4 Deleuze and Guattari (1987) write 15 essays, chapters or what they refer to as plateaus, by which they mean an opening onto a territory that sustains itself temporarily, a relatively smooth surface on which nomadic thinking can unfold. Plateau is a concept they borrow from Gregory Bateson's work on what he refers to as steps (or plateaus) to ecology of mind. It also plays a role in his summative volume; see Bateson 1972 [2000], and 1979. In this context, I am referring specifically to Deleuze and Guattari's fourth chapter on postulates of linguistics (pp. 75–110). See also Lecercle 2002, pp. 154–257 where he explicates some of Deleuze's pivotal concepts regarding linguistics and pragmatics. By way of illustration, he reads portions of Dickens, Deleuze, Joyce, cummings, Woolf and Kipling. My focus is communicative rather than literary, yet I find Lecercle's extension of Deleuze's conceptualization of language and linguistics very useful in recasting communication theory in terms of a new pragmatics that makes possible the concept of nomadic discourse.

5 'We call *order-words*, not a particular category of explicit statements (for example, in the imperative), but the relation of every word or statement to implicit presuppositions, in other words, to speech acts that are, and can only be, accomplished in the statement. Order-words do not concern commands only, but every act that is linked to statements by a "social obligation". Every statement displays this link, directly or indirectly. Questions, promises are order-words. The only possible definition of language is the set of all order-words, implicit presuppositions and speech acts current in a language at a given moment' (Deleuze and Guattari 1987, p. 79).

6 In this respect, Deleuze and Guattari's concept of 'order-words' closely resembles J. L. Austin's concepts in speech-act theory and its perlocutionary and illocutionary forces and effects; see Austin 1975. For a more detailed discussion of indirect speech, direct speech and quasi-direct speech, see Vološinov 1973.

7 I am relying on the concept of settlement here rather than on concepts such as solution, resolution, accords, agreements and so forth insofar as settlement has spatial, geographical, topographical connotations that I wish to take advantage of. Resolution, on the other hand, has more cognitive and rationalist implications, that is, figuring out yet another solution to a problem that had been solved earlier and has somehow become unsolved. Of course, there is a set of connotations pertaining to chemistry in which a solution always leaves behind sediment, which is a necessary by-product of a mixture coming to solution. Nonetheless, the spatial, geographical, territorial and topological connotations of settlement are crucial to this project of rethinking conflict as immanent, communication as discourse, and resolution as settlement. Obviously, the tensions between settlement and nomadicity play a pivotal role.

8 Both Freud's psychoanalytic formulation of desire and Lacan's structuralist reformulation of psychoanalysis understand desire to be the result of and to be driven by a lack within a human subject produced by the split caused when a human subject enters the world of language, the world of consciousness, and splits from the world of the unconscious. In effect, Freud and Lacan argue that what is lost in the translation of moving from the unconscious to consciousness can never be recuperated. Deleuze and Guattari, in their sustained critique of Freudian and Lacanian psychoanalysis, think in terms of desiring-production that does away with the distinction of consciousness and the unconscious, and they formulate desire not as a result of what is lost, but rather as the excess and abundance of a life energy into which we are born, preceding the appearance of any particular body and continuing indefinitely, long after the demise of particular bodies.

9 An assemblage is defined as a neighbourhood rather than as a system. A key difference that distinguishes a system from an assemblage is that the former organizes hierarchically or concentrically within itself, whereas the latter organizes rhizomatically around itself, spreading out unevenly. Deleuze and Guattari juxtapose the concept of rhizome to the concept of arborescence. A rhizome resembles a tangled root ball of a plant, or the way in which crab grass grows, that is, from the middle outward, or the way in which a conversation unfolds in non-linear progression. Arborescent growth resembles a tree, with a trunk and branches growing out from the trunk, or a hierarchy with smaller elements contained within larger elements, or other forms of linear progression. A plane of desire consists in flows of desiring energy, and series of cuts, breaks and ruptures that punctuate and code it, forming sequences and series. Lecercle points out that this conception of assemblage avoids the sedentary imperialism of representation and the tyranny of an egoistic subject. For the complete development of his critique, see Lecercle 2002, pp. 174–201. This conception of assemblage is not far removed from Watzlawick, Beavin and Jackson's thinking of analogue and digital communication, the former corresponding to flows of desire, the latter corresponding to cuts and breaks that code a flow.

10 Deleuze and Guattari at times qualify the concept of desire with the adjective 'machinic' in order to emphasize the point that desire is agency without a subject. They are at work disarticulating the supposedly 'natural' articulation of agency and subject. Their point is that such articulations are accomplishments, productions really. The articulation of discourse to desire produces subjects with discursive

identities (i.e. with fixed places within discourse) who are assumed to author original utterances that then accomplish results. By 'machinic', Deleuze and Guattari do not intend 'mechanistic' nor do they intend 'machine-like'. 'Machinic' is intended to signify the energy, force and agency of desire, but desire consisting in partial objects and partial-bodies of things animate and inanimate, that do not constitute subjects. Subjects are not produced until desire articulates to discourse and its slots for the partial objects of desire to congregate, that is, subject positions of discourse. For its part, discourse has subject and object positions, but no bodies until desiring partial-bodies and objects articulate to machinic desire.

11 By 'collective enunciation', which is a concept created by Deleuze and Guattari, I mean that indefinitely large and unbounded domain of all that has been enunciated. Utterances in the process of being enunciated can draw upon all that which can be taken for granted, assumed as given, natural, part of cultural life.

12 'Interpellate' is a concept Louis Althusser 1971 created for his project of re-reading Karl Marx through a structuralist lens. 'Interpellate' is a verb Althusser used to account for how subjects and subjectivity could be understood in a structuralist paradigm that had difficulty accounting for both. For Althusser, discourse hailed bodies as subjects. For example, a police officer calling out, 'You, stop!' Everyone within earshot would probably turn to the voice, assuming they had been hailed, that is, addressed by the voice of authority.

13 Lecercle credits Jacques Lacan as the pre-eminent thinker of the human psyche as a machine; see Lacan 1977.

14 This is the conception of system that Watzlawick, Beavin and Jackson inherited from general systems theory. However, they invoke the concept of system in their pragmatics of human communication in terms of second cybernetics and the cybernetic epistemology/ontology of Gregory Bateson. Watzlawick, Beavin and Jackson were not content with a purely synchronic structure to represent the systemic organization of communication. Their concern was to push the concept of structure beyond spatiality towards temporality. Deleuze and Guattari's post-humanist ontology, however, extends this spatiotemporal form of structure beyond the boundaries of human communication towards assemblages of material bodies of machinic desire. For a more complete and technical discussion of this line of thinking, consult the source from which my work draws heavily; see Lecercle 2002, pp. 184–93.

15 For an extension and elaboration of this line of thinking introduced by Deleuze and Guattari 1987, pp. 232–310, *passim*, see Lecercle 2002, pp. 184–93.

16 I am using the term 'articulate' as a verb rather than as an adjective, recognizing the two senses of that verb, which Stuart Hall not only taught us in so much of his theoretical and political work in cultural studies. One sense, of course, is to utter – to bring into being in the act of speaking or writing. But the second sense, the sense in which Hall often uses that verb, and the sense in which I use it throughout the book, is the sense of being connected or hitched in the manner in which a semi-tractor is articulated to its trailer. Both tractor and trailer can and do move somewhat independent of one another, even though they are always connected to one another. It is in this sense that structure and machine, discourse and desire are articulated. See Slack 1996, pp. 112–27; 2006, pp. 223–31; and Grossberg 1996, pp. 131–50.

17 See Deleuze and Guattari 1977, pp. 1–22.

18 This section on the syntheses of libidinality/desire is obviously relying heavily on the first section of Deleuze and Guattari's (1977) first translated version of 'The Desiring Machines' (pp. 1–50).

19 For an examination of language and the method of dramatization of the political, see (Mackenzie and Porter 2011, pp. 13032, 73–92).

20 These are concepts Deleuze and Guattari created to refer to two types of groups: a 'subjected group' is a group with a stable and fixed identity such that as new members join, they assimilate to and accommodate a group's identity in ways that do not alter a group's identity. Individual identity is subjugated to the group identity. A group-subject, on the other hand, refers to a group whose identity changes with the addition of any new member. A 'group subject' operates as a collage of all of its members.

Bibliography

Adelman, H. and Suhrke, A. (1999), *The Path of a Genocide: The Rwanda Crisis from Uganda to Zaire*. New Brunswick, NJ: Transaction Publishers.

AI(10 January 2005), 'Rwanda: Human rights organization forced to close down', AI Index, AFR, 47/001/2005.

—(4 April 1996), 'Rwanda: Two Years After the Genocide – Rights in the Balance (Open Letter to President Pasteur Bizimunga)', AI Index Africa 47/02/96.

—(April 2000), 'Rwanda: The Troubled Course of Justice', AI Index AFR 47/10/00, pp. 3–6.

Althusser, L. (1971), *Lenin and Philosophy and Other Essays*. London: New Left Books.

Assefa, H. (2002), 'Embody peace', in J. P. Lederach and J. M. Jenner (eds), *Into the Eye of the Storm: A Handbook of International Peacebuilding*. San Francisco: Jossey-Bass, pp. 283–90.

Austin, J. L. (1970), *Philosophical Papers*. Oxford: Oxford University Press.

—(1975), *How to do Things with Words*. Cambridge, MA: Harvard University Press.

Avruch, K. (1998), *Culture & Conflict Resolution*. Washington, D.C.: United States Institute of Peace.

—(2013), *Context and Pretext in Conflict Resolution: Culture, Identity, Power, and Practice*. Boulder: Paradigm.

Avruch, K. and Black, P. W. (1987), 'A generic theory of conflict resolution: A critique'. *Negotiation Journal* 1: 87–96.

Avruch, K., Black, P. W. and Joseph A. Scimecca (eds), (1998), *Conflict Resolution: Cross-Cultural Perspectives*. Westport, Con.: Praeger.

Badiou, A. (2001), *Ethics: An Essay on the Understanding of Evil*, trans. P. Hallward. London: Verso.

—(2003), *Saint Paul: The Foundations of Universalism*, trans. R. Brassier. Stanford: Stanford University Press.

—(2005), *Infinite Thought*, trans. O. Feltham and J. Clemens. London: Continuum.

Bakhtin, M. (1984), *Problems of Dostoevsky's Poetics*, trans. C. Emerson. Minneapolis: University of Minnesota Press.

—(1986), 'The problem of speech genres', in C. Emerson and M. Holquist (ed.), *M. M. Bakhtin: Speech Genres & Other Late Essays*, trans. V. W. McGee. Austin: University of Texas Press, pp. 66–102.

Barthes, R. (1977), *Leçon*. Paris: Seuil.

Barrett, J. T. and Barrett, J. P. (2004), *A History of Alternative Dispute Resolution*. San Francisco: Jossey-Bass.

Bateson, G. (1972/2001), *Steps to an Ecology of Mind*, forward. M. C. Bateson. Chicago: University of Chicago Press.

Baugh, B. (2005), 'Transcendental Empiricism + Politics', in A. Parr (ed.), *The Deleuze Dictionary*. New York: Columbia University Press, pp. 284–5.

Bertalanffy, L. (1950), 'An outline of general system theory'. *British Journal of the Philosophy of Science* 1: 134–65.

—(1956), 'General system theory'. *General System Yearbook* 1: 1–10.

—(1962), 'General system theory – A critical review'. *General Systems Yearbook* 7: 1–20.

Bignall, S. and Patton, P. (eds), (2010), *Deleuze and the Postcolonial*. Edinburgh: Edinburgh University Press.
Bonta, M. and Protevi, J. (2004), *Deleuze and Geophilosophy: A Guide and Glossary*. Edinburgh: Edinburgh University Press.
Borradori, G. (2003), *Philosophy in a Time of Terror*. Chicago: University of Chicago Press.
Bourdieu, P. (1977 [1972]), *Outline of a Theory of Practice*, trans. R. Nice. Cambridge: Cambridge University Press.
—(1990 [1980]), *The Logic of Practice*, trans. R. Nice. Stanford: Stanford University Press.
—(1998 [1994]), *Practical Reason*. Stanford: Stanford University Press.
Braidotti, R. (2005), 'Schizophrenia', in A. Parr (ed.), *The Deleuze Dictionary*. New York: Columbia University Press.
Buchanan, I. (2000), *Deleuzism: A Metacommentary*. Durham: Duke University Press.
Buchanan, I. and Lambert, G. (eds), (2005), *Deleuze and Space*. Edinburgh: Edinburgh University Press.
Buchanan, I. and Parr, A. (eds), (2006), *Deleuze and the Contemporary World*. Edinburgh: Edinburgh University Press.
Buchanan, I. and Thoburn, N. (eds), (2008), *Deleuze and Politics*. Edinburgh: Edinburgh University Press.
Burton, J. W. (1969), *Conflict and Communication: The Use of Controlled Communication in International Relations*. London: Macmillan.
—(1979), *Deviance, Terrorism and War*. New York: St. Martin's.
—(1990), *Conflict: Resolution and Provention*. New York: St. Martin's.
Burton, J. W. and Sandole, D. (October 1986), 'Generic theory: The Basis of Conflict Resolution'. *Negotiation Journal* 2: 333–4.
Bush, R. A. B. and Folger, J. P. (1994), *The Promise of Mediation: Responding to Conflict through Empowerment and Recognition*. San Francisco: Jossey-Bass.
Butler, J. (1997), *Excitable Speech: The Politics of the Performative*. New York: Routledge.
Butler, J. and Athanasiou, A. (2013), *Dispossession: The Performative in the Political*. Cambridge: Polity.
Canetti, E. (1960), *Crowds and Power*. New York: Continuum.
Certeau, M. D. (1984), *The Practice of Everyday Life*, trans. S. F. Randall, Berkeley: University of California Press.
Chomsky, N. (1957), *Syntactic Structures*. The Hague: Mouton.
—(1965), *Aspects of a Theory of Syntax*. Cambridge: MIT Press.
—(1968), *Language and Mind*. New York: Harcourt, Brace and World.
—(1972), *Studies on Semantics in Generative Grammar*. The Hague: Mouton.
—(1995). *The Minimalist Program*. Cambridge: MIT Press.
Christiano, T. (2003), *Philosophy & Democracy*. Oxford: Oxford University Press.
Clark, P. (2010), *The Gacaca Courts, Post-Genocide Justice and Reconciliation in Rwanda*. Cambridge: Cambridge University Press.
Clifford, J. (1988), *The Predicament of Culture: Twentieth-Century Ethnography, Literature, and Art*. Cambridge, MA: Harvard University Press.
Clifford, J. and Marcus, G. E. (eds), (1986), *Writing Culture: The Poetics and Politics of Ethnography*. Berkeley: University of California Press.
Colebrook, C. (2002a), *Understanding Deleuze*. Crows Nest, Australia: Allen & Unwin.
—(2000b), *Gilles Deleuze*. London: Routledge.
—(2006a), *Deleuze: A Guide for the Perplexed*. New York: Continuum.
—(2006b), 'Deleuze and the Meaning of Life', in C. V. Boundas (ed.), *Deleuze and Philosophy*. Edinburgh: Edinburgh University Press, pp. 121–32.

Coleman, R. and Ringrose, J. (eds), (2013), *Deleuze and Research Methodologies*. Edinburgh: Edinburgh University Press.
Crisafulli, P. and Redmond, A. (2012), *Rwanda, Inc.: How a Devastated Nation Became an Economic Model for the Developing World*. New York: Palgrave MacMillan.
Crocker, C. A., Hampson, F. O. and Aall, P. (1999), *Herding Cats: Multiparty Mediation in a Complex World*. Washington, D.C.: United States Institute of Peace.
DeLanda, M. (2006), *A New Philosophy of Society: Assemblage Theory and Social Complexity*. London: Continuum.
Deleuze, G. (1983 [1962]), *Nietzsche & Philosophy*, trans. H. Tomlinson. New York: Columbia University Press.
—(1988 [1970]), *Spinoza: Practical Philosophy*, trans. R. Hurley. San Fransisco: City Light.
—(1990 [1969]), *The Logic of Sense*, trans. M. Lester and C. Stivale. New York: Columbia University Press.
—(1991 [1966]), *Bergsonism*, trans. H. Tomlinson and B. Habberjam. New York: Zone Books.
—(1994 [1968]), *Difference and Repetition*, trans. P. Patton. New York: Columbia University Press.
—(1995 [1990]), *Negotiations*, trans. M. Joughin. New York: Columbia University Press.
—(2001), *Pure Immanence: Essays on a Life*, trans. A. Boyman. New York: Zone Books.
Deleuze, G. and Guattari, F. (1977 [1972]), *Anti-Oedipus: Capitalism and Schizophrenia*, trans. R. Hurley, M. Seem and H. R. Lane, New York: Viking Press.
—(1987 [1980]), *A Thousand Plateaus*, trans. B. Massumi. Minneapolis, MN: University of Minnesota Press.
—(1994 [1991]), *What is Philosophy*, trans. H. Tomlinson and G. Burchell. New York: Columbia University Press.
Deleuze, G. and Parnet, C. (2002 [1977]), *Dialogues II*, trans. H. Tomlinson and B. Habberjam, London: Continuum.
Dellaire, R. (2003), *Shake Hands with the Devil*. New York: Carroll & Graf.
Des Forges, A. (1999), *Leave None to Tell the Story: Genocide in Rwanda*. New York: Human Rights Watch.
Deutsch, M. and Coleman, P. T. (2000), *The Handbook of Conflict Resolution: Theory and Practice*. San Fransisco: Jossey-Bass.
Docherty, J. S. (2001), *Learning Lessons from Waco: When the Parties Bring their Gods to the Negotiation Table*. Syracuse: Syracuse University Press.
Dolar, M. (2006), *A Voice and Nothing More*. Cambridge: MIT Press.
Druckman, D. (2005), *Doing Research: Methods of Inquiry for Conflict Analysis*. Thousand Oaks, CA: Sage.
Elechi, O. O. (2006), *Doing Justice without the State: The Afikpo (Ehugbo) Nigeria Model*. New York: Routledge.
Ellis, D. G. (1999), *Crafting Society: Ethnicity, Class, and Communication Theory*. Mahwah, NJ: Lawrence Erlbaum.
—(2006), *Transforming Conflict: Communication and Ethnopolitical Conflict*. Lanham, MD: Rowman & Littlefield.
Eltringham, N. (2004), *Accounting for Horror: Post-Genocide Debates in Rwanda*. London: Pluto.
Feldman, A. (1991), *Formations of Violence: The Narrative of the Body and Political Terror in Northern Ireland*. Chicago: University of Chicago Press.
Fuglsang, M. and Sørensen, B. M. (eds), (2006), *Deleuze and the Social*. Edinburgh: Edinburgh University Press.
Giddens, A. (1998), *The Third Way*. Cambridge: Oxford University Press.

Gilson, E. C. (2011), 'Responsive becoming: Ethics between Deleuze and feminism', in N. Jun and D. W. Smith (eds), *Deleuze and Ethics*. Edinburgh: Edinburgh University Press.
Gourevitch, P. (1998), *We Wish to Inform you that Tomorrow We will be Killed with our Families*. New York: Picador.
—(2009), 'The Life After', *The New Yorker*, 4 May, 36–49.
Gramsci, A. (1994), *The Antonio Gramsci Reader: Selected Writing 1916–1935*, ed. D. Forgacs. New York: New York University Press.
Grossberg, L. (1992), *We Gotta Get Out Of This Place: Popular Conservatism and Postmodern Culture*. New York: Routledge.
—(1996), 'Identity and Cultural Studies – Is That All There Is?' in S. Hall and P. du Gay (eds), *Questions of Cultural Identity*. London: Sage.
—(1997), *Bringing it all Back Home: Essays on Cultural Studies*. Durham: Duke University Press.
Guattari, F. (2011 [1979]), *The Machinic Unconscious: Essays in Schizoanalysis*, trans. T. Adkins. Los Angeles: Semiotext(e).
Guillaume, L. and Hughes, J. (eds), (2011), *Deleuze and the Body*. Edinburgh: Edinburgh University Press.
Guttman, A. and Thompson, D. (1996), *Democracy and Disagreement*. Cambridge, MA: Belknap.
Habermas, J. (1996). *Between Facts and Norms: Contributions to a Discourse Theory of Law and Democracy*, trans. William Rehg. Cambridge, MA: MIT Press.
Haley, J. (1963), *Strategies of Psychotherapy*. New York: Grune & Stratton.
Hall, A. D. and Fagen, R. E. (1956), 'Definition of system'. *General Systems Yearbook* 1: 18–28.
Hall, S. (1980), 'Race, articulation and societies structured in dominance', in *UNESCO Sociological Theories: Race and Colonialism*. Paris: UNESCO, p. 325.
—(1985), 'Signification, representation, ideology: Althusser and the post-structuralism debates'. *Critical Studies in Mass Communication* 2: 91–114.
—(1986a), 'Gramsci's relevance for the study of race and ethnicity'. *Journal of Communication Inquiry* 10: 5–27.
—(1986b), 'On postmodernism and articulation: An interview with Stuart Hall', ed. Lawrence Grossberg. *Journal of Communication Inquiry* 10: 45–60. (reprinted in Morley and Chen, 1996, pp. 131–50).
—(ed.), (1997), *Representation: Cultural Representations and Signifying Practices*. London: Sage.
Hall, S. and du Gay, P. (eds), (1996), *Questions of Cultural Identity*. London: Sage.
Hallward, P. (2001), 'Translator's introduction', in *Ethics: An Essay on the Understanding of Evil*. London: Verso, pp. vii–xxxvi.
Halvorsen, K. (1999), 'Protection and humanitarian assistance in the refugee camps in Zaire', in H. Adelman and A. Suhrke (eds), *The Path of a Genocide: The Rwanda Crisis from Uganda to Zaire*. New Brunswick, NJ: Transaction Publishers.
Hardt, M. and Negri, A. (2000), *Empire*. Cambridge, MA: Harvard University Press.
—(2004), *Multitude: War and Democracy in the Age of Empire*. New York: Penguin.
Harries-Jones, P. (1995), *Ecological Understanding and Gregory Bateson*. Toronto: University of Toronto Press.
Hatzfeld, J. (2005), *Machete Season: The Killers in Rwanda Speak*. New York: Farrar, Straus and Giroux.
—(2006), *Life Laid Bare: The Survivors in Rwanda Speak*. New York: Other Press.
Haynes, P. B. (2011), *Unspeakable Truths: Transitional Justice and the Challenge of Truth Commissions*, 2nd edn. New York: Routledge.

Herman, E. S. and Peterson, D. (2011), *The Politics of Genocide*. New York: Monthly Review.
Hirsch, A. K. (2012), *Theorizing Post-Conflict Reconciliation: Agonism, Restitution and Repair*. London: Routledge.
Holland, E. (1999), *Deleuze and Guattari's Anti-Oedipus: Introduction to Schizoanalysis*. New York: Routledge.
—(2006), 'Nomad citizenship and global democracy', in M. Fuglsang and B. M. Sørensen (eds), *Deleuze and the Social*. Edinburgh: Edinburgh University Press, pp. 191–206.
Honneth, A. (1995), *The Struggle for Recognition: The Moral Grammar of Social Conflicts*, trans. J. Anderson. Cambridge, MA: MIT Press.
Hopkins, J. (ed.), (2000), *The Art of Peace: Nobel Peace Laureates Discuss Human Rights, Conflict and Reconciliation*. Ithaca: Snow Lion.
Hughes, J. (2008), *Deleuze and the Genesis of Representation*. London: Continuum.
Humphrey, M. (2002), *The Politics of Atrocity and Reconciliation: From Terror to Trauma*. New York: Routledge.
Ilibagiza, I. (2006), *Left to Tell: Discovering God Amidst the Rwandan Holocaust*. New York: Hay House, Inc.
International Crisis Group (20 December 2000), 'Scramble for the Congo: Anatomy of an Ugly War'. New York: International Crisis Group.
Jabri, V. (1996), *Discourses on Violence: Conflict Analysis Reconsidered*. Manchester: Manchester University Press.
Jacques, F. (1991), *Difference and Subjectivity: Dialogue and Personal Identity*, trans. A. Rothwell. New Haven: Yale University Press.
Johnston, D. M. (2011), *Religion, Terror, and Error: U.S. Foreign Policy and the Spiritual Engagement*. Santa Barbara: Praeger.
Jun, N. and Smith, D. W. (eds), (2011), *Deleuze and Ethics*. Edinburgh: Edinburgh University Press.
King, N. (2000), *Memory, Narrative, Identity: Remembering the Self*. Edinburgh: Edinburgh University Press.
Kriesberg, L. and Thorson, S. J. (1991), *Timing and the De-escalation of International Conflict*. Syracuse, NY: Syracuse University Press.
Kristeva, J. (1984[1974]), *Revolution in Poetic Language*, trans. M. Waller. New York: Columbia University Press.
Lacan, J. (1977), *Ecrit: A Selection*, trans. A. Sheridan. London: Tavistock.
Laclau, E. and Mouffe, C. (1985), *Hegemony and Socialist Strategy: Towards a Radical Democratic Politics*. London: Verso.
Lakoff, G. (2002), *Moral Politics: How Liberals and Conservatives Think*. Chicago: University of Chicago Press.
Larson, C. C. (2009), *As We Forgive: Stories of Reconciliation from Rwanda*. Grand Rapids: Zondervan.
Lawrence, B. B. and Karim, A. (eds), (2007), *On Violence: A Reader*. Duke: Duke University Press.
Lecercle, J-J. (2002), *Deleuze and Language*. New York: Palgrave Macmillan.
Lederach, J. P. (1997), *Building Peace: Sustainable Reconciliation in Divided Societies.* Washington, DC: United States Institute of Peace Press.
Lederach, J. P., Al-Mazri, M. and Litwiller, R. A. (2002), 'The Simplicity of Peacebuilding: An Interview with Adam Curle', in J. P. Lederach and J. M. Jenner (eds), *Into the Eye of the Storm: A Handbook of International Peacebuilding*. San Francisco: Jossey-Bass.
Lorraine, T. (2011), *Deleuze and Guattari's Immanent Ethics: Theory, Subjectivity, Duration*. Albany, NY: State University of New York Press.

Lyotard, J. F. (1988), *The Differend: Phrases in Dispute*, trans. G. Van Den Abbeele. Minneapolis: University of Minnesota Press.
Maalouf, A. (2001), *In The Name of Identity: Violence and the Need to Belong*. New York: Arcade.
Mackenzie, I. and Porter, R. (2011), *Dramatizing the Political: Deleuze and Guattari*. London: Palgrave MacMillan.
Marcus, G. E. and Fischer, M. J. (1986), *Anthropology as Cultural Critique: An Experimental Moment in the Human Sciences*. Chicago: University of Chicago Press.
Martin, S-P. (1988), *Open Form and the Feminine Imagination (The Politics of Reading in Twentieth-Century Writing)*. Washington, D.C.: Maisonneuve Press.
Maturana, H. R. and Varela, F. J. (1980), *Autopoiesis and Cognition: The Realization of the Living*. Dordrecht: D. Reidel.
—(1992), *The Tree of Knowledge: The Biological Roots of Human Understanding*, revised edn. Boston: Shambala.
Mayer, B. S. (2004), *Beyond Neutrality: Confronting the Crisis in Conflict Resolution*. San Francisco: Jossey-Bass.
—(2009), *Staying With Conflict: A Strategic Approach to Ongoing Disputes*. San Fransisco: Jossey-Bass.
Melvern, L. (2000), *A People Betrayed: The Role of the West in Rwanda's Genocide*. London: Zed Books.
Morris, M. B. (2011), 'The Courage to Come Forward: Factors Related to Rwandan Women Bringing Cases of Genocide Rape to Women's Courts', PhD. diss. UC Berkeley.
Mouffe, C. (2000), *The Democratic Paradox*. London: Verso.
Moulard-Leonard, V. (2008), *Bergson-Deleuze Encounters: Transcendental Experience and the Thought of the Virtual*. Albany, NY: State University of New York Press.
Murphy, A. V. (2012), *Violence and the Philosophical Imaginary*. New York: State University of New York Press.
Gettleman, J. 'The worst war', *New York Sunday Times*, 16 December 2012, p. 7.
Nader, L. (2001), 'Harmony Models and the Construction of Law', in P. K. Chew (ed.), *The Conflict & Culture Reader*. New York: New York University Press.
Naím, M. (2013). *The End of Power*. New York: Basic Books.
Newbury, C. (1988), *The Cohesion of Oppression: Clientship and Ethnicity in Rwanda, 1860–1960*. New York: Columbia University Press.
Oetzel, J. G. and Ting-Toomey, S. (eds), (2006), *The Sage Handbook of Conflict Communication: Integrating Theory, Research, and Practice*. Thousand Oaks, CA: Sage.
Parker, J., Samantrai, R., Romero, M. (eds), (2010), *Interdisciplinarity and Social Justice*. New York: State University of New York Press.
Parr, A. (2005), *The Deleuze Dictionary*. New York: Columbia University Press.
—(2008), *Deleuze and Memorial Culture: Desire, Singular Memory and the Politics of Trauma*. Edinburgh: Edinburgh University Press.
Pearce, W. B. and Littlejohn, S. W. (1997), *Moral Conflict: When Social Worlds Collide*. Thousand Oaks, CA: Sage.
Peskin, V. (2008), *International Justice in Rwanda and the Balkans: Virtual Trials and the Struggle for State Cooperation*. Cambridge: Cambridge University Press.
Prunier, G. (1998), *The Rwanda Crisis: History of a Genocide*. London: Hurst & Co.
—(1999), 'Opération Turquoise: A humanitarian escape from a political dead end', in H. Adelman and A. Suhrke (eds), *The Path of Genocide: The Rwanda Crisis from Uganda to Zaire*. New Brunswick, NJ: Transaction Publishers, pp. 294–301.
Rawls, J. (1972), *A Theory of Justice*. Cambridge, MA: Harvard University Press.

—(1993), *Political Liberalism*, revised edn. New York: Columbia University Press.
Rabie, M. (1994), *Conflict Resolution and Ethnicity*. Westport, CN: Praeger.
Rajchman, J. (2001), 'Introduction', in G. Deleuze (ed.), *Pure Immanence: Essays on a Life*. London: Zone.
Ramsbotham, O. (2010), *Transforming Violent Conflict: Radical Disagreement, Dialogue and Survival*. New York: Routledge.
Rancière, J. (2004[2000]), *The Politics of Aesthetics*, trans. G. Rockhill. London: Continuum.
—(2006), *The Politics of Aesthetics*. London: Continuum.
Regehr, E. (1996), 'Armed conflict in the world in 1992'. *Ploughshares Monitor* 8: 13–17.
Reidy, D. A. and Sellers, M. N. S. (2005), *Universal Human Rights: Moral Order in a Divided World*. Lanham, MD: Rowman and Littlefield.
Reyntjens, F. (2004), 'Rwanda ten years on: From genocide to dictatorship'. *African Affairs* 103: 208–10.
Richardson, L. F. (1956), 'Mathematics of war and foreign politics', in J. R. Newman (ed.), *The World of Mathematics*, vol. 2. New York: Simon and Schuster, pp. 1240–53.
Rigby, A. (2001), *Justice and Reconciliation: After the Violence*. Boulder, CO: Lynne Rienner.
Rotberg, R. I. (ed.), (2003), *State Failure and State Weakness in a Time of Terror*. Washington, DC: Brookings Institution Press and World Peace Foundation.
Rotberg, R. I. and Thompson D. (2000), *Truth and Justice: The Morality of Truth Commissions*. Princeton: Princeton University Press.
Rothman, J. (1997), *Resolving Identity-Based Conflict: In Nations, Organizations, and Communities*. San Francisco: Jossey-Bass.
Roy, B. (1994), *Some Trouble With Cows: Making Sense of Conflict*. Berkeley: University of California Press.
Sacks, H., Schegloff, E. A. and Jefferson, G. (1974), 'A simplest systematics for the organization of turn-taking for conversation'. *Language* 50: 696–735.
Saunders, H. H. (1999), *A Public Peace Process: Sustained Dialogue to Transform Racial and Ethnic Conflicts*. New York: St. Martin's Press.
Schelling, T. C. (1963), *The Strategy of Conflict*. New York: Oxford University Press.
Searle, J. R. (1969), *Speech Acts: An Essay in the Philosophy of Language*. Cambridge: Cambridge University Press.
Sebarenzi, J. (2009), *God Sleeps in Rwanda: A Journey of Transformation*. New York: Atria.
Semelin, J. (2007), *Purify and Destroy: The Political Uses of Massacre and Genocide*. New York: Columbia University Press.
Semujanga, J. (2003), *Origins of Rwandan Genocide*. Amherst, NY: Humanity Books.
Sen, A. (2006), *Identity and Violence: The Illusion of Destiny*. New York: W. W. Norton.
Shaw, R. and Waldorf, L. (eds), (2010), *Localizing Transitional Justice: Interventions and Priorities after Mass Violence*. Stanford: Stanford University Press.
Sklair, L. (2002), *Globalization: Capitalism and its Alternatives*, 3rd edn. Oxford: Oxford University Press.
Slack, J. (1996), 'The theory and method of articulation in cultural studies', in D. Morley and K. H. Chen (eds), *Stuart Hall: Critical Dialogues in Cultural Studies*. London: Routledge.
Sluzki, C. and Ransom, D. C. (1976), *Double Bind: The Foundation of the Communicational Approach to the Family*. New York: Grune & Stratton.
Smith, A. (2001), 'Rwanda warns of Hutus preparing second genocide'. *Independent* 4: 13.
Smith, D. W. and Somers-Hall, H. (eds), (2012), *The Cambridge Companion to Deleuze*. Cambridge: Cambridge University Press.
Smyth, M. B. (2007), *Truth Recovery and Justice after Conflict*. London: Routledge.
Spengler, O. (1932), *Man and Technics*, trans. C. F. Atkinson, New York: Knopf.

Stagoll, C. (2005a), 'Transcendental Empiricism', in A. Parr (ed.), *The Deleuze Dictionary*. New York: Columbia University Press, pp. 282–3.
—(2005b), 'Event', in A. Parr (ed.), *The Deleuze Dictionary*. New York: Columbia University Press, pp. 87–8.
Steiner, J. (1998), *European Democracies*, 4th edn. New York: Longman.
Strine, M. (1998), 'Articulating performance/performativity: Disciplining tasks and the contingencies of practice', in J. S. Trent (ed.), *Communicating Views From the Helm of the 21st Century*. Boston: Allyn and Bacon, pp. 312–17.
Suhrke, A. and Berdal, M. (eds), (2012), *The Peace in Between: Post-War Violence and Peacebuilding*. London: Routledge.
Temple-Raston, D. (2005), *Justice on the Grass*. New York: Free Press.
Thompson, J. B. (1984), *Studies in the Theory of Ideology*. Berkeley: University of California Press.
Toros, H. (2012), *Terrorism, Talking and Transformation: A Critical Approach*. New York: Routledge.
Tyler, S. A. (1987), *The Unspeakable: Discourse, Dialogue, and Rhetoric in the Postmodern World*. Madison: University of Wisconsin Press.
Uvin, P. (1998), *Aiding Violence: The Development Enterprise in Rwanda*. West Hartford, CN: Kumarian Press.
Uwazie, E. E. (ed.), (2003), *Conflict Resolution and Peace Education in Africa*. Lanham: Lexington Books.
Varela, F. (1979), *Principles of Biological Autonomy*. New York: Enselvier North Holland.
Varela, F. J., Thompson, E. and Rosch, E. (1991), *The Embodied Minds: Cognitive Science and Human Experience*. Cambridge, MA: MIT Press.
Volkan, V. (1997), *Blood Lines: From Ethnic Pride to Ethnic Terrorism*. Boulder: Westview.
Vološinov, V. N. (1973), *Marxism and the Philosophy of Language*. New York: Seminar Press.
Wallis, A. (2007), *Silent Accomplice: The Untold Story of France's Role in the Rwandan Genocide*. London: I. B. Tauris.
Watzlawick, P., Bavelas, J.B. and Jackson, D. D. (1967), *Pragmatics of Human Communication*. New York: W. W. Norton.
Wilden, A. (1987a) *The Rules are No Game: The Strategy of Communication*. London: Routledge & Kegan Paul.
—(1987b), *Man and Woman, War and Peace: The Strategist's Companion*. London: Routledge & Kegan Paul.
Williams, J. (2000), 'International Organization in the International Campaign to Ban Landmines', in J. Hopkins (ed.), *The Art of Peace*. Ithaca, NY: Snow Lion.
Winslade, J. and Monk, G. (2000), *Narrative Mediation: A New Approach to Conflict Resolution*. San Francisco: Jossey-Bass.
Wise, J. M. (2005), 'Assemblage', in C. J. Stivale (ed.), *Gilles Deleuze: Key Concepts*. Montreal: McGill-Queen's University Press.
Woito, R. S. (2003), *Extending the Democratic Peace*. Chicago: World Without War Council.
Wolfe, L. 'How Rwandans cope with the horror of 1994', *The Atlantic*, April 2014, www.theatlantic.com/international/archive/2014/04/how-rwandans-cope-with-the-horror-of-1994/360204/?utm_content=buffer7cd14&utm_source=twitter.com, accessed 4 April 2014, 3:48 PM ET.
Žižek, S. (1994). *Mapping Ideology*. London: Verso.

Index

www.ingramcontent.com/pod-product-compliance
Ingram Content Group UK Ltd.
Pitfield, Milton Keynes, MK11 3LW, UK
UKHW021907150926
475560UK00003B/233

9 781472 524058